How Did
I Get Here?

How Did I Get Here?

The Barry Young Story

Barry Young

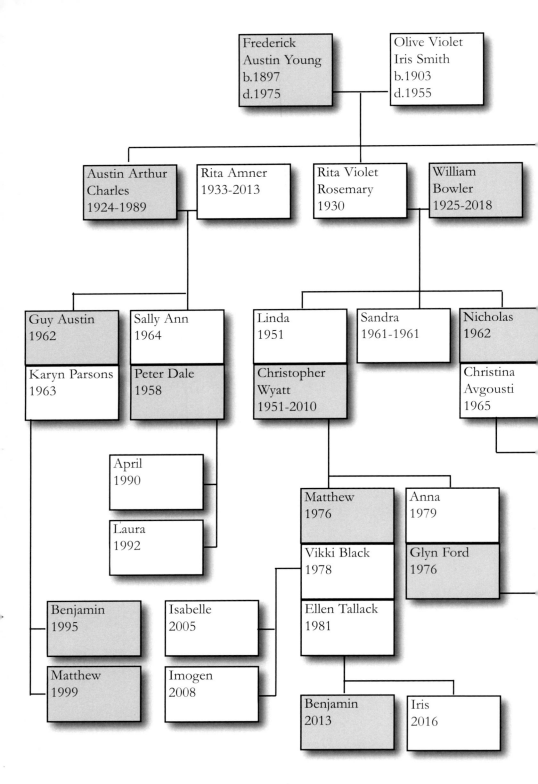

Descendants of Frederick Young and Olive Smith

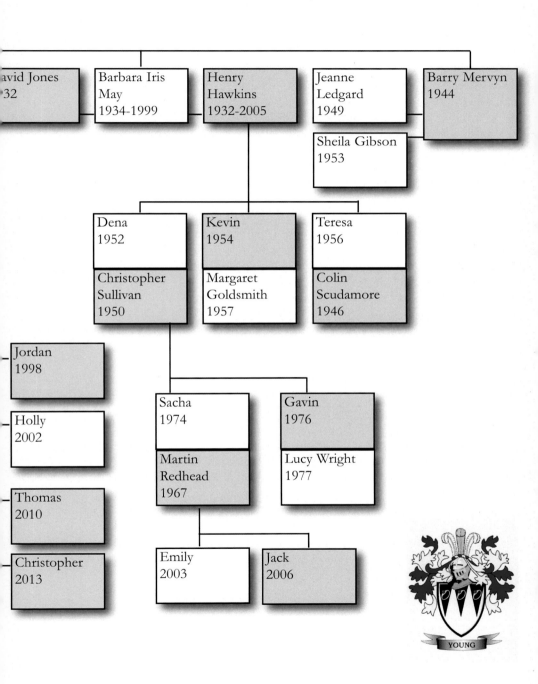

avid Jones
'32

Barbara Iris
May
1934-1999

Henry
Hawkins
1932-2005

Jeanne
Ledgard
1949

Barry Mervyn
1944

Sheila Gibson
1953

Dena
1952

Kevin
1954

Teresa
1956

Christopher
Sullivan
1950

Margaret
Goldsmith
1957

Colin
Scudamore
1946

Jordan
1998

Holly
2002

Thomas
2010

Christopher
2013

Sacha
1974

Gavin
1976

Martin
Redhead
1967

Lucy Wright
1977

Emily
2003

Jack
2006

YOUNG

CONTENTS

INTRODUCTION

What were the circumstances that took Olive Violet and Frederick Austin Young to Barry Island in South Wales in 1944? And what were the consequences of that visit? The answer to question one will reveal itself later. As for the consequences, it is where I was conceived and why I am called Barry. I also have a middle name, Mervyn, although I have no idea where that came from. As for Barry, I am just relieved they didn't go to Porthcawl! My life continued to be defined by circumstances, consequences and indeed coincidences, and it has been all about taking advantage of, embracing and capitalising on them. I have heard people talk about the formative years of their life … I am still enjoying mine!

The consequence of being born in 1944 is that it would seem to have been the perfect time – the end of the war, the carefree days of the fifties, a teenager in the sensational sixties, the quiet roads when I was a salesman in the seventies, all the labour-saving devices of the eighties and the electronic revolution of the nineties – oh, what a time to have been born.

The Speaking Clock, Green Shield Stamps, automatic gearboxes, the Access Card, the end of rationing, seventies disco, colour TV, mods and scooters, Hi-Fi innovations, remote controls, automatic kettles, microwave ovens, electric blankets, the Rockwell 8R calculator, the Ideal Home Exhibition, Filofax, Tesco loyalty card, Space Invaders, hole-in-the wall cash machines, WiFi and Bluetooth … whatever that is!

My family, especially my nephew Chris Sullivan, has been suggesting for years that I write all this down. I was having a beer with Chris at his Staplers home on the Isle of Wight in 2005 when I told him about my life. He asked if I had put any of it down on paper and said I should for the benefit of the family, otherwise it would be gone forever. I have to thank him for putting the seed of the idea in my head, and Chris has gone on to enjoy success as an author himself.

Two of the many thesaurus alternatives for 'circumstances' are 'state of affairs' and 'situation'. Luckily for me, my life has been full of these things. Situations that have led to a state of affairs. Certainly those early circumstances would influence the future of my life and my personality. Life is a rich and varied learning experience, and we have to learn to expect things of ourselves before we can do them. Like a jigsaw, we turn pieces into pictures of our life. My dear friend Damian quotes, "We are the sum of our parts," and here I am at 76, a very happy and contented sum of my parts.

I began this book explaining how circumstances and consequences were to play such an important part in my life and now here they are again. The consequences of the Coronavirus pandemic meant that I would not be going away in my camper van for the foreseeable future. This did, however, provide the circumstances for me to write my autobiography, so on 5th April 2020 I began a whole new chapter of my life as an author. My initial title for the book was 'As I Remember It', giving me two meanings. It would be as I thought of things, and also as I remembered them happening – not necessarily fact. I made copious notes based on this idea, and with A–Z books and notes I made a start. Not being a typist, I hand-wrote the first chapter, but luckily Chris encouraged me to start using my computer and, although it has been two-finger typing, the spell checker, cut-and-paste etc have been a huge benefit. Nevertheless, I realised I would benefit from some professional help with this mammoth task and started a wonderful relationship with biographer Tony Gray. His encouragement, help and expertise have got me to the end. Please forgive me if I haven't remembered every detail of everybody and everything. My story is a 'recollection collection', bringing together elements, events, factors, situations, incidents, occurrences and so many memories. I have also put in life lessons and all those experiences and how I used them to positive effect. Life seems to be full of 'c' words – change, challenge, colour, consider, create, compete, contribute, converse, contentment and many more.

Roald Dahl said,

A life is made up of a great amount of small incidents and a small amount of great ones. It is a good idea to discard all the inconsequential incidents and concentrate upon those that have remained vivid in the memory.

I don't believe I have done that, as many of the inconsequential incidents have also remained in my memory and I wanted to include them. My whole life seems to have been one marvellous adventure and I have loved it all. As the title of the 1976 Top 10 for The Walker Brothers said, 'No Regrets'. Of course, I have made mistakes but, as Elbert Hubbard said, "There is only one way to avoid criticism: do nothing, say nothing and be nothing." I don't have any 'what ifs' or 'if onlys', perhaps because right now I am blissfully happy and contented and, of course, I constantly reflect on the many blessings God has given me.

Writing my autobiography has been challenging, rewarding, enjoyable and incredibly satisfying; it has taken a great deal of discipline, resolve and resilience. I have had to use the characteristics of the mnemonic DAD – Determination, Application, Dedication. I have always said that when I get to heaven, I hope that God has made a video of my life so that I can look back at what has been an absolutely wonderful experience. However, writing this has been just like reliving my life. The ups and downs, the highs and lows, the tears and laughter – all the elements that makes up a life well lived. The writing has also provided me with a superb objective and has been marvellous exercise for my mind. I have been keeping physically fit by walking an average of ten miles at least one day a week, supplemented with sessions of disco-dancing in the kitchen!

I've now had both vaccine jabs but I shall still not be taking any risks with my health, as it is so precious. I did always say that I wanted to live until I was 100, but I changed that to having an objective of living until 2050, as it seems like such a nice round number (numbers that are often used to tell us when some major objective will be achieved). 2050 will be such a date for me, and so I will not be doing anything to jeopardise that goal – I love life too much for that. I have sorted out my will and made arrangements to be buried with my mum at the Church of St Margaret of Antioch in Darenth, where my dad and Barbara are, just half-a-mile from where my life began.

My life, and indeed writing this book, has been a bit like climbing a mountain. If you fly to the top of a mountain in a helicopter, this will not give you the feeling of the kind of happiness that you experience when you have spent many hours walking towards the summit. Happiness is not the opposite of suffering and pain, it is striving towards something, it is suffering through that great task you have set yourself. Happiness is overcoming the obstacles that resist you achieving that goal – that is the part which is the enabling condition of feeling happy.

Make an adventure of all that you do,
Do it with humour and zest,
Looking at life from a broad point of view,
Giving your utmost and best.

Patience Strong

CHAPTER 1: THE EARLY YEARS

My earliest memory is of Christmas Day, 1948. I was just four years old. We were in Mr and Mrs Austin's house, opposite our home in Keith Avenue, Sutton-at-Hone, two and a half miles south of Dartford in Kent. I had opened and was putting together the interlinking rails of a clockwork train set, which had a green engine to pull the carriages around the assembled circular track. I was told that Father Christmas had come down our chimney to leave it next to my Christmas stocking containing sweets, nuts and assorted little treats.

My mum, Olive Violet Iris Young, my sister Barbara May and Mr and Mrs Austin, as well as their daughter (who was Barbara's friend), were in the room enjoying the festivities. Keith Avenue was my first home following my birth on 17th October 1944 in West Hill Hospital in Dartford. Sutton-at-Hone was a lovely area of the Kentish countryside and the River Darent, which started its journey to the Thames just south of Westerham, flowed past just yards away from our house. We played there often, and I am told that one time my sister, who was ten years older than me, nearly drowned me in the river. I never found out if she was trying to!

The wonderful tranquillity and peace were often broken by the Doodlebugs that came over the area. These flying V-2 bombs would drop from the sky when their fuel ran out and devastate whatever was below. Bomber planes on their way to London would trigger a hasty retreat to the Anderson air-raid shelter in the garden. I also understand that we hid under the stairs during these bombing raids, and for years I believed the story that my stork had nearly been shot down. What a tragedy for humanity if that had happened! I can't remember either seeing the Doodlebugs or hearing any of this drama, and of course the war ended a year after I was born.

I had two other siblings. Brother Austin had been born 20 years before me in 1924 and was serving his National Service in India. I have few memories of Austin until I became a teenager, but I will write much more about how important he was to my life later. My sister, Rita Violet Rosemary, was born in 1930 and married George Bowler, moving to his family home just a few doors away on Keith Avenue. My memories of Rita and George begin in my teens and, like Austin, they were to play an influential part in my life. I never knew any of my grandparents.

My dad, Frederick Austin Young, was born in 1897 – gosh, that sounds incredible now as I write it. I really have no memories of him until I was ten years old. What I know is what I have been told. He served in the Merchant Navy and later worked at the paper mill in South Darenth. During the war he worked at the Woolwich Arsenal where munitions were manufactured. In 1942 he was transferred to a new munitions filling factory called ROF Glascoed, near Usk in Monmouthshire, South Wales. I believe thousands of workers were needed at this huge new facility. He had had a good job with a pension, so he decided to move to Wales.

The government arranged lodgings for the workers who accepted the offer of the move. Dad moved in with the Evans family at 28 Freeholdland Road, Pontnewynydd, near Pontypool. He was still there when I next saw him in 1954. My mum was supposed to move to Wales with Barbara and me and, although she made visits, she concluded that the steel works and coal mines were too much of a contrast to the attractiveness and peace of the rural Kent countryside with its orchards, hop fields and better weather. Speaking to the three sisters in Wales many years later, I understand that on one of these visits Mum and Dad went to the popular seaside resort of Barry for a weekend, which was where I was conceived and as I have mentioned, after which I was named. The sisters were also quite blunt and told me they thought that I was an accident. This perhaps explains the ten-year difference between Barbara and myself. Accident or not, I have to thank Mum and Dad, because I have had the most fantastic life.

So, the only family with me at that Christmas train-set opening were Mum and Barbara. Keith Avenue was a wonderful place to grow up. There was a huge oak tree at the end of the road where I would climb and hide. I loved waiting for Barbara to come home from school in Dartford. I

Mum and me in our garden at Keith Ave

Aged 3 or 4 at Keith Ave

would wait in the oak tree or at the bus stop near the shop up at Sutton Corner where we could use ration coupons to buy sweets – a real treat in those days. We had a wonderful dog, a cocker spaniel called Rac, who would follow me everywhere. I had a very lucky escape when I was hit by a cyclist, as the brake lever on his drop handlebars pierced into my face just below the eye – an inch higher and it may have been more serious. (I was to have another very bad encounter with a bicycle many years later.) It was about this time I had scarlet fever and spent six weeks in isolation at Joyce Green Hospital.

The next stage of my life is when Mum, Barbara and I moved to Bexleyheath. My mum sold the Keith Avenue house and bought a haberdashery shop in Mayplace Road. Unfortunately, the business opportunities and profits were not what the seller had led her to believe, and she had to sell the shop, losing a considerable amount of her money in the process. We moved to No 2 Chapel Road, next to the Palace Cinema, not far from the clock tower at the top of the Broadway. Barbara started to go out with Peter Hawkins who lived just around the corner with his parents Nellie and Harry. All four of them were to make an invaluable contribution to my life, and Nellie was to make an early intervention on my first day at school.

On that fateful first day, Mum kissed me goodbye and left me in tears at the school gate. As soon as she was out of sight, I ran away to Nellie's, who consoled me and then returned me to my mum. I have no idea what she said or did, although I did attend on day two and as far as I know didn't run away again!

There were wonderful parties at Nellie and Harry's house at Christmas. All the men dressed up as Arabs, with tea-towels as headwear and sheets for clothing, visiting the local pubs before the party, and fabulous party games were played. A particular favourite of mine that I have continued playing throughout my life is 'Follow the Moon' – the participant (victim) enters a pitch-black room, a white sheet is held up in the centre of the room, and behind the sheet is the beam of a torch representing the 'moon'. The victim is then told to place their face close to the sheet and 'follow the moon' as the torch moves around, up and down behind the sheet. The victim's face follows, with the audience chanting, "Follow the moon, follow the moon." After a period of this, the moon rises to the top of the sheet, the face of the victim follows and as they go over the top of the sheet they are hit in the face with a very wet sponge. The sponge is replenished with cold water and the next participant is invited in. It is brilliant, I love that game. I had my first cigarette and taste of beer at one of those parties. I don't smoke now … but I am still drinking beer.

The Palace Cinema next to our house is where I saw my first films at Saturday morning pictures. The Regal Cinema on the Broadway also had a Saturday morning minors club. The films and weekly episodes featuring Flash Gordon, The Lone Ranger with his trusted friend Tonto, Superman and Roy Rogers all enthralled us, and we would re-enact these characters in our own adventures. I have recollections of sneaking into The Palace via an emergency door that was in our garden (and I have continued my sneaking into adulthood). Something I haven't continued is 'Doctors and Nurses', which I played in our shed with two girls who lived in our street. I have no idea what 'Doctors or Nurses' involved or indeed what we did, I just remember the name. The historic memory at this time was the news

Playing doctors and nurses, aged 5

of the death of King George VI and that Princess Elizabeth was now our queen.

Our next move, perhaps because of Mum's financial situation following her haberdashery experience, was to live in a caravan situated in a wood called 'The Spinney', near Knockholt, about six miles north of Sevenoaks. This was a fantastic experience – well, for me at least, although unfortunately I have no idea what Mum or Barbara thought about it – I really wish I did. I expect many of us wished we had talked to our families more, to learn their thoughts and feelings.

They both knitted and I remember holding skeins of wool on my outstretched hands whilst they wound it into a ball.

I attended my second school, St Katharine's in Knockholt, a few miles from our woodland location. I remember catching a school bus on a corner where there was a telephone box. I expect that was also our communication device. Around six caravans were spread throughout the wood. One of the residents used to paint me like a Red Indian, and I would run throughout the wood in my short trousers, covered in war paint, with hand-made spears and bows and arrows, having the most marvellous time. I would collect dead mice and other wildlife as trophies from my adventures. Barbara wasn't best pleased when I took them home and she would attack me. I always remember my mum shouting, "Don't hit him on the head Barbara."

Barbara married Peter on Christmas Eve 1951. I can't remember if he also lived in the caravan with us, but I do know he built the most amazing rustic fencing around our plot.

I only learnt a number of years ago what happened next. I was staying with my niece Linda and her husband Chris in Horton Kirby. I asked Chris to help me find my woodland home. I knew it was near Knockholt and I remembered the telephone box. The area is a maze of narrow country lanes, and no one had ever heard of 'The Spinney', but with much endeavour we found the school and from there, the red telephone box. We pulled into a farm gateway 200 yards further down the lane. There were a couple of very grand country houses set in huge gardens with large gates. I was going to solicit help from here – I was sure we were not far away from our goal – when I saw a couple walking across a field towards us, so we waited until they reached the footpath stile. I posed the question, "Do you know of a wood called 'The Spinney'?" The couple, Alan and Joy, did not recognise that name but, when I described the caravans that were once there, unbelievably the wood in question was next to their house, just where we were parked! I have maintained that God has had his hand on my shoulder all my life, and that was indeed another wonderful example of my faith and His love.

They invited us for coffee to one of the lovely country houses that I described earlier. They had not moved to the area until the 1960s when

The caravan at the Spinney, with the rustic fencing that Peter built

The family at the caravan – Mum behind me, Peter on the left, and Austin on the right with his girlfriend

they built their house, so they only knew about the caravans and the history of the wood from older local residents. Although they had never heard of the name 'The Spinney', they did, however, now own part of the wood. I have only recently found out a very revealing and enlightening fact. A *University Challenge* question would solve the mystery. What is a spinney? Answer: a small wood with undergrowth.

Alan took Chris and I on a tour. As always, the world seems much bigger when you are a child, but I did recognise many features in the wood. I recalled and related my happy days there: the wild war-painted Red Indian with bow and arrow having imaginary cowboy and Indian battles. Alan showed us the now defunct and overgrown water tap at the entrance of the site, as well as other remnants from the past history of 'The Spinney'. I asked about sanitation and he told us we would have had to dig cesspits. I would imagine Peter helped us with that task. A shocking thing he did tell us was that the caravans should not have been in the wood at all, as the owner did not have the appropriate licence or permission, so one day the council came and towed the half-dozen caravans out of the wood onto the road and left us there. That was the end of our wonderful (for me) woodland home. Although I have no memory of it, my eighth birthday would have been just a few days before.

I had another visit to 'The Spinney' in 2019 with my niece Sally's husband, Peter, where we met Alan and Joy again. Alan took Peter and I on another woodland tour and once again I recalled my memories of those happy childhood days. Peter, who has himself been doing some family research, spoke to St Katharine's School in Knockholt on my behalf. They could not divulge any information to him but suggested I rang them myself. So in 2019, 67 years later, I discovered that I had attended the school from 28th February to 24th October 1952. I arrived there from Woolwich Road Primary School in Bexleyheath and, when I left, went to foster parents in Crayford. Another fantastic piece of information I was to learn was my address whilst at the school: No 2 'The Spinney', Cudham Lane. This was the first time in my life that I have had any real certainty of the dates of events in my life. It was a wonderful, wonderful moment.

Crayford was my third school and almost opposite my new home. The foster parents were not very nice people and did not treat me well. My memories of this awful experience are that I missed my mum, was very unhappy and looked forward to her visits on Sundays. I believe Mum lived with George and Rita in Ship Lane, Sutton-at-Hone, for a while. A strong memory is that Mum was going to send me to Rhodesia. Australia and Rhodesia were recruiting young white blood at the time. During the intervening

Me aged 6 at school

My sister Barbara and I on a day out in London

years it has come to light how badly some of these children were treated. I do not think Mum was trying to get rid of me, I believe she simply wanted a better life and opportunity for me, although I will never know for sure.

I cannot begin to appreciate the anxiety and anguish my mum must have experienced during this period. On her own, with no home, no job and an eight-year-old boy to look after.

In the end I didn't go to Rhodesia. Instead I went to live with Mum at an old people's home in Chelsfield and we were, much to my delight, reunited. My fourth school was in a lovely little village location. I remember we went across the road to the canteen at dinner times. This is where I formed an aversion to fat on meat – there always seemed to be a high percentage of it. My sister Barbara would never eat fat either. I did love the rice pudding with skin on it and other delicious desserts, or sweets, as we called them then, with custard and a skin on the top. I am not sure why we left Chelsfield. Perhaps the old people's home did not like my mum having me there with her, or perhaps she found a better job.

I have no idea how, but she did find another job as a domestic help in a huge 100-room country house, 20 miles away in Abridge, Essex, not far from Epping Forest. Four people lived in Petits Hall in Pudding Lane: Mrs Howard, the elderly owner, Rose the cook, my mum and me. What a contrast this imposing new home was to living in a caravan in a wood. There were croquet lawns and tennis courts all surrounded by their own farm and acres of land. Instead of cowboys and Indians I would ride on tractors with farm workers and build haystacks at haymaking time.

The country house where Mum worked in 1952 (not me in photo!)

My bedroom was at the very top of the house. I remember being very frightened walking along a dark, wide area with rooms going off it and past lots of ottomans, inside which I imagined all manner of things lurking. I walked half a mile down Pudding Lane to catch the No 10 bus to my fifth school, about three miles away in Chigwell. This is where I first remember experiencing school sports day. There were wheelbarrow, three-legged and sprint races. Long and high jump were also featured, and I enjoyed entering all these events. I think my mum came and watched me sometimes.

On some Saturdays I would catch the No 10 bus all the way to London Bridge to have an adventure – yes, all on my own, aged eight! I am sure all these kinds of things contributed to who I am today. Mrs Howard and Rose would go away on holidays, so Mum was allowed to invite Barbara and Peter to come and stay in the big house along with their daughter, my first niece, Dena May. The house had the most beautiful music room with a grand piano and a huge Noah's Ark that housed wonderful wooden animals. This provided hours of enjoyment for us all. We played croquet and generally had a tremendous time.

A significant date I remember is 2nd June 1953, the coronation of Queen Elizabeth II. Mrs Howard had a television set so quite a group of people, including Mum and I, gathered round this very small screen to watch the event.

The summers seemed longer and hotter back then, and this was a wonderful place for me to grow up. However, and I have no idea why, Mum and I moved back to Kent. My memories are very vague from the next period of our adventures. We went back to living in caravans, and I remember sites in Meopham, Herne Bay, and spending winter months at Leysdown on the Isle of Sheppey. How did she find all these places?

At this summer seaside site we were the only people there. I never went to school at all during this time. On 17th October I had my ninth birthday. All Mum could afford to give me was a chocolate cup-cake, those which had chocolate sponge and a hard chocolate top in a silver foil case with a serrated edge. Mum said Barbara would send me a present. Peter was in the RAF, so he and Barbara now lived in airmen's married quarters in Feltwell, Norfolk. I waited anxiously for the postman, and a few agonising days later I was rewarded with a wonderful book from Barbara. I can't recall what it was – it didn't matter – it was a present and something to read on those winter nights on the the Isle of Sheppey.

Two strong memories are the hiss and smell of gas mantles, which were our source of lighting, and Mum receiving a registered letter each week. These had the sender's name and address on the reverse which ended with the word 'Mon'. For years I thought it said 'Man'. Mon is actually short for Monmouthshire, which is where Dad lived, and he never missed sending Mum money each week. So, I was correct in believing the envelope was from a man ... my dad!

In the summertime Leysdown would have been a great place to be, but in the winter months it was not. I have no idea when we left or how Mum found her new job, but I do remember our next home, Rose Cottage in Longfield, about seven miles southwest of Dartford and only a few miles from our first home at Sutton-at-Hone. Mum went there as live-in (with me) domestic help to Mr and Mrs Crouch who ran a coal-yard business next to the cottage. Rose Cottage was the perfect description of this quintessential English cottage – thatched roof, whitewashed exterior, roses growing over a rustic porch – it was beautiful. A bit smaller than Petits Hall, but much more homely.

I joined my sixth school just outside the village. I also kissed my first girl in Longfield (I don't think we had done any kissing when playing 'Doctors and Nurses' at Chapel Road). The village hall put on films each week. I went with a girl who lived opposite Rose Cottage who was older than me – I was nine; she was, I would guess, about twelve. One of the songs played before and after the film was 'Answer Me' by David Whitfield, and I would sing this to her as we walked home. Her house had a wooden porch which is where I enjoyed the first of many goodnight kisses. I was very happy at Rose Cottage; I would love to know if my mum was.

Another significant memory came here in Longfield. One day Mum told me she was going somewhere for the day to get divorced, although I am not sure I understood what that meant at the time.

I really wish I had a better idea – I can't even hazard a guess why – but once again we were on the move. Just a few miles this time to the vicarage at Horton Kirby, the village where Mum and Dad first lived after getting married. As these were to be some of the unhappiest moments of my life, they are hard to recount. Tears are in my eyes just thinking about what happened to my mum here, when she became housekeeper to the vicar and his wife.

I attended my seventh school up the appropriately named School Lane, a short walk away. Living in the vicarage meant I was enlisted into the choir and sang at morning and evening services, as well as attending Sunday School each week. A favourite hymn I remember was 'Sheep May Safely Graze'.

There were some good memories for me here. It was a large house with a garden to play in. We listened to the vicar's radio, with programmes like *Dick Barton – Special Agent* and *Journey into Space* on the BBC Light Programme. I made my first plastic model here, the Golden Hind – I wonder what happened to that? I enjoyed the walnuts from the tree in the garden, made friends with the children from the big house next door and had many great school friends. We played and swam in the River Darent a few hundred yards away. This is the same river just a few miles from where Barbara nearly drowned me some years earlier. Open grass areas, woodlands and the river were our playground. We built soapboxes, sometimes known as taxis, which were home-made wooden constructions with pram wheels. I recall pushing them up a hill nearby and enjoying the thrilling experience of freewheeling down, probably at dangerous speeds, but of course there were far fewer cars on the road in those days to collide with. At the top of Bull Hill was The Bull pub which had an off-licence that sold ice lollies with ice cream in the middle – they were delicious. I entered a soapbox derby at the village fete in South Darenth. I have vague memories of losing a wheel and struggling half a mile back to the vicarage.

Horton Kirby also put on a garden fete. There was a roll-a-penny game, with the old copper coins, when the object was to get your penny to land within a numbered square, and the number would dictate your winnings. I seemed to do very well landing on the number four and winning four pence a few times. So, number four became my life-time lucky number, thanks to that day in 1955. Was this fate at the fete?! I also joined in the maypole dancing, which was always popular at such fetes.

A marquee was erected in a field – we thought it was a circus. It was in fact a travelling evangelical event. I attended but have no memories of what the preacher said. Billy Graham the American evangelist was very popular about this time, but I don't think it was him.

Mum and I did visit Barbara and Peter at their married quarters in Feltwell, Norfolk. I remember this because of an adventure I had there. One evening I said I wanted fish and chips from the chip shop, which was about a quarter of a mile away. Mum, Barbara and Peter said I could not have them, and I had a terrible, terrible tantrum. I was undressed, put into my pyjamas and sent to bed where I was locked in my room, still screaming and crying. That is when I conceived my adventure. I had some money and an overcoat in the bedroom, and I would not be denied my fish and chips, so I climbed out of the upstairs window onto a concrete slab that acted as a porch for the front door and down a drainpipe, ran to the fish shop, bought my fish and chips and ran back. Climbing up the drainpipe (all that cowboy and Indian training came in useful) and onto the slab, I went to climb in the window and was horrified to find that they had shut the window! After I had set off, they wondered why I had suddenly stopped shouting and crying and, when they came up to the bedroom to investigate, they found I was gone and shut the window. This now meant I had to knock on the front door to get back into the house. Much to my anguish, they took away my fish and chips and put me back in the bedroom, confiscating my overcoat and remaining money. I spent half an hour shouting and screaming, calling them thieves, before I eventually fell asleep. I was given my fish and chips in the morning when I got up and have to this day continued to enjoy cold fish and chips!

I recall Mum sometimes went out on Saturday evenings, when she told me she was going to Halifax to see a man about a dog. I had no idea where Halifax was and I never saw the dog. Little did I know that one day I would live just a few miles from this Yorkshire town. I hope she enjoyed some happiness on those Saturday evenings. She was only 51 and certainly hadn't had much enjoyment in her life so far … and things were going to get worse.

I am not sure if it was Mum or perhaps Barbara some time later telling me that the vicar's wife was mad, or something similar. She would get into a cold bath fully clothed, then attack my mum physically when she tried to get her out. I do not know if this was a contributing factor to the events that were to later unfold. Mum became ill – very ill – whilst working at the vicarage. At ten years old I did not fully understand what was happening at the time. I am not sure if a doctor came to see her. I do know I had to come home from school at dinner times to make her a cup of Bovril, which was all I knew how to do. Meanwhile, the vicar did not even go up to see how she was or offer her any food or help, and then would stand in his pulpit on Sundays preaching about being a good Christian. It is unbelievable how badly this hypocrite treated my mum. Eventually Mum sent me to the post office to send a telegram to Barbara in Norfolk. We hastily packed our bags and a few days later Barbara arrived in a taxi to take us away and back to Norfolk. The vicar did not even come out to say goodbye or thank you to my mum.

I have no memory of the taxi and then train journey to Feltwell in Norfolk. I know Mum was taken into King's Lynn Hospital that evening. I never saw her again.

Barbara and Peter told me in the morning Mum wouldn't be coming home. She died in the night. I understand it was peritonitis. I am crying now as I write … my poor, poor mum … how she must have suffered at that vicarage. When I was older I went back to Horton Kirby, with the intention of beating up the vicar, but he was gone – his wife had died and he had moved away.

It was 1955. I was at the front of another new class being introduced as the new boy. It was to be my eighth school. I often wonder if these introductions, being in front of an audience, meeting new people, exploring new places, played a big part in my makeup and had an influence on my future life and I am sure all of this had an effect on my education. Although I really can't remember very much of what I was taught at this stage of my life, I am, however, good at meeting and greeting!

I settled in with Barbara and Peter and Dena in their RAF married quarters in Feltwell. They now had a son, Kevin. Thanks to the fish and chips escapade, I had form, and I didn't get off to a good start. Each of the married quarters had a fire extinguisher at the door. Are you ahead of me? Barbara told me to stop playing with it, but of course I didn't, and just a few days after I arrived, I set the fire extinguisher off inside the house! Barbara was always very house-proud, so for her this was a nightmare, coming just on the heels of the death of our mum. However, maybe because of this she didn't hit me on the head … just as Mum had told her not to all those years ago in the caravan.

I am not sure if it was a birthday, Christmas or just a gift, but I got some roller skates and learnt how to use them. I remember Peter used to tow me round the airfield on the runways with his motorbike. Great fun, if not a little dangerous.

I had other memorable events here. An infection caused a huge boil on the back of my upper leg. I had never had a boil, it was very painful – so painful that I couldn't walk, so Peter took me (or rather, wheeled me) to the doctor's in a pram. I was ten years old, so a rather big baby – and I still am at times! Poultices were applied over the next couple of weeks and I was soon back on my feet and up to mischief again.

Up to this time I cannot remember having had a bicycle of my own. Peter was a keen cyclist and owned a lovely racing bike with drop handlebars. It had no gears, but a fixed wheel, which meant that it did not freewheel and you had to pedal all the time you were moving. Without permission (I certainly don't think I would have ever been given permission), I took the bike one day and set off with a friend onto one of the many unused runways at the base. Having a wonderful time, racing along, one of my feet slipped off the pedal, but the other pedal, because of the fixed wheel, kept rotating and propelled me over the handlebars. I sailed through the air until my face made contact with the tarmac, slid along and, acting as a brake, brought me to a stop. My friend came to my aid and summoned help. He was also astute enough to retrieve my two front teeth, which had been knocked out by the impact, from the runway. My

Missing teeth, aged 10

face was a complete mess, and blood was pouring from the holes in my gums. A military ambulance collected me, my friend and my teeth, and rushed us to the hospital on the base. The doctors and nurses did all they could for me. Unfortunately, I don't think they had the dentistry expertise to reunite my two teeth with the two holes in my gums. (More about my toothless wonder period later.) A lesson learnt that day: "Thou shalt not steal." I never did learn what Barbara and Peter had to say about all this mischief – perhaps they were being tolerant, understanding and kind after our recent tragedy. They certainly were all these things and much more to me then and for many years to come.

Meanwhile I was blissfully going along, minus my two front teeth, although my face was healing. I hope Peter's bike was ok! Like many people I am sure, I wish I had talked about these first eventful ten years of my life to the other participants whilst they were still alive.

The future of my life was in fact being discussed between Barbara, Peter and my dad, as to what they should do with me next. Hopefully Rhodesia wasn't on the agenda. I couldn't continue living with Barb and Pete in their married quarters; they had their own two children and I am not sure if the Air Force would have allowed it. The decision was made: I would go to live with my dad in Wales, 140 miles away.

It was of course a steam train that Barb and Pete put me on at Paddington Station for the four-and-a-half-hour journey to Newport. I had a little brown suitcase containing all that I owned in the world. They told me I was to get off at Newport where my dad would be waiting for me. "How will I know him?" I asked. "Don't worry, he will know you," I was told. Mind you, I don't expect there would be many other ten-year-old boys getting off on their own at Newport. I wonder what was on my mind on that train journey. Another adventure in my life was about to begin.

The little brown suitcase

CHAPTER 2: DAYS WITH MY DAD

A New Home

It was a Saturday and Dad was waiting for me at Newport Station. It was very strange meeting this man I'd never met. We caught a bus to Pontypool, about eight miles from Newport, and a second bus took us to my new home, 28 Freeholdland Road, Pontnewynydd. It was a narrow, terraced house with one front window and a front door that opened into a corridor. A door on the left led into the front room, only used on special occasions. That day was obviously a special occasion, as the Evans family were waiting for us in the front room. Four sisters, Joan, Kath, Min and Nancy; brothers Bill and Joe; Nancy's husband Jim; their two children Garth and Val, and Joe's wife Kit. I spoke to Garth in 2020, who told me that they were all excitedly awaiting my arrival. Dad, or Fred, had been with the family since 1942, and the parents had been alive when he arrived. Garth said he always knew him as 'Uncle Fred'.

The corridor continued to a door leading to the living room, and immediately inside were the stairs. The living room was where we lived and ate. Settees surrounded a large brown oak dining table and chairs which was always covered with a table-cloth. A big coal fire was the focal point of the room, with a coal scuttle and other implements for fire maintenance. Bill had his own special armchair within spitting distance of the fire – he did this with regularity, between puffs on his pipe, and it sizzled as it hit the hot coals. Sometimes his aim was off and it ran down the tiled fireplace. Bill was a lovely man who worked at Branch's, a local builder. I remember collecting his empty tobacco tins, St Bruno and Old Holborn. The irons were also heated over the fire on a metal grille.

On each side of the fireplace were two large cupboards, with double doors at the top, acting as airing cupboards either side of the chimney

23

breast. The house was full of cats – the family loved cats – and the animals used to sleep and have their litters up in those cupboards, presumably because of the warmth. My poor dad had the job of drowning the unwanted kittens, there were so many of them.

A sash window looked out into a yard and up the very long narrow garden. On the windowsill was a radio, our main source of entertainment, and the sisters enjoyed listening to music. I remember Jimmy Young singing 'The Man from Laramie' (No 1 in the charts in October 1955) and other popular songs of the time, including 'Rock around the Clock' by Bill Haley and the Comets (No 1 just a few months later). A door led from the living-room into the kitchen, completing an L-shape around the yard. The scullery was the engine-room of the house, with a gas stove, some food preparation space and a large white sink. This was used for everything from washing up, washing clothes and washing yourself.

Another door led from the living room to a pantry on the right. This had large stone slab shelves and was used like a fridge, as it would be cooler inside thanks to the slabs, which were painted white. So we kept butter, milk, tins of condensed milk etc in there, as well as meat. I used to sneak in and nick a spoonful of condensed milk, which was a real treat – just once a week! I always promised that, when I went to work, with my first week's wages I would buy a tin of condensed milk of my own. I did, and I ate half of it, and I was nearly sick!

A window looked onto the yard and a back door took you into the yard, up some large steps to the garden and the outdoor toilet. This was a whitewashed stone building, inside which the toilet had a wooden seat, but no toilet tissue here – pieces of newspaper hung on a piece of string from a nail in the wall, and there was an old-fashioned cistern with a chain to pull for flushing. Eight of us shared this facility, but I can't remember having to queue very often! There was also a large mangle in the yard. The garden must have been about 100 yards long and six wide, sloping upwards to a gate out onto a road. Almost opposite was the location of my next school, Pontnewynydd Primary School, a large, imposing red-brick building surrounded by black metal railings.

After the tea and cake, the two children Garth and Val, who were a few years younger than me, took me out for a little explore and to Mrs

Werret's shop that, amongst other things, sold ice cream. I had vanilla with strawberry syrup running over it. It was delicious and really nice to make two new friends so quickly.

Back at the house, together with my little brown suitcase I was taken along upstairs. There were three bedrooms: the three sisters, Joan, Kath and Min, shared a large back bedroom that looked out onto the garden; Joe and Kit had a small bedroom at the front and, along a short landing, also at the front, was the third bedroom. This housed a double bed where Dad and Bill slept. A small camp bed had been erected at the bottom of this double bed for me. I slept here until Joe and Kit got a place of their own, when I then moved into their bedroom – what luxury! There was a pot under the bed in the room I shared with Dad and Bill, for the three of us to share during the night if we needed to and, when I moved into my own room, I got my own pot!

Because there was no bathroom in the house, and the toilet was up the garden, on Fridays we would get the tin bath from the yard, boil hot water on the stove in the kitchen and place the bath in front of fire. With the bath full of hot water, the three sisters would get in first, in order of seniority, and between each one another kettle of hot water was added. Then it would be Bill, Dad, and then finally I would get in when the water was like vegetable soup – all sorts of things were floating round in that water. Fortunately, I can't remember whether I washed my hair in it. We used carbolic soap and there was no shampoo.

By the way, there was a rule in the house which the women made quite clear – in an attempt to protect the carpet from wear and tear, I was only allowed up and down the stairs once a day. So, I could come down in the morning and go up at night-time, but that was it. I do remember that Min, the older sister, who was a much softer lady, would allow me to pop up to my room and get something if she was there in the house on her own.

I had something in my little brown suitcase that I had to talk to my dad and the sisters about. I had to tell them that I wet the bed and then showed them the rubber sheet that I had to use. A short time later Dad took me to the doctor and I was prescribed tablets that thankfully stopped the bed-wetting that I had suffered from for years. He also slapped my legs in an effort to stop me biting my nails, but it wasn't until the nineties that I succeeded at that!

25

School No 9

The next week I started at my ninth school. It was certainly the shortest journey to school I ever had – just a walk up the garden, through the gate, across the road and I was there. Through the large black metal gates across part of the playground that was full of fellow pupils enjoying their morning play before the bell rang to start the day. Then inside the entrance was a grand, wide staircase leading to the upper classrooms and dining area. However, I was taken to an office on the ground floor to be introduced to the headmaster, and after the formalities I was taken to my class and here I was again – front of the room meeting my new classmates! It would not be long before I sat my eleven-plus which would decide whether I went to a comprehensive or grammar school and determine the next stage of my education.

Apart from the doctor's, Dad also ensured that I saw the school dentist about my two missing front teeth. I can still taste that pink substance used to make an impression of my teeth and gums. The denture seemed to fill my whole mouth – it was awful, but I was reassured that I would get used to it. The first day I tried it, I was eating my school dinner when I looked down to see the denture in the middle of my mashed potato. I never wore it again. In fact, I didn't have any front teeth until some ten years later.

Playtime activities included marbles, also known in Wales as allies, when we would use large glass gob-stopper-size marbles, throwing smaller ones to try and hit the larger marble to win more for our own collection. We also enjoyed polishing copper pennies by scraping red brick dust from the walls onto the penny and rubbing them to make them look brand-new. In winter we made slides on the ice in the playground. We had races across the playground, and I made a bit of a name for myself as a fast runner. This would be a deciding factor in my position on the team when I started playing rugby. This was rugby union country, so not much football was played, although I would play for a church youth club team a few years later. I quickly started making friends and settled into my new school, and indeed my new home.

We made stilts, probably with Dad's help, using two lumps of wood with an extra piece of wood inserted a third of the way up on each 'leg'. Funnily enough I continued making stilts for much of my life. As children

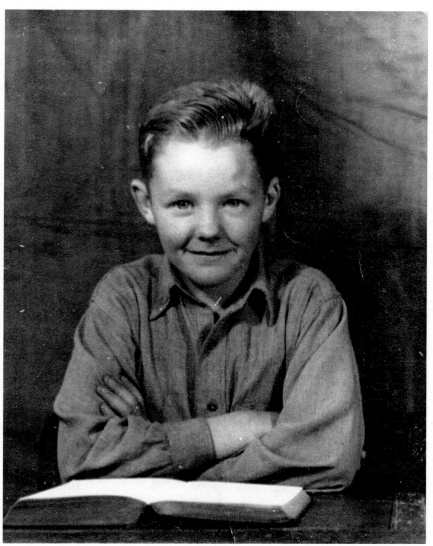

Aged 11 in 1955

we played hopscotch in the playground and on the road outside our house, drawing the grid with chalk. We also played tennis across the road, as there were hardly any cars to worry about.

Leisure Time

As kids when we were not in school, we would be off all day with a picnic and a bottle of lemonade. We headed off into the woods and fields, across the hills in South Wales, with our bows and arrows, gone for the whole day, lost in our adventures. I remember buying 'frozen jubbly' from a shop – these were triangular cartons of orange juice that someone had put in the freezer so that it was frozen like a great big lolly that would last you for hours. We also did a bit of scrumping when the fruit was on the trees.

My bow and arrow was hand-made, using wood from a tree for the arrows, taping a four-inch nail on the end for the point. Playing with these once, I got shot in the arm with one. Someone had to pull the nail out and the blood just poured out, so I went home and was nursed by the women. Later on when I had earned my own pay-packet I did go on to buy a proper bow and arrow, with a quiver and real arrows with feathers.

Often we would swim in the River Usk. It was about eight miles away and lovely to swim in – we would go at weekends and have the most marvellous time, with rope swings from a tree across the river, plunging into the water. I love swimming in rivers. There was a large steep hill on the return journey called Jockey Hill, which we had to push ourselves up on our gearless bikes!

Another place to go swimming was Pontnewynydd Swimming Pool. Like many outdoor swimming lidos, it had a grass area where we could sit with a picnic and a diving board, and it was a marvellous place to spend time. At the beginning of the season the pool would sometimes be frozen because the water was not heated!

On one occasion I caught pneumonia whilst out on one of my adventures, and I had to be taken to hospital in Newport, where my dad used to come and visit me every other night. I was probably there for a few weeks, and it must have been serious enough for people to have been worried about me.

Another game we would play when we were out – and another cause for my dad to be worried – was garden-hopping. In our street there were all these long, thin gardens, about 100 yards long, and between each garden was a hedge or fence. So we would run across them, garden-hopping, like running the hurdles. We were doing this one night and one of these hedges had a metal fence with spikes hidden inside it. I came down on one and a spike went right through the back of my leg. Dad had to take me to hospital, and was not best pleased with me at the time. He was also not very happy when I broke a neighbour's window and he had to replace the glass.

Our friend Terry Gittings lived on our street in South Wales, and he had a knack of playing drums on biscuit tins. I remember him very well, and one day many years later I read in a newspaper that he had married a beautiful blonde dancer who had performed in the *Benny Hill Show*. Then a few years afterwards I was walking past the Grand Theatre in Leeds when I saw her name up in lights. Terry had become her musical director, she was performing in Leeds, and so I walked to the stage door, intending to ask the doorman if Terry was about. Suddenly there was Terry in front of me. He looked up and said, "You're going to take me back aren't you?" and I replied, "Yes I am." We had the most marvellous night, he gave me tickets for the show, and then we all went out for dinner at an Italian restaurant (and I'm ashamed to say it was probably the only time I have ever driven home drunk).

My first and long-lasting friend, Hugh Drinkwater, lived just a few doors from me (we called him 'Hughie'; my nickname was 'Ying Tong', from a song by The Goons, a name which lasted until I joined the army). Later, when I moved to Kent, he came down to visit me a few times and we kept in touch. Sometimes I just ring people up out of the blue, so once, after many years of not speaking, I called Hughie, who sadly told me he was dying of prostate cancer – his whole body was riddled with cancer, although he lived for another five years before he passed away last year.

Back in Wales the sisters would often take me to the Pontnewynydd Pavilion (Pavy) Cinema on a Friday evening. I remember the film *Three Coins in a Fountain*, and the song of the same name sung by Frank Sinatra was No 1 in 1954. We'd also go to the Saturday morning pictures, with the same serials I'd seen before – *Roy Rogers*, *Flash Gordon*, *Superman*, often followed by a cowboy film. During which we'd fling paper pellets into the necks of other boys sitting in front of us, using our elastic-band catapults!

Just up the road there was a little house where a neighbour ran an illegal bookie. Young guys like me were sent to place bets on the horses, mostly by my dad and Bill.

There was one adventure that must have stressed my dad enormously. As children we used to go up this hill behind all the houses called the 'Dumpty', playing football and the like. They had started building a housing estate on it, and one night we went up amongst all these half-built houses to play football. Suddenly we spied a dumper truck, and one of the eight of us said, "Why don't we push this up the hill, all get in and ride down the hill?" So, we did. Several climbed on the front and the back, there was the driver, and others stood either side of him. We set off downhill, but of course we lost control and all of us decided to jump off. However, the dumper carried on hurtling down the hill, turning over like a Catherine wheel and smashed into some metal railings. We all ran away and went home.

I'm not sure if it was Donald who lived next door who gave us up, but an hour later the police turned up, we were all charged and given an £8 fine and a police record. My dad had to take a day off work for the hearing. He must have hated all of this, looking after a kid and all this hassle after all those years of living like a bachelor and looking after only himself. It was a good thing he was patient. We came out of the court and Dad bought me an ice cream sundae. Many years later I paid him back the £8, as I had told him I would one day. The whole event brought shame on the family, and it was the first time Dad had ever had to go to court.

Dad

My dad got up for work at 4.30 am, when he would walk half a mile to the station. The train and then a bus took him to ROF Glascoed, near Usk. Dad and Bill looked after the garden at home and grew a lot of the vegetables and soft fruits that we ate – I enjoyed the goosegogs! There were also some lovely flowers grown. Dad always wore a flat cap, probably because he and Austin were bald by the age of 30. I must have inherited my mum's hair as, now 75, I still have a good head of hair, although, alas, not ginger anymore … but more about 'Ginger' later.

Dad was a very quiet and gentle person, very different to me, but a bit like my brother Austin – they were both quiet, gentle men, whereas my sister and I were both fiery. One of Dad's great lessons to me, that has stayed with me throughout my life, was that if I wanted anything, I would have to earn my own money to pay for it. So when I first got to Wales, if I wanted anything – like a bike, a catapult, or a bow and arrow – I'd have to raise the money for it myself. This was a true 'life lesson' for me – if you want something, you have to save up and work hard, and then you can have it.

Earning Money

As a result I did paper rounds before school, and Sundays were particularly tough with the heavy Sunday papers. I also delivered bread and groceries after school on one of those old-fashioned bikes with a large basket on the front, just like Granville from the TV series *Open All Hours*. I sold the Football Argus, which was pink, outside the cinema and pub in Pontnewynydd on Saturday evenings. When the papers were dropped off, at about 5.00 pm, there were always several boys rushing to cut the strings on the bundles and run down to our pitch to make the first sales of the evening, where men would be waiting for the football results that had been printed in the paper. Sometimes I would be the last one there at 10.30 pm, waiting for the pubs to throw out, so that I could make those last sales when everyone else had gone home. It was also easier to sell when the men came out of the pub drunk – I was only about 11 or 12 at the time.

Once I'd sold the papers, I'd go back to the organiser, hand in the takings and receive my commission. I recall that this man had a record player, and on one Saturday night he was playing 'Heartbreak Hotel' by Elvis Presley, which was No 1 in 1956. This was the first record to make a significant impact on me and the start of my love of music, which continues to this day. Tommy Steele and Guy Mitchell had No 1 hits with 'Singing the Blues'. A record from 1957 I also liked to sing was 'He's Got the Whole World in His Hands' by Laurie London (which was the first record I actually bought).

The organiser of newspaper sales had a large glass conservatory on the side of his house where I was able to keep my first bicycle, which I had bought with my first £15 of earnings – there was nowhere to store my bike at home! It was a brand-new red and white Triumph Palm Beach – oh, it was beautiful, and it was worth all that hard work. Another invaluable life lesson, thanks to my dad, who also had the foresight to open a Post Office Savings bank account for me (I did not realise how important that would be until some four years later).

The money I earned bought all manner of things: a real catapult bought from a shop in Pontypool, after many years of making them with the forked branch of a tree and strong elastic; at the same shop I also bought my beautiful bone-handled Bowie knife, complete with leather sheaf; a Diana air pistol which fired single and double lead pellets; a plastic water pistol, shaped like a spaceship; and a twin-barrelled pirate's gun that fired caps (and I still played cowboys and Indians with it). The sad thing is that, because of all my moving around, I don't have any of my childhood toys.

My C&A jacket

What happened to my train set, Meccano, Dinky cars and the rest?

With my earnings I would also purchase the odd single cigarette, Player's Weights or Woodbines – or if I had no money, I would cut down a tree vine and smoke that! At 12 or 13 years of age I shouldn't have been doing that, but that's what people did back then!

I also travelled on the bus to Newport on my own, where I bought my first ever item of clothing – a blue zip-up jacket with blue and white check shoulder pieces from C&A. I thought it was fabulous, and had saved up the money especially.

Youth Clubs

My leisure time was spent between two different church youth clubs. One was St Luke's, near Abersychan, and I remember that there was a sloping field behind the church which was perfect for sledging in winter. My dad helped me make the sledge, and I would come home wet and cold after a sledging session and then get dry and warm in front of the fire. (By the way, I have suffered with cold hands all my life as a result of Reynard's Disease, and I wonder if it all started back then.)

The other youth club was St James' in Pontypool. This club has two significant memories for me. The first was as the song 'Diana' by Paul Anka (No 1 in 1957) was being played on the youth club record player, I met a girl there called Diana and started singing the song to her before I took her home to Blaenavon, about five miles away (this is where the Big Pit Mining Museum is now located). The next morning, I cycled back to her house and gave her a bracelet, although I have no idea where I got it from, and I don't think I ever saw her again either!

My second memory from St Luke's was playing football for the youth club team – keep in mind that it was nearly all rugby in that part of the world! I had a trial in Pontypool Park (a very famous rugby ground), followed by an away match in Bristol (travelling through the railway tunnel under the Severn) next to the glue factory – I wonder that we were not poisoned by the fumes! I played brilliantly, scoring a goal, and got a write up in the Pontypool local paper about my starring role in our win. Afterwards we were guests at a Bristol City match at their main ground.

At Abersychan I would go to church for Sunday School, although we didn't go to church services. I was also good at religion at school, especially as it was a strong subject in school in those days.

On Sunday lunchtimes Dad, Bill and some of their mates went to The British Legion Club in Abersychan. A real treat for me was meeting my dad from the club, and when he came out he would buy me an ice cream from a coffee bar that had a juke box, the first I had ever seen, before we walked home our Sunday lunch. I always remember afters (dessert) was tinned fruit with bread and butter. Sometimes after lunch Dad would take me for a walk in the wood nearby and we would collect hazelnuts.

Despite my missing two front teeth, I still had some lovely girlfriends during those years. I remember serenading the girls in my class with 'Bad Boy', a hit for Marty Wilde (Kim Wilde's dad), and 'Lonely Boy' by Paul Anka. Both were hits during 1959, and I'm sure the girls swooned at my singing – or is that wishful thinking on my part?! Helen Howe was the next girl I kissed since my experience on the porch in Longfield. I sang to her as well, of course, and I went out with Helen for a while before meeting Beryl Ford. This teenage romance produced a remarkable coincidence some years later.

School No 10

After failing my eleven-plus, my tenth school was Abersychan Secondary Modern, known as 'The British'. It was two miles away, but we walked to save the bus fare. I found it quite daunting going here. At dinner time the older boys at the top of the table served the food, and if you managed to get along with them you got a better serving at dinner! I always enjoyed school dinners, probably because I grew up with them. I remember once some of the older boys threw my cap onto the railway line. (Which reminds me, I once fell down a hole playing on the railway line in the dark – which we shouldn't have been doing – and because it was a very narrow hole, I struggled to get out. I did a very similar thing some years later in the Lake District when I was 45 years old!)

I did well at 'The British', and it was the longest time I ever spent in one school. I was good at maths and science, and I do remember learning about Chaucer. I achieved my best education results there, and my school report for December 1958 shows that I was first in class out of a group of 41 children – not bad after all that educational disruption in my life! This was another life lesson for me – if you work hard and want to learn, you can.

At the age of 14 I received my first recognition and reward for all the hard work, good behaviour, time-keeping and adherence to the rules – I was made a prefect and given all the responsibility that came with this position, which I'm sure would play a part in my future life. I also was awarded the only certificate I have owned all my life, for swimming 10-yards breast-stroke.

My one and only certificate!

I enjoyed woodwork at school and made a kitchen stool. I remember taking this on the train, the Underground and the bus when I went to visit my sister Barbara and husband Peter, and their by then three children, in Bexleyheath in Kent. I would often visit them during school holidays (and at Christmas time I remember the games we played together, such as 'Crow Shoot' and 'The Amazing Magic Robot'). The stool was so good that I made four more stools just like it when I rebuilt my kitchen and installed a breakfast bar in 1980.

I enjoyed and did well in school sports, particularly sprinting. I also played rugby for the school. The larger boys were the forwards and the small boys the backs. The ball was passed out to avoid being tackled by an opposing forward, but when the ball got to me on the wing, I had no one to pass it to, so to avoid being crushed I would fall into touch!

Benny Jones, our PE teacher at school, played rugby for Pontypool. He used a piece of half-inch dowel as a cane on the hand – thankfully I only had the cane at school a couple of times. One of those was an all-class

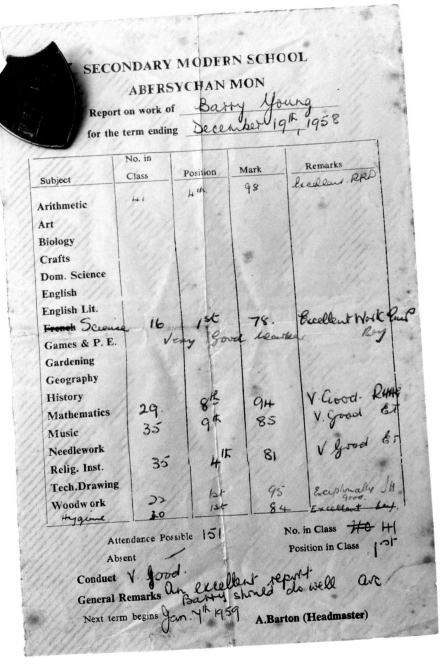

1958 School Report… with my Prefect's badge!

punishment when no one would own up for a misdemeanour. Sometimes, instead of the cane, you had to write 100 lines as punishment, usually in detention after school.

The first school trip I can ever remember was to Bristol Zoo when we went through the Severn Tunnel on the train. It was quite an adventure, and I had certainly never been to a zoo before.

I remember that, at school, thanks to my name, I was always last on the register. My dad always used to say, "Barry, you will die 'young'!"

When it came to the time to leave school, the teachers were very keen for me to stay on for GCE exams. However, Dad said it was time for me to earn a living. The prospects appeared to be either working down the pit or in a steel works. I didn't fancy either. There were family discussions about what to do with me. As my brother Austin had been in the army and Peter in the RAF, it was decided that the best place for me was in the forces – it would give me a home

My dad in his flat cap

and a career, and so another chapter was about to begin for me ... and I was still only 15! I didn't have much of a role in the decision. Anyway, although many people knew what they wanted to do, many people – like me – had no idea at all!

Chapter 3: Junior Signalman Young, 23827617

Peter had suggested the RAF for me, and I had applied and attended the entrance exams in Bedford, but I wasn't successful so I tried for the army – with more success. I chose the Royal Signals, which I hoped meant that I would get to ride motorbikes like the dispatch riders. When I left school I was still 15, so I had to wait until October 1960 for my 16th birthday before I could join up. Austin had left the army and was married to Rita, living in a lovely cottage at the bottom of West Hill in Dartford (very close to the hospital where I was born), so I went to live with them whilst I was waiting to go into the army myself.

I occupied myself and earned some money during this period by working at a second-hand car sales garage in Burnham Road in Dartford, washing cars. This was a really interesting experience. The garage was owned by two brothers who were large guys, wore trilbies and smart suits and drove matching pink Vauxhall Cresta cars. I drove my first cars here, moving them around for cleaning. They had a lovely selection, including a Morris Minor and a huge black Standard Vanguard. They also had a Panther motorbike, a great big heavy thing which sounded fantastic when you started it up. Little did I know that I would later live a few miles from the Phelon & Moore factory where they were made in Cleckheaton.

Rita's dad, Jack Amner, who was a solicitor in London, took me out for days in the city, which was great. We went up the Monument and visited other landmarks and tourist attractions. He was very kind and a real gentleman.

I also worked for my brother-in-law George. He now had a successful carpentry business and was involved in a large house-building project at Fleet Estate in Dartford. He worked on all the second fixing for the houses, and I went to work for him doing all sorts of odd jobs, including

39

driving a dumper truck (which was a much better experience this time!). I loaded it up with flooring board planks and took them to the houses where the carpenters were hard at work. Working on a building site was quite an experience for a 15-year-old boy, I can tell you, but I learnt a lot, especially dirty jokes, some of which I still remember today. Let me tell you this one ... it's ok, only joking!

Talking of dirty jokes reminds me of my dirty books experience (that's what they were called then, although really they were just pin-up magazines). I sometimes used to go up to London in the evenings, and I remember standing on London Bridge smoking a Strand cigarette, just like the advert of the time. The cigarettes were soon withdrawn because the slogan 'You're never alone with a Strand' didn't sell the cigarettes. I obviously was very happy on my own and enjoyed looking around Soho in the evenings. It was exciting, and maybe a bit dangerous, although I never felt threatened. Strip clubs seemed to be the big attraction, including the famous Raymond Revuebar and, of course, The Windmill. I also spent time with an old friend from my days in Horton Kirby.

He came with me on an afternoon just a couple of weeks before I was to join the army. We thought it would be a good idea to have some pin-up magazines like *Spick and Span* to take with me. There was a shop in Villiers Street next to Charing Cross Station and, after perusing the books, I bought two and off we went to Leicester Square. On our way we saw a stall selling more books, so we stopped to look. As we were leaving the stall holder accused us of stealing some books and called a policeman. We pleaded our innocence and admitted that we had books but that we had bought them in Villiers Street. The policeman took us back to the owner, who of course – because he should not have sold such books to boys of our age – denied that we bought the books there. The policeman then marched us off to Bow Street Police Station. We were interviewed in a cell, pleaded our innocence and it was only when I told them I was joining the army in two weeks they decided to let us go – but they kept the books! So, no books went with me to Newton Abbot.

October soon came around and off I went with my little brown suitcase. Junior Signalman Young, 23827617 – it's amazing how you never forget that number – reported for duty. My next home and future were at

Denbury Army Camp, near Totnes in Devon. My memories are of a long barrack room with beds down each side, and of going to the stores and being kitted out with everything from bedding, uniform, socks, underwear, boots and a whole manner of other items, such as sewing kit, mess tins, boot polish etc.

One of my first shocks was to be told we wouldn't be going home on leave until December. So, despite never having had a proper home, I became homesick. After a couple of days I rang my dad for my Post Office Savings book to buy myself out of the army. The fee was £20 for the first three months, then £50 thereafter. So now the massive advantage of Dad opening that savings account I mentioned became apparent, and the fact that I had £20 in it.

Dad and the commanding officer suggested very strongly that I give it a fair try and stay for three months, which I duly did. In the end I won a prize for the best result in the Army Certificate of Education. To succeed at this I had to be good at drill – marching and all of that; to be good at geography – we were dropped on Dartmoor and had to find our way back with a map; able to take a rifle apart and put it back together; had to be able to shoot; and had to continue education in maths, education, science etc. I achieved the best result out of a group of 200 boys.

Some boys cried every night for weeks, but some boys loved it so much (or perhaps did not like their homes) that they didn't go home for Christmas. Reveille was at 6.30 am, when you had to wash, make your bed a very special way (make it look like a TV screen, with lines in it, all wrapped in one blanket – the

Home on leave, 1960

41

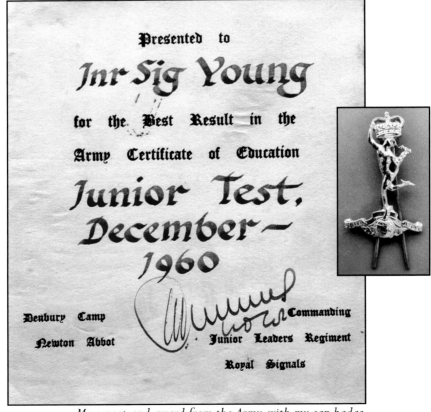

JUNIOR LEADERS REGIMENT, R. SIGNALS,

TESTIMONIAL AND ASSESSMENT OF

MILITARY CHARACTER

No. 23827617 ...... Rank J/SIG ...... Name YOUNG B.M.

NB Gp No .7...... Date due Release .. 25 Jan 61 ....

ASSESSMENT OF CHARACTER . VERY GOOD, .assessed on 3 months service.

Employment Junior Leader Trainee Service Trade ...Nil ....

Testimonial ....

A quiet young soldier who has an alert brain. He is clean and tidy in his habits and can be trusted to work without supervision.

STATION .Denbury.Camp, NEWTON ABBOT. .... R. Signals,

DATE .... Jan 61 ...... Comd. 2 Sqn, Junior Leaders Regiment, R. Signals.

(H. ROTHWELL)

Presented to

Jnr Sig Young

for the Best Result in the

Army Certificate of Education

Junior Test, December — 1960

Denbury Camp

Newton Abbot

Commanding

Junior Leaders Regiment

Royal Signals

My report and award from the Army, with my cap badge

bottom blanket on the bed had to be so tight that, when the sergeant major came along to check it, if a ping-pong ball didn't bounce off it he'd rip your whole bed apart), clean your barrack room job, and then go on parade and march to the mess room for breakfast.

Drill was learning to march. Arms drill was with an SLR (self-loading rifle), which was nearly as big as me! We also had a bayonet scabbard on our belts round our tunics. At the command, "Remove bayonets," you'd put your finger on the button on the top of your rifle; when commanded, bayonets were then pulled out and put in your scabbard, where the sheath was self-sharpening. The first time I did it, I pulled off the sheath and left the bayonet on the top of my rifle. The sergeant major came and shouted at me six inches from my face: "Young, if I see that bayonet again, I'm going to stick it up your arse."

How I remember bulling boots! This involved a hot spoon and candle. We had two pairs of boots each, one daily and one for best. The boots had pimples all over the toes. You held the handle of a spoon over a candle, and then pressed it onto the boot to melt the pimples into a flat surface. You then applied boot polish and spit using a cloth in a circular motion, 'bulling', until you had a gloss-like finish. This took hours and hours at night in the barrack room. Some recruits tried smoothing the toe-cap with an iron and subsequently melted the whole toe-cap! If the sergeant major was not happy, he stood on the toes of your boots and cracked the polish, and you then had to start all over again!

We seemed to spend most of our time getting kit ready for locker inspection. The officer would pull the locker forward if he was unhappy with it and spill everything on the floor. I remember Blanco and Brasso being used for our kit as well.

John Isherwood is the only person I remember from those days and he became my best friend. I would love to find him again. I earned the nickname 'Maverick' because I was good at cards. When we got time off we went into Totnes, a lovely town, but I don't think I drank in those days so there can't have been any trips to pubs. I do remember singing Roy Orbison's 'Only the Lonely', No 1 in 1960.

There were all sorts of horror stories from the older boys at the camp that our next move would be to Catterick Camp in Yorkshire, and how easy Devon was compared to up there, which would be rougher and tougher.

Personally I think the army was too much of a shock for what were essentially children – well, I was still a boy. The contrast from my happy carefree days at school to the strictness, discipline and regimented life of the army was enormous. However, I did learn so much and all these things were important and helped me in my life. Perhaps it could have been done (and probably is now done) a little gentler.

I remember very well the passing-out parade. I laid my rifle down and marched out to the front to receive my award for Best Result in the Army Certificate of Education from a top-brass officer. The award was a book entitled *Soldiers of Misfortune* and, as I read it, I thought it was certainly my misfortune to become a soldier! However, I certainly benefited from the experience.

In order to leave the army I had to have a home and a job to go to. Brother Austin and sister-in-law Rita provided the first, and brother-in-law George provided the latter. So I paid my £20 and it was back to Civvy Street for me, and another exciting stage of my life – and I was only 16.

Chapter 4: The Singing Sixties

I am indebted to the generosity of Austin and Rita who offered me a home for the second time in their cottage at the bottom of West Hill in Dartford. It had a front room, a narrow hallway to the living-room, a kitchen with a large sink and cooker, and the stairs heading upwards to two bedrooms and an attic where I later had a snooker table. Across the yard was an outside toilet, but we took our baths at the slipper baths in Dartford every Friday evening. Rita was a shorthand typist for the government in London, and Austin worked for T&B Supplies in Dartford, a trade and retail builders' merchants.

If only I'd had a relation or someone who knew someone involved in the entertainment industry working at the BBC, Pinewood, Elstree, Fleet Street, or in advertising and marketing – but at the time I had no idea what those were. Or perhaps if one or two of them had been starting a group and wanted a singer, things could have been so different now!

Circumstances seem to have directed my life up until then, but I didn't feel hard done by. Without the luxury of any of the above to get me a job in entertainment, or something more glamorous, I had no idea what I wanted to do, so I went to a careers officer in Dartford. He asked me, "Do you like working with your hands?" I am not sure I understood what he meant and thought it might be a trick question, so I said that I did. "Do you like working with people?" he then asked. Again, I thought it best to say yes. "Right, an apprenticeship in engineering for you!"

I joined Evridge Engineering in South Darenth, just a few miles from where I was born, as an apprentice toolmaker. This was a very valued and respected occupation. It wasn't long before I went there that the toolmakers had worn bowler hats. The next six years were to be a wonderful, wonderful time of my life – so much fun, with fabulous friends, and all during the 'swinging sixties'.

If you or your children ever get to this stage of life, encourage them to read Chris Evans's biography *It's Not What You Think*. His book should be on the curriculum, it is truly inspirational. He knew exactly what he wanted to do and went about getting it. I would do this later on in my life, with wonderful results. I never felt a victim of my circumstances, and life can be happier if you are able to adapt to your circumstances with a positive 'can do' and 'will do' attitude – or at least to give it your best shot.

In the factory I was earning £3 per week and I began to learn the necessary skills. All the other skilled men, the charge hand and the foreman, were our teachers. Of course there were pranks played on apprentices, complete with greasy handles, machines switched off at the mains etc.

Later, when I was perhaps 18 and had gained some experience, I had my own gang and we played our own pranks. For one such prank, I climbed up to the top of the large tree in the factory yard, lowered a rope, and my pals tied a push-bike onto it. I then hauled the bike up into the tree, untied the rope and came down. When we all came out after work, the owner found his bike at the top of the tree – a great laugh for us all, but it nearly earned me the sack!

There was a large washing area, and when new men started Johnny and I would pretend to fall out and start a fight ... much to the consternation of our victim. I recall many visits to the managing director's office with the foreman and union shop steward to be sacked but, luckily, I was good at my job and was told, "Barry, let him into your gang".

On a Saturday evening Rita and Austin sometimes took me with them to visit friends who had a record player, which was great fun – it was very kind of Rita and Austin to include me. We had lovely days out on Sundays to the seaside, to places like Whitstable. I remember swimming at Eastbourne, which was great because it had a steeply shelved beach so that you could almost dive into the water. It must have been very embarrassing for Rita and Austin as I walked along with my portable transistor radio blaring out the latest hits, particularly because they were both very reserved and gentle people. How I would love to discuss all these things

"Barry, let him into your gang"

with them now! Back at home we would listen to the radio – Austin was a huge fan of the radio programme *The Goon Show*.

I enjoyed my first holidays in the 1960s. My sister Rita, brother-in-law George and their daughter Linda, aged nine, took me with them to Paignton in Devon on a couple of occasions, staying in B&B accommodation. It was a novel and exciting experience for me. We had visits to Cockington village, with its quaint thatched cottages and lovely old pub, Brixham, Dartmoor and also Dartmouth. We went swimming in the sea at Anstey's Cove, near Torquay. I had a brilliant time.

Our next trip in George's Citroën DS was to Blackpool. We stayed at the very posh Headlands Hotel on the south shore – what an experience that was, complete with waitresses in black and white uniforms, all very grand to me. We had a marvellous time going up the Tower, enjoying the thrilling rides at the Pleasure Beach and swimming in the sea.

It was all a delight, but the best was to come when we went to the Lake District where we stayed at the imposing grey stone Windermere Hotel.

What a place – I will never forget the huge Victorian toilet in the bathroom, which was across the corridor, mounted on a large wooden plinth like a throne. It was so impressive, when sitting you felt like royalty. George was very adventurous and a day out in the car took us on what is known as one of the most demanding and challenging car journeys in the Lakes, across the Wrynose Pass, which runs through incredible mountain scenery. Then, if that wasn't enough, George took us up the notorious Hardknott Pass, a 1 in 4 gradient with hairpin bends and no places to stop or pull in. I believe it was used by the police for advanced driver training. I filmed our journey on their camera as we were thrown from side to side. Later in life the Lake District mountains became my favourite walking area. I spent many, many happy and exciting days in those wonderful fells.

My first scooter with with my nieces and nephew – Teresa, Kevin and Dena

My first scooter was a pale blue Vespa 125 from Autowheels on East Hill, Dartford. (When I was in Kent in 2019, I was delighted to see that they were still there, and I had a great conversation with the shop owners.) There was no room at Austin and Rita's home for my scooter, so, a bit like I had done with my bicycle, I had to keep it in next door's yard covered by a tarpaulin. I also had to make wooden ramps to get it up the kerb and step. I soon met other scooter boys at Autowheels as well as in and around Dartford, and joined their gang and made new friends with some 'mods'.

I was never really a bona-fide mod, although I did have some of the clothes, such as a parka with fox furs sewn around the collar, and of course the long aerial (ex-army tank) fixed on my scooter with a fox tail on the end. Linda sold me a complete fox fur to sew onto my parka – she tells me she had got it at a jumble sale and doubled her money! Kevin remembers my shiny winkle pickers, and after seeing The Beatles' Cuban heels I got a pair of those as well. I still have my Beatles jacket. When riding we sat right on the front of the seat with our feet sticking out at right angles – if your winkle pickers touched the floor when going round corners, you knew that was the limit to lean over. The winkle pickers were useful for that at least, but I'm sure they contributed to my bunions! It was at this time that we all started using the word 'fab'.

I think I had been with Austin and Rita for about six months when my brother-in-law Peter advised me that I should move to proper digs (lodgings). It was not fair on the young married couple to have a teenage boy living with them. He had found me digs in Leysdown Avenue in Bexleyheath, but the problem was the digs were going to cost £3.50 per week and I was only earning £3.00 per week.

I went to the bosses at Evridge Engineering and told them that because of my new financial circumstances I would have to leave. Much to my delight, they offered a solution – because I was a good timekeeper, an excellent worker and a bright boy, I could stay on as a trainee. Unlike the apprentices, I would not go to college once a week and not receive indentures at the end of the seven years. However, they would always give me a reference to prove I had the necessary skills, *and* I would be paid £7.00 a week. *Wow*, I was rich. Circumstances had rolled the dice in my favour again.

I moved in with a lovely couple, Mr and Mrs Clark. The house had a drive up to the house for my scooter, which was good news. It was further to travel to work, but that was no great hardship until the winter came. The winter of 1962/1963 was very bad, known as the 'big freeze', just like my hands (I mentioned earlier about suffering with Reynaud's Disease). As a result, I sometimes got home in tears with the pain. With this condition, as your hands warm up (usually in a bowl of warm water), you experience the 'hot aches' as the blood starts to return to your fingers – all very painful!

I would use stick-on letters to put the names of girlfriends on the sides of my scooter – on Vespas these were referred to as 'blisters'. It was a bit of a nuisance, and it was a real bit of luck when I changed from Margaret to Barbara because at least I didn't have to replace all the letters! Marlene wasn't quite so easy – Marlene was very posh, and we were a bit like Dennis Waterman and Suzy Kendall in *Up The Junction*, a brilliant film about the sixties in which Dennis rode a beautiful Lambretta. A very unfortunate accident ended our relationship, and my Vespa 125. I was taking her back to her parents' lovely big house in Wansunt Road, Old Bexley – the same road on which Dorothy Squires and Roger Moore lived – when we were hit by a car cutting across traffic lights. We were very lucky not be more seriously hurt, although Marlene did suffer a bad leg injury.

I met another of my girlfriends in Knole Park in Sevenoaks. I remember singing Joe Brown's hit 'A Picture of You' to her. She lived in a large tower block in Deptford, but the relationship didn't last long I'm afraid.

I replaced the 125cc with what was to become an icon in scooter history and my pride and joy, a brand-new Vespa GS 160. It was gorgeous, white with red detailing. I had the side blisters, front mudguard and the toolbox lid chromed, and I adorned it with front and rear carriers, d-bars, cadillac bars, red leopard skin seat and spare wheel covers, a floor mat, tank aerial with fox tail, red fly screen with ginger across it and tassels hanging from the end of the handlebars. Yes, now my nickname was 'Ginger'.

The remarkable thing about the 1960s was, when you went anywhere you could leave your beautiful scooter outside a coffee bar or club in Soho, without any worries. We would go up to London to the 2i's and Le Macabre coffee bars, or through the Rotherhithe Tunnel to the Kursaal at Southend. We had brilliant days out at the seaside in Margate, Broadstairs and longer day trips to Stonehenge.

I learnt a very painful lesson on one of these days at Broadstairs. We spent the day on the beach in our swimwear and, being fair skinned, I became badly sunburnt. When I returned home, everyone was in bed, and the only thing I had to try to relieve the burning and ease the pain was Vaseline, which I applied liberally. I cooked like a chip in hot fat!

When I caught chicken pox, because they were older, the lovely people I lived with were worried and so they asked me to move in with their

Hanging out at Stonehenge

daughter – more circumstances! So I moved in with Mr and Mrs Cosgrove at 44 Pembury Road, Bexleyheath, and went straight to bed in the lovely large bedroom at the back of the house, overlooking the garden. I was in bed for the next couple of weeks and Mrs C, as we agreed I should call her, cared for me wonderfully, bringing me my meals in bed and soothing my red itchy spots by applying calamine lotion. After a couple of weeks, I was back on my scooter and back to work.

By this time I was about to enter the most wonderful period of my life. I have heard it said, "If you can remember the sixties, you weren't there." Well, I was there, and I remember it well – very well. It was one of the most fantastic periods of my life, just like those carefree days at school.

Looking cool in the corduroy suit I bought from Carnaby Street

The Beatles, scooters, mods, mini-skirts and lots of girlfriends, even with those two missing teeth! Dartford Heath was the venue of choice to take girls for heavy petting sessions ... I wonder where you are now, Barbara, Margaret, Linda, Leslie, Marlene and that other girl who was a singer in a group that I went to see – did you go on to be famous?

My favourite films we saw at the time were the Hammer productions of *Dracula* starring Christopher Lee and Peter Cushing. I especially remember going into the cinema with Margaret and coming out with Barbara – my memory is heightened because this was the first time I touched a stocking top and suspender – now this was 'heavy petting' ... well, it was to me at least! Another memorable film of the time was *Psycho*, which I went to see on my 16th birthday and, because I looked younger, I had to show my birth certificate. There were moments when I wish I hadn't been let in, because the film scared me to death.

Life at Mrs C's was wonderful: she woke me each morning at 6.00 am with a cooked breakfast, and sent me off with a lovely packed lunch in a tin box which also fell prey to the pranksters. If I didn't keep an eye on it, I could find it nailed to a bench! I remember Mrs C always gave me an orange, and I even made a special knife to cut it open with – I still have the knife and even now start each day with an orange, thinking of Mrs C. She did all my washing and ironing, changed the bed and I would come home to a smashing meal every day.

Mr Cosgrove worked at H. Samuel's the jewellers up in London. Their children were Pauline, aged 15, who was at college, and five-year-old Michael who went to a local school. Pauline went on to become a window-dresser.

My best friend in the sixties was Johnny Taber who lived near me in Bexleyheath and was more of a rocker than a mod. I helped him get a job with me at Evridge Engineering. I went with him to buy a new motorbike at Pride & Clarke in Brixton, where he bought a BSA Bantam. Our group of friends had a mixture of motorbikes, scooters and different clothes. Johnny and I took turns going to work, one week on my scooter and one on his Bantam. One of the motorbike guys had a fantastic Triton, a combination of a Triumph engine and a Norton frame. He took me for a ride and one time we did a ton coming down Shooter's Hill in Welling –

without helmets! We became friends with another man at the factory, Mac Hatley, who had a car and lived near us, so during the winter we would pay him to take us to work with him. Luxury indeed when snow was on the ground. Sometimes we would do a 'through', which was to work all day, all night and all the next day, usually to fulfil a rush job – and of course, giving us great overtime wages!

I think it was about this time that I decided to have a new front teeth denture made, which I soon got used to, but I nearly lost it in a bit of road rage. Johnny and I were coming home from work on my scooter when a motorist started to pull out in front of us. As we went past the front of his car, I shouted abuse at the driver and my teeth shot out and landed on his bonnet. Johnny jumped off and retrieved them for me, so thankfully this time I was able to put them back in, unlike the runway incident many years previously.

I remember a camping adventure that Johnny, another good friend, Ian, and I went on. His dad drove us down to St Margaret's Bay, between Dover and Deal, supplied all the gear, helped us put the large family tent up and then collected us the next weekend. The campsite was next to a pub and, as we had started drinking by this time, the pub was a real bonus. (My first drink, half of lager and lime, had been with another good friend from the factory, Brian Scorer in The George in Bexley village.) The other advantage of the campsite was the railway station, which was on the main line. In the mornings we would catch the train to Deal and have a drink in the buffet car on the way, where we usually began with a game of crazy golf. We met two girls at the campsite, but poor Johnny spent his evening whittling a bar of soap whilst Ian and I enjoyed an evening of kissing and cuddling with the girls in our bedrooms.

I regularly worked on Saturday mornings. It was overtime and so paid time-and-a-half, which was welcome because I had the HP (hire purchase) to pay on my scooter that had cost almost as much as a new Ford Anglia. The gang used to meet on Saturday afternoons, either at the Wimpy Bar or The Silver Lounge on the Broadway in Bexleyheath – frothy coffee was the drink at that time. Then we would go off to Danson Park which had a wonderful open-air lido, or the boating lake if we felt energetic.

In those days the red buses of London had an open back which meant that you could get on and off easier and quicker. Because I enjoyed showing off, the slightly dangerous thing I liked to do was to leave the moving bus right outside The Silver Lounge so that all the girls could see me. Stupid, but effective!

Just a bit further up the Broadway was Jennings Music Shop, where we could listen to the latest records in booths. One such record was 'It's Not Unusual' by Tom Jones, No 1 in 1965, and a tune that Barbara also liked. Jennings also sold musical instruments, so I bought a couple of mouth organs or harmonicas (I have never been quite sure of the difference). I also bought a pair of bones, some castanets, a set of maracas and a metal kazoo – I must have still been hankering after getting into a group. Each week I would buy the *New Musical Express* and *Melody Maker* to keep up with the latest pop news.

On some Saturday afternoons Johnny, Mac and I would go up to The Valley to watch Charlton Athletic. Nicknamed the 'Addicks' or 'Red Robins', their players included Billy Bonds, Sam Lawrie, Stuart Leary and Harry Gregory. The Valley was a natural bowl that made for great viewing, and so we stood up in those days. We also played in a snooker hall above Burtons in Bexleyheath (some of these snooker halls were right seedy places), and I bought an aluminium cue to play with – a good example of me wanting all the latest things.

I didn't realise at the time how exciting this period of not just my life, but also of social history, would be. It included: the birth of Carnaby Street, with just a few shops like Lord John; the first disco in Soho, *La Discotheque*, in Wardour Street; purple hearts and bombers to keep you awake; mattresses around the sides of the dance floor if you needed to lie down; coming out on Sunday morning and going over to the East End for breakfast; Petticoat Lane bagel shops and Tubby Isaac's at Aldgate, which was also a late-night venue on the way home. Rolls-Royce cars would pull up, and the chauffer would buy plates of jellied eels for the occupants – maybe stars from a West End show.

Coffee bars like the 2i's and Le Macabre in Soho were popular destinations for us on our evening rides out. We had our own fabulous coffee bar at the top of Gravel Hill in Bexleyheath where I put money into a juke box for the first time (the first of many, I might add) to play the record 'Wonderful Land' by The Shadows, a No 1 in 1962.

The selection of places to go locally was vast and varied. A row of four terraced houses linked together made a fabulous venue, forming a maze of rooms all with speakers playing the music of the moment. Chislehurst Caves also made for an atmospheric music and hanging-out venue, with people wandering around with lit candles.

There was plenty of live music to see. I was in the queue outside the Co-op Hall in Gravesend waiting to see The Hollies when the news came down the line that President Kennedy had been assassinated. The Hollies had been formed in Manchester and were one of the top groups to see live, and an answer to the Mersey Beat sound so popular at the time. Graham Nash went on to be part of another of my favourite groups, Crosby, Stills, Nash & Young (no relation).

I saw The Beatles live at Woolwich Odeon and Finsbury Park Astoria, and Helen Shapiro at Dartford Granada. I well remember shouting out, "I love you Helen," but alas, it didn't get me any heavy petting on Dartford Heath! One of the mod groups, The Small Faces, appeared at Dartford's Scala Ballroom – they were enjoying chart success with 'What'Cha Gonna Do About It' at the time.

It wasn't unusual to go out to a coffee bar on a Saturday evening and end up at someone's house for a party. I am reminded of one such party in Barnehurst where they were playing a Top 10 record in 1963, 'Hey Paula' by Paul and Paula. Again, it was quite safe to leave all our beautiful scooters outside the house – amazing when you think of it now. This was all so fantastic and exciting, I loved it. I have a big, big smile on my face as I write. What wonderful memories.

Friday nights were usually a ritual of having our hair done by Roger Holmes, a friend and hairdresser on Long Lane, watching *Ready Steady Go!*, and then off to St Michael's Community Centre in Wrotham Road, only a mile from my house. I learnt to twist here to Chubby Checker, who was in and out of the charts in the early sixties with 'The Twist' and 'Let's Twist Again'. Two great girls taught me to jive to the appropriately named 'Let's Dance' by Chris Montez who had a Top 10 hit, both in October 1962 and also in 1972. The Who played live here one Friday night, and a

My Friday night dance tutors

couple of the band came in when I was in the toilet – a claim to fame moment ... for them, I mean!

One week I took a Friday afternoon off and went up to London to the studios of *Ready Steady Go!* in Kingsway. I hoped my parka and fabulous chrome Vespa GS 160 would impress, but my clothes were not mod enough for television I'm afraid, and I didn't even get to meet Cathy McGowan! A life lesson here: it is better to try and fail, than not to try at all. This mantra would be invaluable for the rest of my life. (I did sometimes consider buying a bubble car, either a BMW Isetta 300 or a Messerschmitt bubble car, but I stuck to my GS 160.)

Once a week I would take my lunch up to Rita's house, just up the road from the factory, to spend time with her. It was during one of these visits that she suggested and encouraged me to go away on holiday with Johnny. We agreed Blackpool as the destination and the Warwick Hotel, just along from the Headlands where we had stayed last time, would be our accommodation. Johnny and I bought matching-style tailor-made suits from Burtons the tailors – his was light grey, mine charcoal, complete with Hush Puppies boots with an elastic gusset. There was much frivolity among blokes in the factory, and because we were both virgins, our trip was the subject of much anticipation!

Tailor-made suits

We were travelling from Euston to Blackpool and when we got to the station Johnny said he wanted to visit the kiosk outside. I had no idea what he wanted, but to my surprise he came back with a packet of Durex each, something that hadn't even crossed my mind. I was very happy with heavy petting and after the life I had already had I was petrified of getting a girl pregnant. We certainly met and made friends with a lot of girls on this holiday (and one of them became my wife a few years later). The very first night, we found ourselves with two girls, snogging in a seafront shelter across from the hotel. They were just walking past on their way to Pontins Holiday Camp up the road where they were working, but the Durex packet remained intact.

Our first dates were with two girls from Leeds, one of whom was on holiday with her parents. They were only there for the week, but before they left we swapped addresses. Johnny and I did all the Blackpool things: the Tower, Stanley Park, the tram to Fleetwood, rowing boats on Fairhaven Lake at Lytham, the Pleasure Beach and rides, including the Wild Mouse, the Grand National, the Big Dipper etc.

As in the Headlands, the waitresses at the hotel wore black and white uniforms. After the two girls from Leeds had gone home, we started dating two waitresses who were friends and students working in Blackpool during the summer holidays, one from Leicester and the other from Ashby-de-la-Zouch (a fabulous name, but we had no idea where it was). I fell in love with Julie and started travelling up to Blackpool to see her at weekends, and then Leicester when she went back home. She had beautiful long hair, so I would sing, "Let it hang down on me," from the hit 'Hang on Sloopy' by The McCoys, No 5 in 1965.

On my first visit to stay at her parents' home, I had one of my embarrassing moments. At breakfast on Saturday morning we had a fresh half of grapefruit, my first ever! It had not been cut completely through, but I did not know you could hold it whilst pulling out the segments with your spoon, so I was sweating and still struggling when the eggs and bacon arrived.

Johnny came with me on one of my weekend trips to Leicester. We took the coach from Victoria and then a bus to Julie's house and when we arrived at about nine on the Friday evening, we knocked on the door. Julie

With Julie and her beautiful long hair

answered the door and looked in amazement to see me there. "Didn't you get my letter? I've dumped you!" and closed the door. So we went back into Leicester, where we were moved on from the train station as vagrants and wandered the streets. We found a launderette with a vending machine and spent the night drinking hot chocolate and trying to sleep on benches 12 inches wide. A guy finishing his night shift came in to do his washing at 6.00 am, so that was the end of any chance to sleep. Our return coach was not until Sunday afternoon, so we managed to find a B&B for the Saturday night. After walking round Leicester, we went to a football match between the home team and Northampton, nicknamed the 'Cobblers' after the shoe-making industry in the town. It was a long day on Sunday, but we eventually returned home. I of course was heart-broken and, much to the dismay and amusement of the blokes in the factory, my Durex were still unopened!

Thanks to Rita's encouragement, we became more adventurous – it would be European coach tours next. To pay for these trips, Johnny and I got work from my brother-in-law George lagging lofts with rolls of fibreglass insulation on Saturday afternoons. It was an awful job – hot and itchy, and the dust got in your eyes – but it paid for our trips abroad. We also became Littlewoods pools collectors, so on Thursday evenings we would go around the local area collecting the customers' coupons and money and leave them next week's coupon. Then we would go to the main organiser, Mac Hatley, to hand in the coupons and takings. Again, not always fun in the winter, but we focused on the reward. Another life lesson here: if you do the things you have to do, when you have to do them, you will be able to do the things you want to do, when *you* want to do them.

With our savings, our sights were set on foreign lands. We went up to Petty France to obtain passports, got our foreign currencies and embarked on a European coach tour. We flew from Southend to Ostend where we stayed for a few days and visited the Atomium (which is a brilliant, remarkable structure, and I have been back since). The coach then took us into Austria and Switzerland, over the famous St Gotthard Pass. I remember the coach had to negotiate hairpin bends in a sort of three-point turn. Johnny and I always had the two backseats, so we were suspended out in mid-air over the drop whilst this manoeuvring was going on.

We had a wonderful week in Diano Marina, a whole new world to us. We made friends with the rest of the passengers, including two girls from Lichfield – but again the Durex went home unopened. We swam in the sea and in the pool, then moved along the coast to overnight in Nice where we visited the Casino; then onto Lyon, Montélimar, where we bought some nougat; finally Paris, up the Eiffel Tower (just like Blackpool, only bigger!), and saw the *Mona Lisa*, Arc de Tromphe, Notre-Dame, Montmartre, and then back to Ostend – *all* of this for £50 – yes, £50 – incredible, wasn't it?

As I look back I am reminded of how kind, generous and wonderful Austin and Rita, Rita and George, and Barb and Pete were to me, and the many reasons I will always be grateful. I spent a lot of my life with all of them in one way or another, especially Barb and Pete – they really were exceptional, considering they had three children of their own. I was more like a brother to the children, Dena, Kevin and Teresa, than an uncle. By this time Peter had a successful plumbing business.

The family in 1963 at Barbara and Peter's house

When I lived in digs I spent a lot of time at weekends with them, and they took me out with them to the coast and places of interest. Pete taught me to drive in his Mini Pickup. We went up to Wales to visit my dad, always stopping at places to eat and drink along the way. Pete even let me take my driving test in his brand-new pale blue Ford Corsair. It was an automatic because Barbara wouldn't drive with gears. (This was before the law changed – back then you could drive a car with gears, even if you had passed your test in an automatic, but that is no longer the case.) Barbara and I enjoyed a lot of the same music and I was able to play my records on their radiogram, which was also a beautiful piece of furniture. Barbara was a big Johnny Mathis and Nat King Cole fan (as I am now), and we both liked Dusty Springfield and I would take my Beatles albums to listen to.

I had such great fun with the three kids – I bought a Grundig reel-to-reel tape recorder from a chap at Evridge, and we all had a lot of fun with that, recording voices etc. I also owned a transistor radio which had a microphone input, so I bought a mic with a long lead and we could put it under a table and start talking to someone, without them knowing where the voices came from – giving them the shock of their lives! Perhaps hankering after show business, I would often practice being a DJ with these gadgets.

I often babysat for the children, and on one occasion I had a girl to take along with me. Sneakily I had previously left a note, on which I had written a message saying, "Sorry we've all had to go out." So we ended up alone, all the time Leslie not knowing that I had set it all up!

About this time, I was growing my hair long. One day I arrived at Barbara and Pete's to find a note on the door from Peter which said, "You're banned until you get your hair cut!" I used to secretly see the kids just up the road, with my long hair sticking out from under my flat cap – which we wore on scooters in those days.

Banned due to my long hair!

Meanwhile, at work I was learning new skills and working hard to become a professional toolmaker. At the factory there were duckboards, slatted wooden platforms to raise us off the floor so that we would not get cold, wet feet or become covered in grease from spilled coolant. Coolant is a white, almost milk-looking substance that fills the sump, and when cutting it sprays out of a tube onto the cutting tool to keep it lubricated and to stop it over-heating – otherwise the heat created from the friction of cutting into stainless steel became too much.

Work would give us a barrier cream to form a barrier over our hands to protect our hands from all the grease. It was pink and we took a big blob from a tub, and then we would finish the day washing all this stuff off with Swarfega.

A great film that depicts factory life is *Saturday Night and Sunday Morning*, a 1960s film starring Albert Finney. In the movie he works a lathe and washes his hands in the coolant. I copied his character, and he became something of a hero for me – he always wore an identity bracelet, and so I bought one and had it stamped with 'Ginger'. He also wore his watch the wrong way around, and to check the time he had to look at the inside of his wrist – so I did the same for years.

Other great 'kitchen sink' films that I enjoyed included *A Kind of Loving*, starring Alan Bates and June Ritchie (filmed near my home, in Osset), and *Live Now, Pay Later* with Ian Hendry. Ian played a 'tally man', going round door-to-door selling household items for a few bob a week. I remember a classic sales patter he had – he knocked on the door and a gruff woman answered, asking, "What do you want?" He replied, "Your chimney is on fire," so she rushed out, and as she checked the chimney he unrolled a carpet down the hall. When she came back and said there was no chimney fire, he answered, "This must be your lucky day – no chimney fire and you have a new hall carpet." This is what we in the business called a puppy-dog sale!

In addition, when cutting there would be swarf – all those cuttings removed from the lumps of metal can coil into springs etc, pretty dangerous when it flew in all directions, hot and sharp. When grinding something (rather than cutting) it sends off sparks, tiny little steel splinters, and I was forever getting them in my eyes. I would have to go to First Aid who might wash the splinters out in an eye bath, and these tiny splinters felt like a house brick stuck in my eye! On one occasion they didn't get a splinter out and it went rusty in my eye, so I had to have an operation to remove not only the splinter, but also the rust. Luckily this didn't impact my vision at all.

I took up football again, playing for the factory team on Saturday afternoons, and bought a pair of boots. On Friday lunchtime we played cards at the pub round the corner and the two games we played most often were 'Shoot' and 'Nap' – both wicked games which you could easily lose your money on!

At work we used to have to clock in and out with a card – punch it in when we arrived, and then move it from one rack into the other. If you were ever caught doing it for someone else, you'd be sacked on the spot. The factory had a brazing and welding department, so I could ask to use the tools to weld and modify the exhaust pipe on my scooter, replacing it with twin copper pipes, which sounded great. With my scooter I was sometimes sent out on errands from the factory down to Rochester and up to Isleworth, near Richmond, to deliver or pick something up. If it was near Richmond, I would go home, leave my scooter there, and travel up by train.

Along with hard work, as I learnt in my school days and indeed in the army, good time-keeping was an important element of success. I was working all the overtime I could and, along with the pools collecting and loft lagging, I could afford those trips abroad and the fabulous times we were having enjoying all the coffee bars and music venues. (Remember, if you do the things you have to do … etc.)

Another wonderful innovation at the time was pirate radio, playing all the latest hits, and I would sing along with the factory radio. I loved listening to my transistor radio whenever I could and would ride home late at night loudly singing the latest hits by artists such as John Leyton, Adam Faith, The Beatles, and The Dave Clark Five singing 'Glad All Over' – and I certainly was … feeling glad all over!

Johnny and I did all sorts of things in the 1960s. We went up to London to see a live showing in a theatre of the Indianapolis 500, and we saw Larry Grayson in his own show, long before he hit the big time. We had a favourite joke shop on Shaftsbury Avenue run by Alan Alan, a very prominent member of the Magic Circle. It was a tiny shop, packed with jokes and magic tricks. We bought all sorts – the disappearing cigarette trick was a beauty, and the imitation dog poo and imitation sick were also great! I don't think I ever used one, but stink bombs were another popular joke item.

I remember we used the sick when we got on the train at Charing Cross, heading back to Bexleyheath. We climbed into an empty carriage and put it on the seat opposite us. Several passengers went to join us until they suddenly saw the sick. I also put it in the sink at Barb's where Teresa saw it and complained about it to her mum, who thought Teresa had been sick and comforted her. The dog poo also worked on trains, buses, in the factory and, the best gag of all, behind the lavatory pan at Barb's. She was very house-proud, so you can imagine how she reacted when she saw this – a great gag!

The next coach trip that Johnny and I took included Rome, Sorrento and Florence. I always remember the heat that hit us when we got out of the aeroplane. Of course in Rome we were shown all the usual visitor sites, but it was often what we did on our own that created the strongest memories. Very late one night, along with another couple, we walked down to the Trevi Fountain. It was so atmospheric with just a few people there. Suddenly a large black limousine pulled up, a guy got out of the back, took his beautiful black suit jacket off and walked down to refresh his face in the fountain. It was like a scene from a movie.

We moved on to Sorrento, and while there we went on a guided trip to Pompeii. The same four of us walked down to Herculaneum, where we thoroughly enjoyed the lack of crowds and more intimate atmosphere. Another brilliant trip was the Amalfi Coast road, visiting Positano and the very beautiful Ravello. The chair lift on Capri was a stunning experience, and of course we were shown Gracie Fields' home. Then onto Florence for some culture, although unlike today I had no interest in art back then, so I didn't really appreciate what we were seeing. Nevertheless, the whole trip was superb, and all for £80 – outrageous, isn't it? No wonder we had to work overtime!

I am so sad that my dear friend Johnny isn't with us anymore. I would love to reminisce about these wonderful times with him and to thank him for all the fabulous photographs he took of those happy days, including his absolutely brilliantly creative and classic photos at Stonehenge. Johnny and I were nicknamed the 'Likely Lads'. Of course, we met people on these holidays and, as is the custom, addresses were exchanged and invitations given, "You must come and see us." Well, Johnny and I would come and see you! A wonderful example of this was a visit to a lovely couple, Jim and Shirley Rae, from Wallsend near Newcastle. What a fantastic weekend we had with their wonderful hospitality. In the evening we went to the Miners' Welfare Club, which was a revelation to us, packed with people and great entertainment and bingo. I remember Shirley liked me to sing 'Eleanor Rigby', a Beatles No 1 in 1966, which I did on the way home. They took us to Whitley Bay, which I have been back to many times (more of that later). We went to look at the shipyards, where a ship named the *Sir Winston Churchill* was almost ready for launching at the Swan Hunter yard, Wallsend. The highlight of the weekend was the Miners' Gala, which had everything from fancy dress competitions (with miners in prams dressed as babies) to whippet racing and everything in between. I tried to find Jim and Shirley on a recent holiday in Whitley Bay, without success, but I will try again on my next visit.

Lawrence Godley, another friend from the factory, made up a great threesome. He had an added benefit of owning a green Austin A35 van. We had some fun times together, especially as by this time we were visiting fewer coffee bars and more pubs where we would drink 'light and bitter' (more about that later). We also went greyhound racing at Walthamstow and Crayford, and Lawrence later took part in some stock car racing at Brands Hatch (I was to return to Brand's Hatch much later under very different circumstances).

Sunday evenings were spent at The Black Prince on the A1 at Bexley, which was a brilliant R&B venue. I actually stood at the bar next to Rod Stewart and Julie Driscoll who, along with Brian Auger and Long John Baldry, were all part of Steam Packet. Others we saw here included The Animals, The Yardbirds, Zoot Money with his Big Roll band, Alexis Korner, The Pretty Things (a local group) and many more great rhythm and blues bands.

My friend Brian lived in Swanley where there was another great music venue, and I can recall that one of the records playing there was 'Baby Love' by The Supremes, No 1 in 1964. Nearby, Crockenhill Village Hall was another venue to see local groups. All of this took place before the advent of mobile discos.

Georgie Fame and the Blue Flames played many of these south London venues, and his No 1 hit, 'Get Away', from 1966 was used in a Shell advert promoting an early frisbee called a 'getaway disc' which you got when you bought petrol – I still have mine!

We also saw groups like Screaming Lord Sutch, Brian Poole and the Tremeloes. A local group, Bern Elliott and the Fenmen, would play at local pubs, including The Jolly Fenman near Eltham. I recently bought their CD, *The Beat Years*, which demonstrates their Mersey Beat style – they enjoyed some chart success with 'Money' in 1963, and appeared at Dartford's Scala Ballroom, Crayford Town Hall and another of our favourite venues, The Railway Tavern in Dartford. As the name implies, this was right outside Dartford Station and made it a perfect venue to get to on the train from Bexleyheath. The record I remember from there is 'Yesterday Man' by Chris Andrews, No 3 in 1965.

I remember one return journey from Dartford vividly. The green Southern Trains had single compartments seating about 12 on bench seats, with running boards and large brass handles to help boarding. I had chatted up a girl and was taking her home, so we climbed into a compartment on our own – Johnny got in next door. The train set off and so the girl and I started snogging. We were travelling at about 50 mph when we heard a tapping at our window. Looking up, we saw Johnny outside the moving train! He had used the running boards and handles to get out of his compartment and move along to our window – quite incredible, and another one of the fantastic memories of this wonderful friend. I also remember that the girl scratched my back until it bled – now that was not 'heavy petting', as the Americans called it, but 'harsh petting'! I had to keep my shirt on in bed so I didn't get blood on the sheets, which would have taken some explaining to Mrs C.

Pirate radio was growing in popularity at the time, providing us with an endless stream of fabulous music. Many of our well-known DJs were making a name for themselves on ships which broadcast stations like Radio Caroline and Radio London. John Peel, Tony Blackburn, Johnnie Walker, Kenny Everett and Emperor Rosko were entertaining us with jingles, fun and great records. I tell you, this was a brilliant time to be alive!

In 1964, when I was 20, I developed an urge to travel and decided to work my way round the world. I started making my plans – the route was going to be very flexible with some planned destinations: down through Europe, taking in France, Italy, Greece and Turkey, then on to India. My sister Barbara was busy applying for visas for me, although she had a problem getting me into Burma, so the route was open to change. I knew for certain I wanted to get to Australia where the Snowy Mountains Scheme between Melbourne and Sydney, a huge project, offered employment. It was said if you didn't drink too much and didn't gamble you could quickly earn enough money for your ticket to America. I went up to London to the Centre for Tropical Diseases to receive my yellow fever inoculation. I advertised my beloved scooter in the *Exchange & Mart* and sold it to a man who had won the football pools and wanted it for his son. What a buy for them, but it broke my heart. This big adventure prompted Teresa to call me "My hero," something she still calls me to this day.

Then I fell in love ... and once again circumstances took over and everything changed.

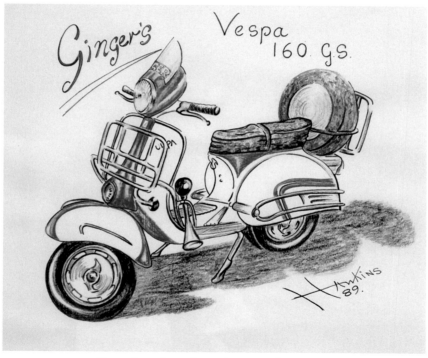

My pride and joy, drawn by my nephew, Kevin.
The first outing on my Vespa GS 160 was a 360-mile round trip to Wales to visit
my dad, the Evans family and all my friends. When I arrived my face was filthy
from all the traffic grime and I ached all over. It certainly was an arduous
adventure, but got my scooter run in nicely!

CHAPTER 5: UP NORTH

Following the unceremonial dumping by Julie, I had made contact with the other girl I liked from our Blackpool holiday, Jeanne from Yorkshire. We had been communicating by post and, following many letter exchanges, I had begun to fall in love with her – if that is possible by letter.

So Johnny and I accepted an invitation to stay for a weekend at Jeanne's home in Yorkshire. We took the coach from Victoria and Jeanne and her dad, Peter, met us at Leeds. They took us home to meet mum Pauline, and Jeanne's younger sister Anne, who all entertained us with Yorkshire hospitality, taking us out and about and feeding us very well. As traditional, the men went to the pub before lunch on Sunday, and when we came home to a roast dinner, I remember that we were served with an enormous piece of Yorkshire pudding. I thought to myself, "I am not going to get much else on this plate," and so I sat courteously waiting for the meat and veg to arrive … except I noticed that everyone else was applying gravy and tucking in. Johnny and I duly followed suit. We were to learn that this was the way it was done in days gone by, to fill you up and make up for the lack of what was, back then, expensive meat. The gravy was a tasty, thick onion mix. In the south we had been used to a small amount of Yorkshire pudding with the meal. In time I was to learn all sorts of customs and different ways in the north.

The record at the time which I sang all week in the factory was 'Friday on My Mind' (which of course is what I had) by The Easybeats, which was No 6 in the charts in October 1966.

This was the first of many visits to Yorkshire for me and the end of my round the-world plans, but at least I wouldn't catch yellow fever! Peter lent Jeanne and I his VW Beetle – they were massive VW fans and helped

71

run a local VW owners' club. If Johnny came up with me, Jeanne would fix him up with Kath, a good friend of hers, and the four of us visited Ilkley Moor and the famous Cow and Calf Rocks, as well as many other local places of interest.

On one occasion when I was going up to Yorkshire to see Jeanne, instead of spending money on the coach, I decided to hitchhike. (I still hitch regularly now – the bus drops me a mile from where I live and, when coming home from a night out drinking, I often thumb a lift and rarely fail to get one – most people who pick me up are women! Sometimes I stumble when I look round to see who's stopping. One night I was coming home, about halfway up the hill, when a car pulled up and offered me a lift; a man whose wife had passed me on the way home had sent him out to come and pick me up – there are some lovely people out there!)

So anyway, I took the tube to Barnet, next to the A1, and I started thumbing for a lift. I managed to get a ride to Doncaster and another to Wakefield, but I ended up arriving very late at night, so Jeanne's dad Peter came and picked me up in Wakefield. I spent a lot of the weekend worrying about getting back home, although I managed it successfully. However, I only did it the once.

Jeanne and I were very much in love and wanted to be together, although at the time she was only 17 and I was 22 – both of us were very young, which was to have consequences later. (I was young in the head and didn't have the maturity to pay a mortgage, to run a home etc …) At one stage her parents did threaten to make her wait until she was 21, and neither of us wanted that. There was no way her parents were going to let her move to London, so I made the decision to move to Yorkshire. There were no ties to keep me, and I didn't even think or worry about a job because I had confidence in myself – perhaps another life lesson. (I would have loved to have stayed in London with all the swinging sixties stuff going on, but Jeanne's parents were not happy with her coming down south, and I really don't blame them.)

I did, however, always have it in mind that this would be a temporary move and that when we got married, we would move back south. I think I made this clear, but I didn't want to be apart from her, I didn't want to do any more hitching, she wouldn't come down to me, and so I headed up north.

72

My engagement to Jeanne with
Lawrence, Dena, Barbara, Jeanne, Shelagh and Johnny

Lawrence (my great friend from the factory) helped move me to Yorkshire in his Austin A35 van. Off the three of us drove (Johnny, Lawrence and I) with all I owned, including *the* little brown suitcase. I didn't have a lot of stuff at the time (and in fact I carried on not having a lot of stuff until we got married and had a house with a spare room etc).

It was very hard and sad to say goodbye to the Cosgrove family, especially Mrs C who had cared for me so well – what a lovely woman she was – but I was to see her many times again.

I settled in Yorkshire with Peter, Pauline, Anne and of course Jeanne for a few months, and the two of us were blissfully happy. It squeezed the family home, but they didn't make me feel unwelcome, and they were probably happy that Jeanne had not left home (and possibly hoping that it might all blow over and she would come to her senses eventually). I remember that Jeanne and her sister Anne had a record player and I bought an LP by The Four Seasons, their *2nd Vault of Golden Hits*. They are still a favourite group of mine today.

I thought the move north offered me a good opportunity to look for a job outside the factory. I saw an advert in the *Yorkshire Evening Post* promising all sorts of wonderful things – it was very attractive and, although I can't remember the details, the ad promised the moon! I went for an interview in Leeds and along with several others was offered a job, so I started a week of unpaid training.

In fact, it was all unpaid – there was no money until you sold – and the job was selling volumes of the *Encyclopaedia Britannica* door-to-door. This idea of being paid on results was to stand me in good stead later in life – a life lesson to 'Learn and Earn'. This first week was spent learning the 'spiel' and the tricks of the trade from my sales manager, Paul Ferrari (what a great name – as a manager he had a car, but it was not a Ferrari).

We spent the mornings knocking on doors looking for young couples with children, when we would make an appointment to go back in evening when the husband was at home. In the afternoon we went bowling and ate some food. The aim of the evening call was to go back and sell the first edition of 26 volumes, showing a beautiful book and a free gift (which would be a lovely bound copy, complete with gold writing, of something by the Brontës, for example). The sales patter would focus on the benefits of the volumes to the children, and the cost might be as little as a shilling a day paid in instalments ('funny money', as we called it).

When I went in with Paul Ferrari, one young couple said that they could really do with a new washing machine. At this Paul stood up and said, "Mr Young, we're leaving … pack up Barry … if these people think more of a washing machine than their children's education …" Of course the young father told us to stop, we sat down, and we got the order (or rather, Paul Ferrari got the order and the commission, not me). At the end of the day all the new sales trainees met up at a local pub, where I said I was sorry but I couldn't work like that and left.

As a result it was off to the Job Centre, which was a whole new experience for me, as I'd never had to queue up with all these people out of work before, looking at the job boards. I managed to get some engineering interviews, including one for David Brown Tractors ('DB', as in Aston Martin) who had an enormous factory producing tractors – they were the UK's version of Massey Ferguson. My first job had been in a small rural building which had probably been a cow shed in a previous life, so I was used to a much smaller scale – DB was like an aircraft hangar, with huge noisy machines. It took two buses to get there from where I lived, so I scrubbed that idea!

Then I got a job milling at a small local firm in Ravensthorpe. As I was a tool and cutter grinder, this was not my speciality and I wasn't very good at it, and so I was not that happy. I don't think the bosses were that happy either, so I didn't stay long – two or three months at the most.

Peter told me about an engineering exhibition at the Queen's Hall in Leeds where exhibitors were hoping to find new customers. I went along and saw a stand that manufactured speciality cutting tools of all special shapes and sizes – tools that you couldn't buy off the shelf. I picked one up and was looking at it, when a guy asked if I wanted to buy some. I replied, "No, but, looking at these, you could do with a new tool and cutter grinder." He then said, "Why, are you a tool and cutter grinder?" I told him that I was, and that I was looking for a new job, so he introduced me to the foreman and he invited me along to the factory in Bradford on Saturday morning for an interview.

The two owners were Eric and Gordon Bowers, and George Pocock was the foreman. They asked me whether I had my indentures, so I explained that I hadn't completed the apprenticeship (as explained above). Instead I said, "I tell you what I do have." "What?" they asked, and I held out my hands. "I start Monday, and if by Friday you don't like what I've done, don't pay me and I'll leave." Eric said, "Give lad a job!" Another life lesson – put your money where your mouth is!

It was a very long commute for me to the factory in Thornbury, Bradford – I had to take three different buses, heading out at 5.30 am. for a 7.30 start, and then ending at 5.30 pm. (or 7.30 with overtime), so it meant for very long days. Fortunately, they were happy with my work and

I stayed at Bowers for two enjoyable, happy years. They were a nice family company, so work had a good atmosphere.

To avoid the long commute I decided to move to a bedsit in Oak Villas which, although it sounded grand, was actually a terrible place in the Manningham Lane district of Bradford. There was a large hole in the mattress and another one in the window, and because the room had a very frail Yale lock on the door, I was frightened of leaving anything in there. There were half a dozen rooms with a communal bathroom and kitchen – it was pretty grim, but the room was close to where I worked, and I only had to catch one bus to get to Bowers. Jeanne stayed with her mum and dad.

It was quite common for the men to come to the factory in their overalls with a jacket over them. The overalls were colour-coded, and I wore white for a toolmaker. I had my lunches with some of the lads at the greasy spoon café just up the road. We usually came back for a game of football in the yard outside the factory.

It was at this time that I bought Jeanne's uncle's VW Beetle – he was due to buy a new car, so I bought this one from him second-hand. It was like a tank in build and colour, an early 1960s model. The wings of the vehicle must have been an eighth-of-an-inch thick steel – it really was a brute – but it was reliable.

Having the car meant that I could move back to Mirfield where Jeanne lived with her parents. I must have looked in the local paper for people offering lodgings, and ended up with two choices, both in walking distance. One was with a bloke in his thirties who lived on his own and had an immaculate house – it was absolutely beautiful, and he said that he would do all the washing, ironing and cooking. The other one was with a West Indian couple who had three children – they were offering the same, but the thought of living with three kids put me off. So, I moved in with Leslie who worked at a local blanket manufacturers in Mirfield.

I had my car, job, fabulous digs and a lovely girlfriend. I had two enjoyable years there and made lots of friends. Paul Grieves lived just across the road from the factory. He was always late, even though he lived closest. Later Paul became a councillor, took an interest in the community and then became mayor of Skipton for a year and ran a successful alarm business.

Jeanne was still living with her parents in Mirfield studying shorthand and typing at Dewsbury College and went on a course for a week at Leeds University. When she came back, she told me about this chap who had been trying to force his attention on her. Apparently he came into her room one night and she couldn't get rid of him. I was very jealous and possessive, and Jeanne knew where this chap lived because he gave her his address. I asked Ian Wilson, who worked with me at Bowers, to come and help me sort this bloke out. So, we went to his house, where the chap's dad said that he was out playing rugby. We waited, and sure enough this big rugby player turned up with his equally large mate … so Ian and I drove off!

I joined the VW Owners' Club and we attended some great weekend events. They would organise games, such as a passenger in the car picking up sticks from the window, driving between two poles, driving in and reversing out. We also spent time with Jeanne's friends from Dewsbury where she was studying.

This was the 'flower power era', which Jeanne and I embraced. Jeanne had a fantastic pink crocheted mini-dress and I had plenty of colourful clothes, and we would wear flowers in our hair – although I'm not sure what the locals in the pubs thought, as I don't think they had seen much flower power. Scott McKenzie was No 1 in August 1967 with 'San Francisco (Be Sure to Wear Some Flowers in Your Hair)'.

Lawrence would come up to see us and Jeanne fixed him up with a friend, so the four of us went out in his A35 van. There was a fabulous pub out on moors at Midgley called The Black Bull with lovely large settees, and I can picture us all sat there singing along to 'Reach Out, I'll Be There' by The Four Tops – No 1 in 1966.

I went out with Peter and his mates on Sunday lunchtimes where I learnt to play dominoes and exchanged my drink of light and bitter for just bitter. In all the pubs and entertainment venues in the south, a favourite drink for men was light and bitter – the bitter in the south wasn't that brilliant, so the barman would pull a half of bitter and then pass a bottle of light ale to you. The light ale had sparkle and lightness to make the bitter more palatable. (The same thing happened with brown and mild – a bottle of brown ale brought some life to the mild ale.) However, when I moved to Yorkshire and asked for light and bitter, it was as if I came from Mars! So I learnt to drink Tetley bitter, which was so beautiful that you didn't need anything else. Tetley also made a mild and, as their bitter was quite strong, I sometimes had a pint of mixed, which tempered the bitter and made it less sharp. I remember on one occasion I went into a pub at lunchtime and asked for a pint of mixed. The barman said fine, but they only sold bitter – so he pulled half from two different pumps and asked, "Is that mixed enough for thee?"!

As for the dominoes, they had been more of a toy to me before, but here they would sit down at Sunday lunchtimes and play it seriously, matching numbers, as well as a game called 'Fives and Threes', a popular Yorkshire game with dominoes. We went to one pub out on the moors and Peter asked the landlord for a set of dominoes. He replied, "They are bricked up behind that chimney – I ain't having dominoes here, they always end up fighting!"

The Flower Pot pub had bells on the walls behind the seats to summon a waiter to order drinks, and some of the pubs even had men-only bars, which were popular back then. I also remember The Station at Drighlington, Travellers Rest, Upper Hopton, Top Withins and The Moorcock out on the Pennines, as well as many others in and around West Yorkshire. I really enjoyed these Sunday lunchtimes – it was a new thing for me.

Of course now that I was in Yorkshire I had to learn a new language, with all the different words and phrases they used and how they pronounced them. Instead of, "Something for nothing," it would be, "You don't get owt for nowt." A good example for a different use of a word is 'teacake'. I had always known it as a biscuit with a marshmallow inner, covered in chocolate – that's what I thought. But in Yorkshire, a teacake is like a hot-cross bun (and a long bun is similar, but long and thin). You could order either for breakfast, but I had to learn the difference, especially as I was used to the marshmallow variety! The other incredible thing was that you could buy a terraced house for £250!

A guy at Bowers shared with me a route for exploring the Yorkshire Dales, and of course I fell in love with the hills – they were so grand, majestic and beautiful. I still use that route to take visitors today, visiting places such as Ilkley, Bolton Abbey, Barden Tower, Burnsall, Grassington, Arncliffe, Malham, Malham Cove, Janet's Foss and the magnificent Gordale Scar. A phrase that is thrown around in Yorkshire is that there are more acres in Yorkshire than words in the Bible – which only goes to prove a Yorkshireman bothered to count 'em!

I wrote earlier about my teenage romance in Wales with Beryl Ford, and it was here at Bowers that the coincidence occurred. We had a Welsh tea lady, Gwen, and one day I asked her where in Wales she was from. "Pontnewynydd," she replied, and was amazed when I said I used to live there and went out with a girl called Beryl Ford. Then she amazed me by explaining that Beryl was her sister's daughter – Gwen, just like me, was 200 miles from home – what an incredible coincidence!

At about this time, people were starting to emigrate to Canada. They were looking for skilled toolmakers and Billy Philips, the Scouser, moved there along with other people from Bowers. The Canadians were offering great opportunities. However, I saw a job advertised at the Rheinmetall factory in Düsseldorf, Germany. I went to Manchester for an interview and was promptly offered the job, but I turned it down because the place sounded frightening – I was worried it was going to be a massive industrial set-up. Jeanne didn't much fancy it either, so we stayed where we were.

I'd lived with Leslie in Mirfield for quite a time, but at some stage Leslie moved to be closer to the blanket factory where he worked, so I had to find somewhere else to live. There was a chap at Bowers, Derek, who lived with his son, who said that I could lodge with him on the Holme Wood estate, a huge council estate. I was very happy there, and used to take Derek to work in my VW Beetle. Sadly, one morning I came out and my VW had been stolen. The police eventually found it in Wakefield, but the thieves had driven it so hard and damaged the engine. Paul Grieves (who worked in the factory with me) was a bit of a mechanic and he and his mate Alan had a part-time repair business. They stripped the car down, bought some new parts and got the VW going again.

Paul also had a Mini Cooper and would take me from Bradford to a café near Skipton called The Tomato Dip, a place for bikers as well as the general public – remember, there was no motorway in those days, so no service station, and everyone just stopped at cafés like this. Paul frightened me out of my wits in his Mini, flying round the bends on the way to the café.

George, Rita, Linda and Nicky came up to see us in 1968 and stayed in a local hotel. Jeanne and I took George and Linda to Batley Variety Club which had been opened in 1967 by James and Betty Corrigan. Quite amazingly, this small Yorkshire town became the Las Vegas of the north. We had front row seats to see a favourite singer of mine, Scott Walker, part of The Walker Brothers, who had No 1 hits in 1965 and 1966. They split up in 1967 and Scott was by then pursuing a solo career. He too had a No 1, this time in May 1968, with the beautiful record 'Joanna'. I still love his music and voice today. (Writing this has prompted me to buy Maureen Prest's book *King of Clubs* to learn the history of Batley Variety Club and remind me of the fabulous nights we had there.)

Our wedding was planned for 7th September 1968 at St Mary's Parish Church, Mirfield, with the reception at The Marmaville Hotel just down the road from church. We had bridesmaids and a page boy chosen and, of course, who else but my best friend would now become my best man – Johnny. We booked The Woodlands in Gildersome, not too far from the wedding venue, for my family and friends. Jeanne and I would also spend our honeymoon night there … and Jeanne had gone on the pill, so my Durex would not be required – it made them redundant, and probably out of date by now!

I mentioned earlier that I had always said when we got married we would then be moving to the south. I am not sure Peter, and particularly Pauline, were totally happy about the whole thing, especially as this meant their daughter would be moving 200 miles away down to London. Anyway, it was now time for me to move back down south and find us somewhere to live. Once again, circumstances determined that I moved back to Kent.

CHAPTER 6: MARRIAGE, MORTGAGE AND MUSIC

In May I came down to Kent to start house-hunting. Very sadly Barbara and Peter had separated whilst I was in Yorkshire – a sad event, given what they had meant to me. Barbara was living in an upper-floor maisonette in Slade Green, not far from Dartford, with Dena, Kevin and Teresa. It was a pleasant spot where all the houses surrounded a green. She kindly offered to let me stay with them while I looked for a place for Jeanne and me.

Three bedrooms accommodated the five of us – one for Barbara, Dena and Teresa shared a room, I slept on a camp bed in Kevin's room. I went back to having great fun with the kids who, as I mentioned before, were more like sisters and a brother than nieces and a nephew. Dena recounts a story about her mum telling me to put the light out. I duly obliged by taking her standard lamp outside and putting it in the middle of the green, much to the kids' amusement! Barbara later married again to David, a lovely kind man.

Normal service resumed with Johnny and Lawrence, and we continued our adventures. I do have a memory of one not-so-pleasant end to an evening out. I returned home very drunk, got into my sleeping-bag, fell asleep and, when I woke up, I was immediately sick inside the bag. I felt so ill, I just turned over and went back to sleep. Barbara quite rightly went mad. The kids didn't think much of it either. Despite her own situation, Barbara was still my big sister and was very kind to me. I wish I had told her how much I loved her.

When Barb and Pete had lived in Watling Street, they had a Refuge Assurance agent called Bryan. He and his wife Shelagh had become friends, and Barb was still in contact with Bryan. He and I met up and had a couple of conversations about mortgages, life insurance and a job for me. Bryan enjoyed the job and suggested that I would be suitable for the role, so after an introduction and the necessary interviews I became an agent for the Refuge Assurance Company. Thanks to the company's name, sometimes I would knock on a door and when I said that I worked for the Refuge, the owner would say, "The bin's round the back mate!"

I used a lovely old sit-up-and-beg bicycle to do my rounds, collecting weekly insurance premiums and selling new policies, such as endowments and life insurance etc. The *Encyclopaedia Britannica* experience came in useful here, especially, "It's only a shilling a week." I expect my earlier experiences starting at numerous schools and meeting new people all helped me with my confidence, communication and conversation skills – this really is the essence of getting on with people, getting them to like you and buy from you.

Now that I had a job, income and could get a mortgage with the company I worked for, I started house-hunting. Cycling round Bexleyheath for work helped me see properties for sale, and I eventually found a top-floor maisonette in Burr Close, a short walk from Bexleyheath Station. I thought this would be ideal for Jeanne, because we hoped that she would be working in London. (I cannot recall whether Jeanne viewed the flat and approved it, but the purchase went ahead nevertheless.)

As I mentioned, my friendship with Johnny took off where it had left. He was still working with Evridge Engineering and was now going out with Barbara, a secretary who worked in the company office. Johnny helped me, not only with the wedding plans, but also the new home. As for the wedding, Johnny helped me choose a new suit, and our other great friend, Lawrence, agreed that he would drive a hired mini-bus full of all my guests up to Yorkshire.

There was lots of nervous excitement as the wedding approached, with all the usual last-minute plans – not just for the wedding, but also the move into our new home. We had to buy furniture, carpets and all the usual items for a house. We bought a bed from the Co-op in Dartford (more about this bed later, as it moved round with us).

Johnny and I went up to Yorkshire a few days before the wedding, which was set for 7th September 1968. We had a wonderful wedding

Jeanne looked beautiful in her wedding dress

present from Johnny's parents – his dad would film the event on his Super 8 movie camera (more about this film later).

Jeanne looked beautiful in her wedding dress; I was so happy. My dad was there, with Barbara, Dena, Kevin and Teresa, who was a bridesmaid. Also present were: Rita, George, Linda and Nick; Lawrence and his mum; Johnny and his parents, as well as his brothers, Bob and Billy; Mac and Florrie; Bryan and Shelagh, plus many of Jeanne's friends and my friends from Bowers, including Ian and Julie Wilson and Henry and Cynthia O'Hare (both of these couples would play important parts in my life).

It was a wonderful reception. We had all the usual speeches, cake-cutting, dancing and drinking, and then headed off to our Woodlands Hotel room for a very apprehensive and nervous honeymoon first night. I am delighted and proud to say I was 23, Jeanne 19, and, despite all those intimate sessions I had in the sixties, as I have already mentioned, we were both virgins. (I think I had been so frightened of getting a girl pregnant and all the trouble that might have brought.)

We settled into married life at Burr Close and began to put our own mark on the home. It had a little garden and a shed where I kept my bike. A lovely lady called Elsie lived in the ground-floor maisonette, and she was very helpful and friendly. There were plenty of other nice neighbours, including a smashing young couple across the road with whom we became good friends. We had parking just outside the flat for my VW Beetle. Jeanne was offered a superb job in London as a shorthand typist working for Lord Thomson of Fleet, who owned *The Times* and *Yellow Pages*. Before she started, we went up to London so that she could familiarise herself with the journey.

Johnny was still working at Evridge Engieering and one day told me that the bosses would like to see me. They offered me a job at a second factory at Powder Mill Lane in Dartford. They knew me, I knew them, so the money offered was very good, with plenty of overtime into the bargain. So I left Refuge and went back to factory work, where it was great working with all my old mates again.

It was brilliant to be able to take Jeanne to all those wonderful places I used to go to. Johnny and/or Lawrence would often come along, and this became another of those wonderful periods of my life. We often went to a local pub a short walk away on Long Lane called The Yacht, where we played 'Bat and Trap', a traditional bat-and-ball pub game from Kent.

Often we would head to Greenwich where there were two fabulous pubs on the side of the Thames, The Yacht and The Trafalgar. Jeanne loved going up to Carnaby Street and Petticoat Lane, and I enjoyed showing her all the London sights such as Hampton Court and Hyde Park. Several times we watched The Hollis Brothers performing their sand-dance in Leicester Square (they were buskers who put sand down on the road and performed an Egyptian-type dance). We liked to go dancing at local venues like The Bali Hai nightclub, next to Streatham Ice Rink, dancing to records like Marvin Gaye's 'I Heard It through the Grapevine' (No 1 in April 1969).

Lawrence will tell you that when he used to pick us up to go out, they often had to wait while I finished ironing Jeanne's hair. I loved her long straight hair and she would lay her head on the ironing board so I could flatten it. Lawrence was by now going out with Eileen, a lovely girl from Otford, and the four of us had some great times together.

The Top Rank Suite at Croydon was another fabulous venue, and we went here with Linda and Chris. Linda knew the singer and, apparently, one moment I had disappeared and the next thing they knew, I was on stage with her!

There was always something going on. In 1968 Jeanne, Johnny and I went up to London to see the CND 'Ban the Bomb' marches and demonstrations, including one that ended at the American Embassy in Grosvenor Square.

We were still in touch with Mac Hatley, whom we had worked with at Evridge. He now worked for SASCO, an engineering company on Princes Road in Dartford. They made precision moulds for the plastic injection moulding industry. Some of the moulds could take two skilled toolmakers months to make. He told me it was a better hourly rate and a great company, so I joined them. Once again, it was a bit like the company in Ravensthorpe in Yorkshire, and I was a little out of my comfort zone. Mac and the other men were very supportive and helpful, so I soon grew into this new area of expertise. I was involved with the mould used to manufacture the Gillette G2 handle, as well as another mould to make syringes. This is where I was introduced to CNC machines and spark erosion technology.

My Beetle was going strong, so I decided to paint it orange. Much preparation went into ensuring an excellent finish. Lawrence and Johnny helped me remove bumpers etc. My brother Austin, who was still working at T&B Building Supplies, although now at their Mayplace Road, Bexleyheath site, recommended Valspar paint. Undercoats were applied and then the beautiful orange. The second and final coat was applied on a Sunday morning. It looked fabulous, but then disaster late in the afternoon … it rained and pitted all the paint. So now it really did look like an orange, but we all liked it, and so we kept it that way. The paint job was admired wherever we went. In fact, Jeanne and I, along with Peter and Pauline and hundreds of other VW devotees, attended a large VW rally up in the Midlands. The top dogs from Volkswagen were there and a few years later VW launched their own orange Beetle!

In 1970, my love of music, combined with my frustrated desire to be in entertainment, resulted in me buying a mobile disco – which was quite a new innovation back then. I bought it from a guy called Terry McDermot, and it had twin Garrard record decks, a linear amplifier, two Vox speakers and two huge lighting cabinets.

To go into business as a mobile disco I had to sell my orange Beetle and buy a vehicle suitable for transporting all the gear. So I purchased a brand-new green Bedford Viva van. As for the records, I had a few 45s but I had to go out and buy all the latest hits. Once I had everything in place, I started touting for business in local pubs. Most of them were very happy to stay with the live music, but I managed to persuade the landlord at The Lord Kitchener in Wrotham Road to let me do a spot in the interval on Saturday night. We agreed a fee of £4, only to be paid if I was any good.

With my neighbour acting as my roadie, we arrived early on Saturday evening to set up behind the band, ready to move into position at the interval. I will remember forever the first record I played, 'Down the Dustpipe' by Status Quo … although I should say, tried to play. The audience were soon on their feet and enjoying dancing, as sometimes live bands aren't always that great for dancing to. Then halfway through, the disc stuck, the dancing stopped and everyone looked at me, including Jeanne and my friends.

Fortunately, I had another record cued up on the second turntable. I apologised for the problem and introduced the next record, meanwhile trying to discover what was wrong on turntable one. I wasn't short of advice from members of the audience – one guy suggested putting two or three two-shilling pieces on top of the needle. I still have that record with the first half of it very worn. With the dancers back on the floor, the unthinkable happened – the second record stuck! Surrounded by people trying to help, fed-up dancers and some unfriendly comments, I decided to call it a night and apologise to the audience and the landlord. We had to wait until the band finished and left before I could remove my gear. My first booking was certainly memorable!

On Sunday morning I investigated the problem with the turntables and identified the issue. The turntable arm had a restricted movement – it had a free area of movement from the arm rest to the centre of the record, but the restriction stopped the arm from flying about and going any further than the centre and damaging the stylus. In transit to the pub, that area of free movement had moved and was restricting the arm going any further than halfway across the record. The remedy was to lift and move the arm manually against this restriction, until the needle was over the centre of the disc. Memorable Maxim – "Check your equipment."

I went back to see the landlord on Monday evening and told him that I had rectified the problem – would he give me another chance, for no money, to make up for last week's trouble? He agreed, the next Saturday went without a hitch and I got a regular booking. At last, I was in the entertainment business.

Meanwhile, in my day job at SASCO, ever the entertainer, I organised a work's coachtrip to the coast. I canvassed interest and bookings and booked the coach but, as the date approached and money was to be paid, people started backing out and leaving me with a half-empty coach. The trip was no longer financially viable and so I had to cancel it.

On Jeanne's 21st birthday we organised a party at our maisonette. Her mum and dad, plus several other Yorkshire friends, came down. Also packed into our small home were our neighbours, including Elsie, my

The mobile disco

landlady Mrs C and of course Johnny, Lawrence, Mac and Florrie. I set my disco up in our bedroom – I have no idea what we did with all the furniture, but it was a fabulous evening. A strong memory of this time, probably because of the distinctive smell, is the paraffin heaters we used for heating our home. We would put one in the middle of the lounge and refer to it as our central heating!

During our time at Burr Close, Jeanne and I had been up to Yorkshire on several occasions, staying either with her mum and dad or friends of ours. I began to fall in love with Yorkshire and the people. I don't want to generalise, but I do think they are friendlier in the north. I continued to enjoy Sunday lunchtimes with Peter and his friends, and the VW club and other activities there all helped.

The disappointment of the cancelled coach trip made up my mind. We would go back to Yorkshire. Jeanne was pleased, and of course her mum and dad were delighted.

So we now spent time travelling to Yorkshire house-hunting. On one such day in 1969, I remember that the Emley Moor mast had fallen down

– this was a massive TV mast, built from nine-foot diameter tubes, held up with wires which had all frozen during winter. In the end the weight of the frozen wires pulled the mast down. It is now an important telecommunications station, a concrete structure which can be seen for miles around.

Burr Close was put on the market and quickly sold. Lawrence once again hired a big van and with his and Johnny's help we were off to Yorkshire. The England World Cup Squad were No 1 in the charts with 'Back Home' and Free were at No 2 with 'All Right Now'. Jeanne and I felt like it was back home and hoped our future would be all right now.

A Christmas booking at the golf club

CHAPTER 7: THE BUTTERFLY HOUSE

We had asked the estate agent Dysons in Cleckheaton for a house with a view and were given two to choose from. We sold the maisonette for £4,200 and bought 16 Moorfield Avenue for £3,600. Jack Amner (my sister-in-law Rita's dad, with whom I'd had the days out in London) did the conveyancing for us and, although he warned us about a new motorway (the M62) that would be built just half a mile away, and that the open fields at the rear (*the* view) had been open-cast mining and could not be built on for at least 25 years – which at our age of life sounded like a very long time – that didn't put us off! I wasn't worried about the motorway, as the wind usually comes from the

The *view, 1991*

west, over the Pennines, and as the M62 is half a mile to the east, we only hear it when the wind comes from the east. Hartshead Moor services and exits are very close, which was great when I was doing a lot of travelling. Since then the view at the back of the house has been sold by the farmer to another for growing wheat, with the assurance that no houses will be built there. It is also greenbelt land.

The house was one of a small close of eight pairs of semi-detached homes built in 1963 to a very modern design, for which the architect won an award. Semi-detached with a flat roof sloping into a central gutter, the pair looked like a butterfly, so this was how the houses came to be known locally – 'The Butterfly Houses'. They were good-sized houses, and we bought a second-hand upright piano, painted it white (it was the thing to do at the time!) and placed it in the hall, which gives some idea of the size of the house.

We had lovely neighbours in Ken and Renee Bedford – Ken became invaluable with help and advice on gardening, DIY and particularly the use of his ladder!

The view meant that we hadn't looked very hard at the condition of house and we soon began to realise that lots of sanding down and repainting were required, as well as in some cases replacing rotten woodwork on window frames etc. The top half of the house was clad in red cedar board, which had not been well looked after, so this became a mammoth job to maintain. Firstly we had to sand all the cladding boards down, including the gaps between, and then paint them with red Cuprinol preservative – it was a nightmare job, but the view was brilliant!

Next it was on to the white window frames, with lots more sanding down and undercoating and then, on the advice of father-in-law Peter, a top coat of white lead paint (which was banned some years later because of the dangerous lead content). A few years later I had to replace the old roofing felt, a very expensive experience, but we replaced it with some new modern long-lasting product – or, so I was led to believe, 'guaranteed' – but then that also had to be replaced. The original builder had gone bust by that time, so I had to pay for another new roof … but the view was great!

Moorfield Avenue then and now

A small front and rear lawn were easy to maintain, and on Ken's advice I bought a Qualcast hand-push lawnmower. It was great to have a garage with the house, especially for my mobile disco gear.

Jeanne and I soon settled with lots of help from Peter and Pauline – so now it was time to look for a job. George Pocock, the foreman at Bowers where I had worked, had moved on to a newly set up company, Bradford Tool & Gauge. They were manufacturing special-purpose cutting tools for the automotive industry, such as drill reamers, subland drills and custom-made cutting tools. It had been set up by three partners – two brothers, Bill and John McGraff, and Bill King. John and Bill were both salesmen who had worked for rival leading companies in the cutting-tool industry, Osborne Tools and Clarkson Cutting Tools. Bill was an entrepreneur with various other business interests, including being a director at Bradford City Football Club.

George heard that I was back in Yorkshire and contacted me via a friend. I went to see them and was quickly taken on as a tool and cutter grinder at their location on Lower Ernest Street in Bradford. I enjoyed being back with many old friends that had also joined BT&G, along with many new ones, including old Albert, who would take his set of false teeth out and put them in the pocket of his overall. A great saying in Yorkshire is, "There's nought as queer as folk." It was very obvious that, with the industry contacts that John McGraff and Bill King had, and the determined business skills of Bill McGraff, that this company would be going places. The three directors and I would regularly go for a couple of pints after work, usually at The Yarn Spinners, a Webster's pub on the bottom of Manchester Road, during which we formed a great friendship.

Meanwhile, I had decided to try to make more of my mobile disco career, so I had some leaflets printed. I called it the 'Barry Young Disc Show' (my first attempt at marketing), and I took them round all the working men's clubs (which were very big in the north, providing members with snooker tables, dart boards, entertainment and bingo). Although it was never in my mind that this would become a full-time business, I guess I had this frustrated entertainer part of me, and Jeanne was always very supportive.

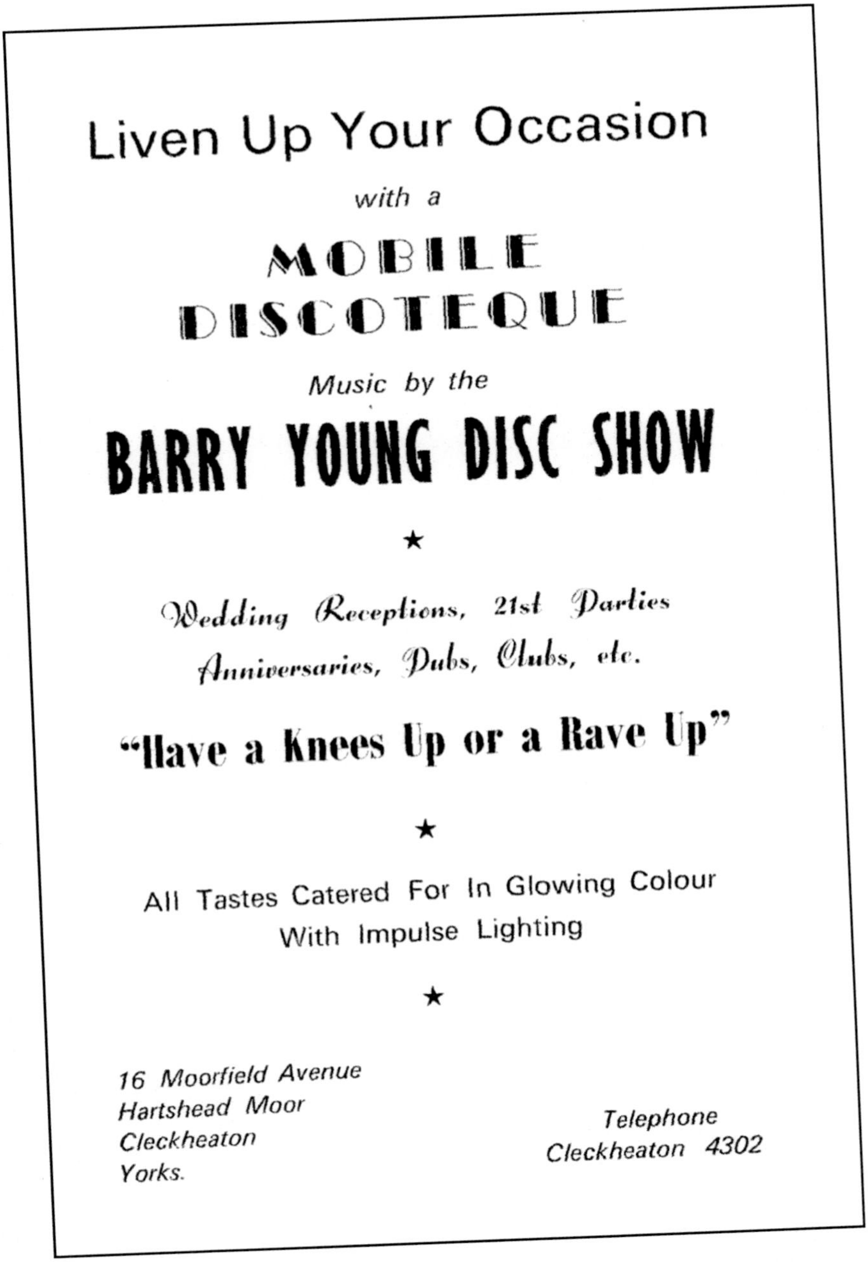

Liven Up Your Occasion

with a

MOBILE DISCOTEQUE

Music by the

BARRY YOUNG DISC SHOW

★

*Wedding Receptions, 21st Parties
Anniversaries, Pubs, Clubs, etc.*

"Have a Knees Up or a Rave Up"

★

All Tastes Catered For In Glowing Colour
With Impulse Lighting

★

*16 Moorfield Avenue
Hartshead Moor
Cleckheaton
Yorks.*

*Telephone
Cleckheaton 4302*

The leaflets — note no STD codes back then!

I secured a booking at a local club. My disco and I were not what they anticipated – they were expecting a show band playing the latest disco hits! That evening was a learning lesson for them and me, which taught me a great Memorable Maxim – "Know your audience, what they want, and that they understand what you are selling." I did my best between the bingo and the pie and peas, and some younger people did dance, but the men just carried on playing snooker and darts.

I also decided to acquire a theatrical agent to get me bookings. The Arena Agency was run by Barry McManus, from whom I was to get some good and interesting bookings. I invested in a new 100-watt Marshall amplifier from Shaffers Music Store, as well as a new 100-watt Fane bass speaker that had been manufactured in Batley. Peter helped me build a cabinet for the bass speaker which supplemented the other two, which meant I could now play larger venues. Peter also made me a fabulous wooden box to hold my 100-odd single records.

Private parties were great bookings to get, more friendly and intimate, but of course I had to cater for a wider cross section of ages with broader music tastes. I had to provide music for ballroom dancing, including the waltz, quickstep, foxtrot, cha-cha etc. I was still using 'Twango' as my signature tune and ending the evening with 'Na Na Hey Hey Kiss Him Goodbye' by Steam, a Top 10 hit in 1970.

I started to acquire more LPs – dance bands, like Ray McVay and His Orchestra, old-fashioned party dances with Sydney Thompson ('Lambeth Walk', 'Knees Up Mother Brown', 'The Hokey Cokey' etc) and *The Best of the Old Tyme Dancing* with Sidney Bowman and His Olde Tyme Dance Orchestra. A great LP for parties was *Time Gentleman Please* with all the old favourites to sing along to, such as 'Don't Dilly Dally' and 'Down At the Old Bull and Bush'.

A big favourite with audiences at Christmas time (and I think still one of the best Christmas LPs) was Phil Spector's *Christmas Album* with all those great artists like The Ronettes, The Crystals, Darlene Love and Bob B Soxx and The Blue Jeans, all singing those fabulous Christmas tracks.

I also ensured I had appropriate music for a variety of audiences and occasions, with LPs from K-tel and Ronco, the precursors to the *Now That's What I Call Music* brand. Easy-listening LPs were invaluable at parties –

artists like James Last, Perry Como, Nat King Cole, Dionne Warwick, Percy Faith, Ray Conniff, Manuel and His Music of the Mountains, Glenn Miller and Andy Williams – these were all the kind of music to play when food was being served, or for smooching at the end of a mixed-age group party.

All this sort of music was to be useful for another regular booking I had. John McGraff, Director at BT&G, was a member at West Bowling Golf Club, Bradford. He arranged an initial booking for me on a Saturday night, which went so well it became a monthly event. The big hit I played a lot here was Clodagh Rodgers' 'Jack in the Box', which she sang at the Eurovision Song Contest.

Barry McManus got me a lot of work in many other pubs and clubs in the area, and I am reminded of many of the venues Barry sent me to by records I played such as: Three Dog Night's 'Mama Told Me Not to Come' at a pub in Dewsbury; Dave Edmunds with 'I Hear You Knocking' at a club in Cleckheaton and 'My Sweet Lord' by George Harrison at The Shaftesbury on York Road, Leeds.

Luckily Billy Philips, my friend from work who had returned from Canada, was helping me in those days, because some of these places could be bit rough at times, although they certainly enjoyed the many times I played 'My Sweet Lord' (No 1 in January 1971). I remember being threatened at a youth club because I wouldn't play 'Tell Laura I Love Her' by Ricky Valance (a No 1 back in 1960). At the time all the kids were up dancing to hits of the 1970s, like 'Spirit in the Sky' by Norman Greenbaum and 'In the Summertime' by Mungo Jerry, and I didn't want to interrupt them with a slow, sad ballad. However, I did play the tune later, after the guy told me what would happen if I didn't!

There were two very memorable bookings from Barry. The first was at an American airbase near Harrogate. I was in the bar lounge, which was just like those fabulous chrome and glitz places from the movies, with beautiful leather bar stools along the length of a stunning bar. I only had to play for 30 minutes and then break for another 30, so I had a brilliant evening sitting at the bar, chatting to the service men and women between my spots, just like being in the States.

The second great booking was at a millionaire's daughter's 21st birthday party. It was at a huge mansion over near Ripley, with a massive marquee in the garden. They had hired a steel band, with which I alternated, and when the steel band packed up at midnight the host offered me some extra money to play on. Poor Jeanne had to go to sleep behind the equipment as I played on until 4.00 am on the Sunday morning.

Another memorable booking was arranged by Julie Wilson, the wife of my friend Ian from BT&G. She worked for the Provincial Building Society and in 1970 they opened a large new building in the centre of Bradford. Julie secured me a booking at their opening night. However, it turned into something of a horror story. The location I was to play in was on the top floor, but the lift wasn't working. Very fortunately my roadie, Billy Philips, was with me. This building was maybe 15 storeys high, and we had: three loudspeakers, twin record decks, a 100-watt Marshall amp, a box of singles, a case of LPs, a case of cables and leads etc and two huge lighting cabinets. These had to be carried up to and down from the top floor! Those disco lighting cabinets always took a lot of lugging about, but they did add to my presentation and create an excellent atmosphere as they pulsed to the music.

Jeanne and I had a fabulous night out with Barry. He had booked Tony Blackburn for an evening of personal appearances in the Yorkshire area and invited us along. It was a terrific experience for me, as I remembered his broadcasts from the pirate stations Radio Caroline and London in the sixties, as well as listening back in 1967 on the morning he launched Radio 1 with 'Flowers in the Rain' by The Move. It was a memorable night … I wonder if he remembers me?

Meanwhile Jeanne worked as a temp in a secretarial capacity and then started her own temping agency in Cleckheaton. Peter helped us decorate the offices and it was exciting when she opened. I don't think temps were as big in the north as in London, but she made a great success of it.

By now Batley Variety Club was in full swing. Special-priced tickets were available at work, which meant we could see a top-line four-hour show, featuring big-name artists, for five shillings. With chicken and chips in the basket for next to nothing, it made for a brilliant night out, and we saw some wonderful acts, including The Bachelors, Mike Yarwood, the hypnotist Martin St James, Joe Brown, Gene Pitney, Neil Sedaka, The Grumbleweeds, Charlie Williams, Roy Orbison and many more. We often went with Bill King and his wife (which was great because, if there was a queue, Bill would go down to the front, put a fiver in the doorman's hand, and the four of us would be ushered in and to a table down at the front of the auditorium). Great days! We were spoilt for choice with entertainment venues: Wakefield Theatre Club, Carlinghow Working Men's Club and the Fiesta Club in Sheffield.

I was still enjoying my Sunday lunchtimes with Peter and his mates. I remember going to a fabulous nightclub in Brighouse called The Ritz, which apparently had the largest sprung dance floor in Europe. I think we saw PJ Proby one Sunday lunchtime, and we certainly saw John Paul Joans because I have his record, which I love, 'The Man from Nazareth', which I think is a great record (in fact I am playing it now as I type – fantastic voice).

Jeanne and I made friends with many of the VW Club members and, although we didn't have the Beetle anymore, we were still going to club events. In 1970 the national VW Owners' Club were having their annual rally at Billing Aquadrome near Northampton. Peter and Pauline were still members and booked me into the event, where I did the Saturday night disco in a marquee. It was a great weekend, and the memorable records that night were Deep Purple's 'Black Night' (No 2 in the charts in August 1970) and 'Band of Gold' by Freda Payne (No 1 a month later).

One of the club members was Mike Ware, who owned a very special VW, a Karmann Ghia, which was a lovely car and the envy of many club members. Mike had worked at Leeds Bradford Airport before moving to the airport on Jersey, where he also took on a B&B business. Jeanne and I went to stay for couple of weeks, hired a car and had a wonderful time on this gorgeous island.

Our visit was made even better by a trip to Sark in a small speedboat owned by one of Mike's friends. We set off on Saturday morning, moored up in the small harbour and walked up to the lovely Stocks Hotel for lunch. We had a look round part of the traffic-free island and then back to the hotel later in the afternoon for a couple of drinks before setting off back to Jersey. Unfortunately (and unnoticed) fog had enveloped the island and there was no way we could go back in such conditions. We had a nice meal and then drank our way through the night. The lounge became a refuge and sleeping location for other stranded sailors. I well remember there were five of us and each round of drinks cost just £1 (plus an extra 2 shillings if you bought a pack of cigarettes – I still smoked in those days). It was the most fabulous experience that I shall always remember. In the morning, the fog had lifted and we were able to sail back on a beautiful calm, sun-kissed sea. What a weekend.

Mike Ware was a Leeds United fan, so I went along with him and his friends to some home games. We also went down to Villa Park for an FA Cup semi-final against Manchester United, but I have a painful memory of this day. At half-time I went to the gents and, as I zipped my trousers up, I trapped my foreskin in the zip. I expect some male readers may have tears in their eyes right now thinking about it – I certainly did at the time. There was blood everywhere as I tried to extricate the end of my penis from my trouser zip without drawing attention to myself. After managing this delicate operation and wrapping my wounded willy in my handkerchief, I returned to my seat to be quizzed about where I had been. They, without success, tried not to laugh at my distressing misadventure.

I particularly liked Allan Clarke (nicknamed Sniffer), who was a similar player to Jimmy Greaves. Both played a bit like me – I was an inside forward, I didn't want to do a lot of work and would hang around in the box, but if you gave me or them the ball we would put it in the net. Leeds enjoyed great success under Don Revie and were marvellous to watch. One of their players, Paul Reaney, was to become a friend later in life.

You may remember that back in the sixties I played quite a bit of snooker with Johnny, above Burtons the tailors in Bexleyheath. After marrying Jeanne I lost interest as I had much more interesting things to do with my time. I even sold one of my cues, although I kept the aluminium one. I was out in the front garden one evening when Charlie Wild, a neighbour opposite, walked by with a snooker cue. I asked him where he was going to play – Hartshead Moor Working Men's Club just round the corner.

I should say at this stage that after four years our marriage wasn't going well. I realise now we were both too young and I in particular was very immature. I lacked understanding of what a partnership should be. I think maybe, because this was the first time in my life that I had control over my own situation, I had become very selfish and self-centred, thinking only of myself. I didn't help things when I bought Jeanne a Kenwood Chef for Christmas – or was it our wedding anniversary? Both as bad.

The state of our marriage deteriorated when I asked Charlie Wild how I could get into the club to play snooker. He told me, in a broad Yorkshire accent, that I would have to be proposed, seconded and then go before the committee. I did all of this, paid my subscription and I so became a member of Hartshead Moor Working Men's Club.

Charlie took me round on my first visit to play. Above the bar was an interesting trophy, a snooker player holding a cue on a lovely wooden base. I was curious and was told that it was the Christmas Knockout Trophy. This cocky cockney upset a few there that night by declaring that I would win it that year. By then it was July and I was informed that last year's winner had his eye on winning it for second year in a row. I started immediately on my quest. So after my evening meal I would go round to the club to practise, just for couple of hours, but every night … then I started going on Saturday and Sunday lunchtimes for a couple of hours … all of this time leaving Jeanne to her own devices.

I came home from work one day to find the *Yellow Pages* open at the Marriage Guidance Council office in Bradford. Jeanne and I went a couple of times, and the counsellor agreed with me – that I was a selfish, inconsiderate, uncaring individual and that marriage should be a give-and-take relationship. Jeanne's friends told her she should be tougher with me. She never suggested perhaps playing badminton or something similar together, but whether that would have changed the situation or my attitude, I don't know.

In December I came home from the club one evening to find Jeanne had gone. Peter and Pauline had taken Jeanne away to their home. I went there pleading, but they said she did not want to see me. I arranged to meet Peter in a pub near where he worked in Mytholmroyd, but it was no use, she wasn't coming back.

A few weeks later I received an even bigger shock – a letter from a solicitor advising me of divorce proceedings. I was in a terrible mess, alone in Yorkshire, and I didn't know what to do. I certainly looked very hard at myself in the mirror, and I was not pleased with what I saw. But it was too late.

Leonard Birch Snooker Trophy

The good news – I did win the 'Leonard Birch Snooker Trophy' ... but I lost a wife.

I didn't contest the divorce, although I did go to the court to listen. It was not a pleasant experience to hear all the evidence against me read out loud. The finances were agreed and settled. I was in a mess mentally and, as during our marriage Jeanne had handled all the domestic and household affairs, I didn't know how to use the washing machine, how to cook or even where the vacuum was. "No wonder she left you," you might say, and of course you're right. Although that is how it would have been at home for her when she was growing up and she would have been used to this way of things, her friends told her she was too soft with me. I really needed to be told that I was not a very nice person and only thought of myself. The divorce certainly did that.

I met Jeanne a year or so later, and of course said how sorry I was. She said I would probably make someone a good husband next time. I wondered if there would be a next time. This was not to be the last contact with Jeanne (that would happen some ten years later).

I had a difficult period recovering from this experience. I sold my mobile disco as I had lost my enthusiasm for it. The consequences of all this turmoil meant circumstances would again play a part in the next chapter of my life.

Chapter 8: Moving On

Remembering and writing the end of the last chapter was difficult and demanding. Prior to Jeanne leaving, we had booked a long weekend trip to Istanbul – one of these things you see in the papers, a special all-in deal. To avoid wasting the cost of the trip, I asked another good friend at BT&G, Ray Speight, if he wanted to go with me. I think it only cost £29 each! We stayed at one of the top hotels, the Pera Palace, which was so smart it even had one of those lifts with metal gates and an inner door. We sailed on the Bosphorus, the border between Asia and Europe, and at the time they were just constructing the suspension bridge to join the two. We also visited the Blue Mosque, Topkapi Palace and the Grand Bazaar.

I was still suffering from the marriage break-up and didn't feel like going out at night, but Ray did visit a belly-dancing venue and enjoyed himself. I remember sitting at the hotel bar and drinking 18 bottles of Pepsi. When he came back, I was as high as a kite from all that caffeine.

I had also planned a trip to the USA, so again I asked Ray if he wanted to join me. At that time the AA were one of the first companies to offer cheap flights to the States, and a return from Heathrow to New York was only £80. I had arranged all of this, including Greyhound bus tickets that were £40 each for three weeks' unlimited travel all across the states. So the total cost was £120. When Ray and I got to New York we boarded the Greyhound bus and got off 55 hours later at Flagstaff, Arizona (although thankfully we were not on the coach for 55 hours in total, as we spent time in St Louis and Oklahoma City on the way!).

At Flagstaff we were to get a connection to go up to the Grand Canyon. We had arrived at 4.00 am but the first bus was at 8.00 am, so we filled in that time with a bottomless coffee cup, playing pool with the locals, and then caught the bus (we had a small case each and left them in a left-luggage locker for the day). Then we spent the day at the Grand Canyon, came back and continued our journey on the Greyhound bus down over the Hoover Dam, through Reno, then all the way down to San Diego on the border with Mexico. We walked over the border into Tijuana in Mexico and spent the day there. The roads were just dirt, but it was an exciting and interesting place, that's for sure!

We also went to Las Vegas on the way down to San Diego, arriving at about 2.00 am. We found a motel, checked in, and then went out. In 1972 there were very few hotels on the Strip. We visited Caesars Palace, which was the main place back then in its early days, and we got chatting to a guy who worked there as a pool attendant – he said if we wanted a swim, to see him and he would get us in free. So the next day we were sat around the pool in Caesars Palace, but it was so hot it burnt your feet just to get from the chair to the pool! We stayed there for about three days, taking a proper tourist trip to the Hoover Dam. In Vegas we liked the Circus Circus hotel, where you could walk in and everyone was so busy feeding these gaming machines that no one took any notice of people performing trapeze all day long in the big top – instead everyone was glued to the slot machines!

We met a young couple whom we got on well with. If you did play the slot machines, you could ask for a free drink, so we did. In the morning you could even get a free breakfast. I only did slot machines; I looked at and watched the tables of roulette and blackjack, which were pretty impressive, but I didn't gamble there. We also visited the Sands Hotel, among others.

In Tijuana we had met a teacher, Mike, from Michigan who had bought a leather cowboy hat. Chatting to him, we told him that we were off to LA and then San Francisco, so he said, "Let me share an idea with you. I'm going to San Francisco in my car and I'm happy to take you with me up the Pacific Highway, through Santa Barbara and Monterey." He told us he was staying in Anaheim for two nights, which would give us a day to visit Disneyland. We even managed to see a baseball game on the first night. 8.30 am saw us going into Disneyland, and when we came out at 8.30pm we still hadn't done everything!

So we took up his offer and got in the car with him; Ray in the back and me up front, driving up the Pacific Highway, past all these beautiful places. Then Mike said, "I tell you what will make it more beautiful ... get that pouch and pipe out Ray, fill it with the grassy stuff and hard brown stuff and then set light to it." It was a Tuesday afternoon, about 100 yards in front was a black and white police patrol car, and we were just passing it round. I just started laughing – my first and last hash-smoking experience!

When we got up to San Francisco he hid one of us in the trunk. "I'll book a motel with one double room to save some money," he said. In the room I remember we could put a dollar in a machine and the bed vibrated! "Right, we're going out now," he said, "get the pipe out again Ray." So we went out, but after one bottle of beer I was gone! We had a great night with this guy before he left us to catch our bus. We had a few days in San Francisco, when *Deep Throat* was showing at the cinema and couples were queuing up to see it, so we went too. We visited a bar afterwards and played poker dice where we met some great locals and had a fantastic evening. We visited Fisherman's Wharf, went up and down the hills on the tram, down the steepest street with the famous hairpin bends and halfway across the Golden Gate Bridge. We went to a strip club where they advertised co-eds in large neon signs: young girls who had just graduated. We didn't go to Alcatraz but saw it from the Golden Gate Bridge.

After San Francisco we went east, through Salt Lake City, Cheyenne, Denver and St Louis. Whenever we stayed anywhere it was usually in a motel, which was reasonably cost-effective. Many times we slept on the coach overnight, so we didn't need a bed; we would then wash our socks in the restroom at the back of the bus and hang them out of the window at the back to dry. Greyhound bus stations would have showers, left-luggage lockers etc. In the US people even moved house by Greyhound bus – because most rented places come furnished, people don't have any furniture to take with them, just half a dozen suitcases etc. I remember we met some people moving from New York to Baltimore.

From St Louis we went south, following the Mississippi down to Memphis, Tennessee. I wish back then I had been more into blues and country music, as I am now! We carried on down to New Orleans for about three or four days where we stayed in a YMCA, visiting Bourbon Street, the focus for Mardi Gras, with all the jazz and strip clubs. There is one bar that has a swing that comes out of the top window, complete with dummy. (Later in life I went back to New Orleans in very different circumstances.)

We then picked up the coach and went round the coast to Miami, before we got back on the bus to Washington DC where we visited all the sites via a little train that we could hop on and off – the Smithsonian Museum, White House, Lincoln Memorial etc. I remember we visited one building where this woman was excited about something 200 years old … the Americans have a different slant on history to us in the UK! We stayed with Ray's aunt, who had an apartment in Washington and a boyfriend, and they took us out in the evenings to cabarets, bars etc. On the first night in the flat, when it was bedtime, Ray's aunt said to us, "Oh by the way boys, this box here, if there's any problem, the gun is in here." It was a loaded handgun!

We went up to New York for three or four days to finish off. We saw as many of the sights as we could – Times Square, Central Park etc. We caught the Subway out to a park that overlooked the Hudson, and then we decided to go back by bus to see more, but the bus went straight through the centre of Harlem and we didn't see a white person for half an hour – quite a shock to us then! That street eventually becomes Fifth Avenue, and suddenly there was Tiffany's and all the top designer names. We went down 42nd Street, renowned for musical theatre, although every other building was a strip joint. It is a heck of a city.

In total we covered 9,000 miles and 29 different states, all for £120 plus expenses. We flew home to the UK from New York. Incidentally, I gave up smoking on the return flight, just like that, and never smoked since.

I carried on working at BT&G and playing snooker. After my success winning the trophy, I was picked for one of the club teams, the lesser B-team that played in the Heavy Woollen District League. Every other week we played away matches which were handicapped and, being a new player, I was given a 30-point start, which is probably why I won the trophy! It was all very serious – no messing about like the places above Burtons. Of course, the opposing player might also have a 30 handicap, so we started equal, or it might be the opposition's best player on scratch (or anywhere between). I had some great nights playing away matches, which meant visiting other clubs all over the area, which also improved my local area knowledge.

Howard Sharp was in the first team and we became very good friends and practised together. I went to the snooker championships in Manchester and bought a book by John Spencer who had been World Champion in the 1970s. Memorable Maxim — "Mix with successful people, or at least read their books!" My game improved immensely as a result. I also went with Howard to Carlinghow Working Men's Club, a very smart venue, to see the World Amateur Champion Ray Edmonds playing an exhibition afternoon. Howard and I had visited other snooker venues to play and practise — he was much better than me and helped me a lot. A very well-respected local player was Joe Johnson who went on to win the 1986 World Snooker Championship.

On another occasion we went to The 148 Club on Chapeltown Road, where the Leeds Carnival is held each year. The 148 was a strip club in a small, terraced house. We sat at front and the girls could talk to you, they were that close — it was quite an experience, and incredibly embarrassing. Howard is still embarrassed about this evening out, even now!

Henry O'Hare, a friend from BT&G, was about to play a very significant part in my life. When Henry and Cynthia, who had been good friends of ours, split up, Henry asked if he could stay with me for a while until he got sorted, so he moved in. Henry was a member of Bradford Pothole Club, and each year the club would open Gaping Gill, a huge natural cave near Ingleton, where they would set up a winch and lower people down 300 feet into an incredible cavern. Henry said he would take me. He had a sports car, but unfortunately on the way we had mechanical problems in Keighley and had to abandon our trip. I returned in my own car, but by the time I arrived there they had stopped taking people down. (A few years later I did eventually get down Gaping Gill, but more about that later.)

Moorfield Avenue had (and still has) a lot of very friendly neighbours. I have mentioned Ken and Renee next door, and there was Charlie Wild across the road who with his wife Hazel ran a hardware store in Cleckheaton – very useful with help and advice. Two doors away were Edwin and Betty Fielding. Perhaps because they knew of my marital situation, their son David and his girlfriend took me with them to see Hawkwind at St George's Hall in Bradford in December 1972. Hawkwind had a No 3 hit with 'Silver Machine' that year, and I remember it particularly because I suffered from a migraine attack at the time!

I got my first migraine attack when I was about 16, after I had been to an open-air lido on a bright sunny day. My sister Barbara suffered from them, as had my mum, and Barbara's daughter gets them. I was very frightened at the time. My sister would go numb all down one side of the body and couldn't stand up. I seem to get an hour's warning, when I lose vision in one eye, can't read, feel sick and giddy, and from that moment, one hour to the minute, the pain will start. I've had them throughout my life, including one fairly recently. In the early days of attacks I would scream and shout, get angry, vomit and crawl on the bathroom floor. Now I go to bed and lie quietly, take some tablets, relax and go to sleep, which helps me to get over it. People say all manner of things cause migraines, but my trigger seems to be bright lights or stress, and I can't attend firework displays. What annoys me and my fellow sufferers is when people say they have got a migraine, when it is just a bad headache – they are very different!

There were to be several life-changing consequences of Henry coming to live with me. At the time, my life simply involved going to work but, with no marriage and no mobile disco, I was sad and moping about. Henry said to me, "Come on Barry, you've got to stop moping about. You need to get out." He knew the manager of a disco nightclub in Bradford, The Pentagon, on Westgate, where he could get me an audition. It was a top venue in Bradford with two floors and the main disco on the ground floor, and a top DJ, John Khan. I was given the job of the more romantic top floor (complete with booths for kissing and cuddling and smooth smoochie music) – ideal for me and my LPs.

It was a demanding and tiring period of my life – up at 6.30 am to be at work for 7.30 am, through to 5.30 pm (plus two hours of overtime on Tuesdays and Thursdays), then home to try to get some sleep before arriving at the club at 9.00 pm where I would play until 2.00 am in the morning. The kitchen would save the staff something to eat from the menu, such as chicken and chips. I would come home to bed at 3.00 am and do it all over again the next day … all for £4 a night. But the money wasn't important, getting out and playing music was.

Sometimes I would fill in for John Khan downstairs, which was brilliant. There would be 'go-go' dancers on the stage with me, a wonderful atmosphere, with a large audience dancing to records like 'Love Train' by The O'Jays and 'Wade in the Water' by Ramsey Lewis (only a minor hit in 1972, but a stunner of a record, and a great LP too). The manager Beno was a great guy, as were all the bar staff, waitresses, bouncers and regulars – it was a fabulous place to work. All the guys, me included, went to the same hairdresser, Vlad's in Sackville Street.

Baz and Cherry

The best consequences of Henry's suggestion to audition at the club were about to unfold. One of the waitresses was a lovely girl called Vera who, like a lot of us, would go to The Pentagon on their nights off. On one such occasion she brought her house mate with her, a beautiful girl called Sheila. They shared a house together in Heaton. The next night, when Vera was back at work, like a school kid I told her how much I liked her friend Sheila. Vera said she would take her to the Oddfellows pub on Sunday night where all the people who worked at the club met up when The Pentagon was closed. Vera said she would fix me up with a date with the gorgeous Sheila. The DJ organised some games, so I roped Sheila in to compete in one of them, involving couples skipping together and, without stopping, the woman having to feed the man with a banana at the same time! Only one other couple entered and we were robbed – the winning couple stopped as she fed him, and the prize was a bottle of brandy!

At least Sheila knew then what I was like – fun-loving but competitive – and what she was letting herself in for by going out with me. We started seeing each other regularly. Apparently that first night she asked me how old I was. I told her, and also that I had been married before, but this didn't seem to put her off. She was 20, I was 29.

Two early dates we had were very memorable. In June 1973 we went to see David Bowie at St George's Hall in Bradford. Despite the volume, I will always remember the clarity in Bowie's words, his diction, and you could hear every word he sang – and of course see the fantastic costumes and watch the stage presentation with The Spiders from Mars: Mick Ronson, TJ Bolder and Woody Woodmansey, all brilliant. I went out next day and bought the LP, *Aladdin Sane*, which was No 1 in the charts. We were so impressed, a few weeks later we went to see him again at the Leeds Rollarena on Kirkstall Road. Again, it was fabulous.

In July we went to my niece Linda and Chris's wedding in Kent. It was a great opportunity to introduce Sheila to the family. The reception was at The Black Prince where I had spent so many Sunday evenings listening to all those blues bands back in the sixties. I found my diary from 1965 the other day, and the entry for 14th February reads, "Black Prince in evening, Animals plus two other groups." ('Don't Let Me Be Misunderstood' was at No 3 in the charts that week.)

I wonder how I felt at this time. I can remember the events, but not the emotions … but of course, it was nearly 50 years ago. I remember singing the 1962 Top 10 hit for Tommy Roe, 'Sheila', all the time – sweet little Sheila. We were in love, we got on great and I think I had learnt some lessons.

Sheila worked at Bradford University in the computer department on Tumbling Hill Street working with punch cards. If I wasn't DJ-ing, I would pick her up after work and we would go out before I would take her back to her flat in Heaton. If I was working overtime, Sheila would meet me at work. I loved this because I could show her off – she was gorgeous.

Sheila had two older brothers, Alan and Peter, who had moved on. Her mum had died, like mine, and her father had remarried. They shared a house with her stepbrother and Sheila shared a bedroom with her stepsister. However, she was unhappy with all of this and so moved out and got her own place in Heaton, in a shared house. Because she had left home, the people where she worked had taken her under their wing. They included Maureen and Jim, and Ann and John, so Sheila spent a lot of time with them, staying overnight at weekends.

It soon became obvious to me that I would have to be approved as a suitable suitor by these friends. They were real party animals and also very much into cycling. We went out on nights out with them, which was a wonderful time for me, as a whole new world opened up. The Hill Top pub was the favourite on Friday nights, where we all played darts (I invested in some darts of my own, as most of the others seemed to have their own sets), but many other pubs also featured, including The Boars Head and The Waggoners at Wibsey, near to John and Ann's house – where I understand at some stage Sheila had been banned for being sick in the ladies, which was not at all surprising, as when I met her she drank Cherry B. In fact, I affectionately called her 'Cherry' all our married life.

When the pub closed, about eight of us would go back to John and Ann's and continue drinking, usually from John's wine bucket. We played darts in their narrow conservatory and listened to music on his fantastic music system. I vividly remember sitting in their lounge in total darkness, listening to both sides of Pink Floyd's *The Dark Side of the Moon*. Another fantastic entertainment venue we all went to regularly was The Amsterdam Bar in Huddersfield.

Jim and Maureen were keen cyclists and also famous for their hospitality at their fabulous cottage in Queensbury, conveniently just 100 yards from another great pub, The Junction. Bicycles were a big feature for them, and it was not unusual for some of them to ride up to the Lake District after work and then back in an evening, stopping off at a well-known café in Gargrave. I remember Jim inviting all the visiting Irish cycle team to stay at their place for the weekend, bikes everywhere.

After a Sunday lunchtime session at the pub, Sheila and I were invited to go back with them and several others for something to eat. The drinking carried on into the evening. Ann, when alcohol took over, was a renowned exhibitionist and always keen to remove her clothes to dance. This evening The Rolling Stones provided the music and, with the lights turned off, I was the spotlight operator using a cycle lamp. Someone came to the front door, so I then took on the role of usherette and used my torch to show them to seats on the floor. It was all quite something! I remember I used to go into work on Monday mornings with all these incredible stories. I was having the time of my life – this was all a different world for me!

I never went away with them, but Sheila had done so – wild weekends camping on the side of Windermere, cycling round the area, water-skiing, and of course BBQs and drinking. We weren't involved with their regular cycling outings, but at Christmas their club organised a fancy-dress cycle race called 'The Batman and Robin', a circular course of about ten miles which involved visiting three pubs on the route to drink a half-pint at each. One year I entered the race on my old sit-up-and-beg insurance agent's bike dressed as Frank Spencer. We got to one of the three pubs where I took my bike in – it was absolutely heaving, and all the spectators, punters and racers asked why I was bringing my bike in. So I ended up doing a short Frank Spencer impersonation in the pub! I am not sure how, but this impersonation had become a party piece for me over the years and, much to the embarrassment of family and friends, it still is!

Anyway, I passed muster with this amazing group of life- and fun-loving people, and a few months later Sheila moved in with me. It was a big step for both of us! The amazing thing was that, even though she was only 20, she even enjoyed my easy-listening LPs, artists such as Andy Williams, Ray Conniff, Percy Faith and one of my favourites, 'A Man and a Woman' – very apt, perhaps? Sheila also liked cats, and at the time I had Button who had come up from Bexleyheath with Jeanne and I.

Before Sheila moved in, I was having a clear-out of the stuff associated with Jeanne, including photos and our wedding video. Very fortunately, Henry stopped me and said he would look after them. He said they were part of my history and how right he was.

I saw Henry a few times after that, and then he disappeared – with that film. My dad, sisters, nieces and nephews and many old friends were all on that film, so I *had* to find it. I tried everything I could to find Henry. One day I decided to employ a company that specialised in finding people (by this time I'd separated from Sheila as well). This organisation thought that they had found someone who knew Henry and had written to her, but she had not replied. In the end I asked for her address and walked to her house in Huddersfield. A woman answered the door and said, "Bloody hell, it's Barry Young!" She explained that she and Henry used to come and stay with me and Sheila and she had kept meaning to reply to that letter. Henry had gone off to Canada and abandoned her, but she was still friends with his brother – so she contacted him, who was still in touch with Henry. We then discovered that the film was in her loft! I had to wait for quite some time, even offering to help her, but she said she would sort it. Eventually I came back from one trip to find that she had left a message on the answerphone: "Some good news Barry, we have found your film!" I was absolutely delighted. I collected it, had it converted to a DVD and now I have it safely in my possession. It is wonderful to see it: the fashion, the cars and of course family and friends, some sadly no longer with us. Once again my tenacity and persistence paid off.

Meanwhile, at The Pentagon I was playing great records like 'The Jean Genie' by David Bowie, 'Hell Raiser' by Sweet and 'Stuck in the Middle with You' by Stealer's Wheel. All good for dancing to, and I would often join the customers on the floor for a bit of boogie disco.

Having been approved by the friends, my next step was to meet Sheila's family. Sheila arranged for us to call in one evening to briefly say hello. They lived in Rawdon, on the other side of Bradford, and I met her dad Don and stepmother Joyce. They were very friendly, down-to-earth people. They were going to have a wonderful influence on my life, which is still impacting me now nearly 50 years on, but I'll explain later.

Sheila and I were enjoying our life together. I remember someone asked her if she was using the same cooker as my ex-wife, and she got great enjoyment telling them, "Yes, and I'm also sleeping in the same bed!" I would drop her off at work and meet her afterwards, and sometimes she came with me to work at The Pentagon. We were also having great fun with her university friends and their capers. I put a Philips cassette player and speakers in the green van so that we could enjoy our music as we travelled.

Near the factory was a wholesale fruit and veg market. I'd buy a whole crate of oranges or carrots in bulk, and then break the boxes down and then sell them in lots to the guys in the factory to make a bit of money (ever the entrepreneur).

Bill McGraff, one of the directors, had a holiday home near Windermere where he taught us to water ski. He also took us to the Waterhead Hotel where he pulled up in his boat, moored up and had Sunday lunch. The directors of the company took us to Batley Variety Club where we saw more great shows – Gene Pitney was a regular there, and Louis Armstrong made his only ever UK appearance there. Bill McGraff also took us to Cinderella Rockerfella's in Leeds, owned by Peter Stringfellow.

Sheila and I had our first holiday together in Morocco. We visited Tangier, Rabat, Marrakech (including the gardens where Churchill used to paint), Meknes, Fez, Tetouan and Ceuta (an autonomous Spanish city).

Sometime in the 1970s I was offered a job at a new nightclub opening in Bradford called Scamps. I was booked to do the opening night, a large, lavish, champagne affair. All the top brass from the owners, the Star Group, were there, and it was a memorable evening for me, that's for sure. I took to the stage and over the microphone welcomed everybody to The Pentagon, the club where I used to work – I thought some people were going to faint! A young lady came dashing across the dance floor, but by then I had regained some credibility using self-effacing and humble humour. I'd seen a comedy where they used the phrase, "I don't think anyone noticed, I think we've got away with it," but I am sure the top brass noticed. However, once the music started, the evening was a great success and my blooper was forgiven and forgotten ... I think! I wouldn't work there for very long, as a new chapter in our lives was about to begin.

I must have behaved myself when I met Sheila's dad and Joyce, because we were invited to visit them at their caravan in the Yorkshire Dales. I said earlier they were to have a wonderful influence on my life. It began when Sheila and I went up to see them on a Sunday at Appletreewick in Wharfedale, a beautiful little village where they had a caravan on a small site run by the farmers Mr and Mrs Mason. The Craven Arms was the quintessential Yorkshire Dales pub just up the road in the village. There was also another pub called The New Inn, run by John Showers, who had a sign that read 'The First No-Smoking Inn in the World'. It certainly got him a lot of media attention and free publicity!

The River Wharfe ran along the bottom of the field, with some marvellous swimming pools and a Tarzan rope to swing from an embankment and drop into the river – it was brilliant. Yes, I had been told to take my swimming trunks (budgie-smuggling speedos) and, although I was 29, I was like a kid again. I ought to warn would-be Tarzan-swing participants that on another occasion my hands slipped down the rope, hit the knot at the bottom and I dislocated my finger. Luckily Joyce was a nurse and put the finger back into place, but the pain was terrible. She made a splint with two parts of a peg, and the finger is still badly disfigured today and a constant reminder of happy days plunging into the River Wharfe.

This was just the beginning of my 'enlightenment'. All these things were new to me – dinner parties, drinking wine, VHS tapes, CDs ... I was moving in more cultured circles, and the 'enlightenment' was that I suddenly found out why God had given me legs. The world is a bigger place than I thought! We can climb mountains and hills, we have eyes to see the beauty of the countryside, we could stay in beautiful hotels in the Lake District, eat a cheese course at the hotel where a whole Stilton was brought out and spooned from ...

At lunchtime with Sheila's dad and Joyce we went up to the pub, which had fabulous stone floors, an old oak bar and settles, wonderful Yorkshire ales, and a 'Bull Ring' (a game with a ring tied to a piece of string – on the wall of the pub is a large hook and punters have to stand back, take the ring on the string and swing it to try to get it onto the hook). I was full of enthusiasm about swimming in the river, so Don said that after our drinks they would take me to another lovely spot. We drove to a delightful village called Arncliffe, where for many years *Emmerdale Farm* had been filmed. We walked up a valley following a stream until we came to a spot where the stream cascaded over rocks into an inviting pool for swimming. Unfortunately, with no sun on it, it proved to be too cold for swimming, and this was to prove to be significant – because we didn't swim they suggested instead that we walk on up the valley, onto the fell and return down the ridge to our cars, which is what we did.

This walk was another massive part of my enlightenment – I had never walked much further than from my car to the pub door. Reaching our turning-off point, we began to ascend the fellside. I had only ever looked up at hills – I didn't know you could climb up them. Halfway up I broke into song. With my arms in the air, I belted out, "The hills are alive with the sound of music." I ran and sang, I was in a whole new world, a whole new experience, *walking*. Now nearly 50 years later, the utter joy of that experience has not left me and is still as strong. I am still walking the fells, hills and mountains of our beautiful world. I couldn't wait to tell the lads at the factory about my experience, but of course most of them had been enjoying the Dales themselves for years. Nevertheless they were pleased for me.

Sheila and I married on 7th September at Guiseley Registry Office. Our neighbour, Max, was best man, and Jeannie took the photographs. Rita and George came up from Kent, and various family and friends helped make it wonderful day. We had a get-together at Don and Joyce's, and as always Sheila looked beautiful … and I didn't look too bad either.

I remember many years later we were doing the housework together, when Sheila said to me, "Do you know what day it is?" "Thursday," I answered. "No, what date?" We had both forgotten that it was our anniversary. There were plenty of dates that were celebrated, like the surprise party I organised for Sheila's 33rd birthday and my 40th, but more about those happy occasions later.

I get a gorgeous second chance

As 1974 came to an end I had no idea of what a fantastic year 1975 was going to be … and this time it wouldn't be circumstances or consequences that would influence things. This time it would be me, I was going to make things happen, and happen they did!

Memorable Maxim — just ten two letter words: "If it is to be it is up to me."

CHAPTER 9: MAKING MY ESCAPE

Although I was enjoying life at BT&G, I was 30, I had been cutting up lumps of metal for 14 years and I knew that I didn't want to be doing this until I was 65. I still had this yearning to be in show business – I got a 'fix' when I was on stage at The Pentagon and loved the attention and the joy of pleasing the audience with my chat and, most importantly, playing the right records. I had seen many a wedding or party spoilt by a rubbish disc jockey, either saying nothing, saying too much, talking over the start of records, playing the wrong disc at the wrong time, and usually with a friend or partner sat behind them looking fed up!

And then one day when I was 31 my stars aligned and my opportunity presented itself. I saw an advert in the newspaper: "Redcoats Wanted". It all came back to me – Austin and Rita had gone on holiday many years before to a small holiday camp where there were camp hosts and entertainers, and they had told me way back then that this would be an ideal job for me. Remember, I had organised family get-togethers with cricket matches and games, and I was always having fun with the kids, ever the frustrated entertainer. I duly replied to the advert and was allotted an interview at the Midland Hotel on Manor Row, Bradford.

Sheila certainly did not want to be a Redcoat and wasn't really keen to go at all, if I'm honest, but I so wanted this chance to get into show business. Many top entertainers before me had begun their careers at Butlin's, including Ted Rogers, Sir Cliff Richard, Jimmy Tarbuck, Des O'Connor and many others.

I went along with my Frank Spencer beret (my only impression, remember) and was interviewed by Alan Ridgway, the entertainments manager at Skegness Camp. He asked if I was married, and we discussed Sheila not being keen on being a Redcoat. I thought she could perhaps be

119

The Butlin Group of Companies

Butlin's Limited

Central Administrative Offices
BOGNOR REGIS, Sussex PO21 1JJ
Telephone: BOGNOR REGIS 25511
Telegrams: JOLLIDAYS Bognor Regis

Date as postmark

Reply to: RLS/ES. 1497

Mr. B. Young
16 Moorfield Avenue
Hartshead Moor
Cleckheaton
Yorkshire. BD19 6PG.

Dear   Mr. Young,

    Further to your application for employment
within the Entertainments Department we would advise
you that interviews will be held at THE MIDLAND HOTEL
Forster Square, Bradford.
You are requested to attend at 4.00 ᴀ.ᴍ./p.m. on

Thursday 10th April 1975.

    This early indication gives you ample time to
inform us if you no longer wish to be considered for
employment, or likewise, if the time and date are
unsuitable.

                        Yours sincerely,
                        for BUTLIN'S LIMITED.

                        R.L. Stanway.
                        Divisional Manager.
                        ENTERTAINMENTS.

P.S. We would point out that the above is the only
      date on which we shall be in Bradford
      for the purpose of interviews.

Letter from Butlins offering me an interview

120

a chalet maid instead of a Redcoat, but Alan told me that this would be out of the question, as camp staff were housed in a separate area from the campers, but the entertainments staff had chalets amongst the campers and ate with them. So no, Sheila could not be a chalet maid. He did, however, have a possible solution. Rocky Mason, the entertainments manager at Filey Camp, had a vacancy for an assistant entertainments manager. Perhaps he could arrange for Sheila, whilst still being a Redcoat, to work in Radio Butlin, which would mean that she would have no direct contact with the campers.

I was now in a dilemma. I wanted so badly to be a Redcoat, messing about, throwing people in the swimming pool, making campers laugh at my Frank Spencer impression (which, by the way, helped me get the job). On the other hand Alan's proposal did mean we could both go and I would be paid another £1 a week, taking me up to the fantastic sum of £16, with all food and accommodation included (although with only one evening and one day off a week).

Alan suggested Sheila and I went over to Filey to discuss everything with Rocky Mason. After some coaxing from me, that is exactly what we decided to do, and Rocky was happy for us to take up the roles. It would be a 20-week season starting in May; I would work alongside Rocky and Sheila would work with two other girls in Radio Butlin. As assistant entertainments manager I would need a dress suit, frilly white shirt, bow tie etc, and smart casual and suits during the day. Sheila would get a Redcoat uniform.

We came home and started organising ourselves. We both gave our notice – the directors of BT&G, who had become good friends, were sorry to lose me but knew it was what I really wanted to do. The season was only 20 weeks … did they (or I) think that I would go back?

Sheila and I went shopping to get the new outfits I needed. The dress suit and other trousers had flares, the fashion at the time (perhaps I should mention that by this stage I had stopped wearing short trousers). Max and Eileen kindly agreed to feed our cat, Beano, while we were away (Beano had replaced Button, the cat that had belonged to Jeanne and me and had come up from Bexleyheath with us but had since sadly died).

We bought various bits and pieces to try to make our chalet more homely, such as a small kettle, radio etc. Each block of chalets had a communal block of bathrooms and toilets. I can't remember if we took a chamber pot with us, but otherwise it could be a cold and sometimes wet and windy walk to the toilets in the middle of the night! The entertainments staff were shared out, so each block had a least one Redcoat in residence, and the Redcoats also sat in the dining rooms with the campers (more about this later).

So in early May 1975 off we went to Filey. YES! At last – the entertainments business proper! I was not happy about not being a Redcoat, although the role as assistant entertainments manager was to be very beneficial later in life, as it was to teach me an awful lot about organisation, coaxing and so much more.

With so many well-known entertainers beginning their careers at Butlin's, many of the Redcoats were hoping to do the same. Bingo was big with the campers and I would bribe the aspiring entertainer Redcoats by letting them do a bit of their act, playing guitar, singing, telling jokes between calling the bingo, *if* they marked out the lines on the football pitch for me. Instead of white paint we used creosote, which did the job by burning the grass and was cheaper.

On Saturday I would be given the programme for the week, which listed all the shows, events etc – there were hundreds of events to provide something for everyone (well, just about everyone). I then had to designate a Redcoat to organise and host the event. For example, First-Sitting Guests' Football, so put Tony on that, then Angela on the Bonny Bouncing Baby Competition, John on snooker etc. With 10,000 campers and 2,500 staff (of which only 25 were Redcoats), it was a massive juggling act!

We had all these competitions every week, and punters could come back at the end of the season and compete in the finals to win money and holidays. Funny looking back now, but at the time all this was all my responsibility as the new boy. For example, I'd put Tony on snooker at 9.30 am when 200 people would turn up ... but at 11.00 am I also had Tony refereeing the football, although with 200 entrants he'd be there two days! So I'd have to quickly arrange a replacement.

Saturday was change-over day, absolutely chaotic, with 10,000 campers all moving out, and another 10,000 arriving. The camp had its own branch line and railway station, and people also came by bus, car and coaches. We would help the guests get their chalet keys, and although we were entertainers we were also used as the information desk.

If campers went to a chalet and were unhappy with it, we got it all. These people had worked all week, come to Butlin's for a break, and right away on the Saturday they started moaning ... they moaned all week! They had seen the films, there were no tips on the snooker cues, not enough roller skates, their chalet had a light out, they complained about the food, the weather etc ... But on the last day as they left the camp they'd come in and say, "See you next year!" I guess all year they had someone else moaning at them, and now it was their chance. So we always sorted out what we could.

Rocky Mason was the entertainments manager, George was his assistant, and Liam Kelly a singer who used to hang around with them. These three had been together for many years and I was very much the apprentice. It was all pretty cliquey.

Dennis, who was ex-army, joined later in the season and helped with a popular gag. On Donkey Derby Day (horse racing, but with donkeys), we attracted crowds to the 'Human Cannonball' by explaining that we were going to fire a Redcoat from a large wooden cannon (the barrel was made out of dustbins). So, we had one Redcoat hiding while we put another in the cannon. After a large explosion and cheers the other Redcoat appeared – hey presto, we fired a Redcoat from the canon! It was a great gag. However, Dennis had offered to get the explosives, and thank goodness we tried it first. It was just like Michael Caine in *The Italian Job*, as one of the dustbins disintegrated with the force! We could have been one Redcoat less.

The camp had two dining rooms with two sittings for meals. The Redcoats' day started at 8.25 am to meet and greet all the campers at the dining room doors for breakfast, and again at 9.25 am for second-sitting guests. The Redcoats would swan up and down the rows entertaining the campers until they got a signal over the Tannoy from Radio Butlin, telling them to sit down. The Redcoats were allocated a seat with the campers, I think to indicate that the food was all OK, although I personally thought the food was very good (perhaps it was because of all those school dinners?). The atmosphere in the dining room was a bit like school dining rooms, although at Butlin's the food was served by young waitresses, girls from all over the country. They always looked ever so pale, and by the end of the second week they were usually serving dinner sporting love bites!

I do remember at the beginning of the season the quantity of food was substantial. On Sunday evening it would always be a hearty piece of salmon, followed by a dessert of sponge cake ... but by the end of the season this had reduced to a very small piece of salmon and half a cake! The general manager, who was responsible for food, accommodation, cleaning and security, was I believe an ex-top military man, a major or similar, and he would certainly need those sorts of operational and organisational skills to run a camp like that. With guests and staff, there were something like 12,000 people on the camp at the height of the season. Imagine the logistics for that.

At breakfast Radio Butlin would announce the day's forthcoming activities, which was one of Sheila's jobs. This might also include the announcement of the wet weather programme. Most events were normally planned to take place outdoors but, suddenly if it started to rain, Sheila would announce, "Ladies and gentlemen, due to the inclement weather, we will be holding ..." Quickly events would have to be rearranged in the ballroom and other inside areas, so I had to change the whole programme at the last minute to reorganise these events. The announcement would go out all over the camp through the large Tannoy speakers.

The Redcoats' and my day began at 8.25 am at the dining room doors and ended with 'The Last Waltz' at midnight in the Viennese Ballroom (except Tuesday nights, more about which later). Sheila worked shifts with the other two girls in Radio Butlin and enjoyed going to the beach in her time off. She looked smashing in her uniform and sounded great over the Tannoy. On early shifts she would be responsible for gently waking the campers at 8.00 am with "Good Morning Campers" (just like Gladys Pugh in *Hi-de-Hi*). "Breakfast for first-sitting guests will be served at 8.30," she would say, followed by some appropriate music. This of course was a critical announcement, and only once did we wake up late and Sheila only did her bit at 8.15, but it was never mentioned, so I think we got away with it.

The whole Butlins gang

Sheila settled into her role. She was very well liked and gradually began to enjoy the job and, because she didn't report to me, there was never a conflict or any animosity from the other Redcoats. She did get asked all sorts of questions and told stories from the campers as she went to and from our chalet, including one man who was keen to show her the pus on his septic thumb and a lady who wanted her to repair the door on her chalet! Redcoats were all things to all people.

Just like me, everyone working at Butlin's seemed to be escaping from something ... perhaps a broken marriage, not having a job etc. I was escaping from the factory, where I had been cutting up metal for 14 years. There were lots of people in broken relationships etc.

Everyone got on well, and I was much closer to the Redcoats than I was the management! It all felt just like *Hi-de-Hi*, with many stories and characters just like the TV programme. We had a projectionist who would fall asleep ... or was drunk ... and not change the reel of film, so I'd get a call that the roll of film was just clicking over. I am not sure whether the 'kids' uncle' really loved kids, our two dancers reminded me of the show's

Barry and Yvonne and they hated it if I put them on creosoting the football pitch lines!

We had one day off a week and one evening. In the evenings we would go for a run out to a pub somewhere, and I remember a cassette we played a lot was by Fox who had a Top 10 in 1975 with 'Only You Can'. Their charismatic Australian lead singer was Noosha Fox – I thought she was gorgeous and have just bought a couple of Fox CDs. Try 'He's Got Magic', you can sing and dance along to that one!

On our day off we had originally planned to go home every few weeks but then decided that if we did we might not come back. I was loving the job, but living in a small chalet and sharing ablutions with hundreds of campers was testing for us. I was still frustrated at not being a Redcoat and we were missing our cat, family and our friends. The chalets were pretty sparse. Bed, small wardrobe, wash basin and fridge – that was about it. We were not supposed to use electrical appliances, but we got ourselves various adaptors to power the hair dryer, iron, kettle etc from the light fitting.

However, we did have some marvellous times on our days off, visiting Scarborough, Bridlington, Whitby, Flamborough Head and Robin Hood's Bay. I found out early on it was a very good idea to make friends with the dining room manager who would make up a wonderful picnic for us on our days off. Don and Joyce were among the visitors who came to see us on our day off, and we would entertain and show them round and give them lunch at our table.

We made many great friends amongst the entertainers. Bob Webb was a resident singer and, as he and his wife were in the adjoining chalet, we would often enjoy him rehearsing. I always remember his fabulous flares.

Butlin's was just about how I imagined it and more. It was very tiring, demanding and exhilarating, and it was fabulous value for campers, as it provided all their food and entertainment. There were films and shows in the Gaiety Theatre, plays at the Empire Theatre; they had places to dance, eat and drink. Entertainment included bingo, wrestling, snooker, darts, table-tennis, football, netball, trampoline, the donkey derby on Thursdays, indoor and outdoor swimming pools with a weekly gala, roller skating, family sports and church services; competitions included fancy dress, mother and child, talent shows, the most glamorous grandmother of

Great Britain, even Butlin's junior national yo-yo competition; and, of course, the amusement park with free rides.

It was mine and the 25 Redcoats' function to arrange and host all these events throughout the week. No wonder I experienced a bad migraine attack – it was awful. I have said that if I had owned a gun I would have shot myself, the pain was so severe.

I did enjoy my role in the evenings. I would put on my dinner suit, complete with bow tie, cummerbund and frilly shirt, and walk round the camp to all the entertainment venues. I'd get a drink from the bar and then ring in to Radio Butlin to say, "I'm in the French Bar if you need me." (I think the French Bar was the longest bar in the country – it was certainly the longest I had ever seen and needed an awful lot of people to operate it.) They might then say there was a light out over the dart board, for example, so I'd have to deal with that. I also had to make sure that Redcoats were all dancing and mixing with the guests. Another job was to liaise with Redcoat patrols for baby-crying. They would go up and down the chalet lines listening for babies crying. So, if they heard a baby on Blue Row No16, they would go to the nearest phone, ring the control centre, who in turn would tell me. Radio Butlin would then interrupt their broadcast, or arrange large notices in the cinema which the usherette would shine her torch on, or interrupt a show with an announcement.

Tuesday night was cabaret night from 10.00 pm until 2.00 am. It was my job to meet the artist at the gate, as I did with Frankie Howerd when he turned up in his Roller and I took him to 'band call' where, with the resident group who backed up their act, they went through their 'dots' (their music) – for example, when he'd tell a joke the band would give him a roll on the drums. Then I'd take the act to their dressing room in the theatre, and introduce them to the Redcoat hostess who would give them drink and food etc.

I remember Frankie Howerd had a look in the theatre on the way to the dressing room where there was a huge red grand piano which had been covered with small mirror squares to make it look glamorous. Frankie said that when the spotlight shone it would glint on the piano and so people would look at that, not at him. I called Rocky Mason and asked him what to do. He told me to go to the dining room to fetch a bag of flour and also

It was a massive juggling act for the programme of events

Tuesday night was cabaret night

Sheila and I with Bob Monkhouse at Butlins

get some lacquer from the hostesses. Then I was to spray the mirror with lacquer and then blow the flour onto the mirrors. Next day I had to clean it all off, but Frankie Howerd was happy and performed as planned!

Other stars included Ted Rogers, Frank Carson, Roy Castle, Bob Monkhouse (known as 'The Governor') – they were all doing the circuit of the six or eight camps. We also had Ken Dodd, whose reputation was that he went on and on and on ... At Butlin's the night finished at 2.00 am, but he was still telling jokes as everyone was going to bed.

On Sunday evenings Bill Maynard, a friend of Rocky Mason, was a regular on the cabaret spot. I read that, when he was going through a bad period in his career, he found great inspiration from Norman Vincent Peale's *The Power of Positive Thinking*. As a result Bill strives each day to do one thing which he fears, no matter how small. What a brilliant book this is, and what a great Memorable Maxim from Bill.

The male Redcoats, who started the season young and fresh-faced, soon discovered that their Redcoat was like a magnet – grannies, young girls, middle-aged women, wives … they were all interested. The boys came in fresh-faced but went home exhausted, having learnt a lot about the world!

On Thursdays Paul Reaney, a Leeds United player and an England international, would come to play football with the kids. I'd meet him at the gate and take him for lunch where, as assistant entertainments manager, Sheila and I had our own table in the dining room. I would compère and commentate on the match. Paul became a friend and bought Sheila and I a present at the end of the season. (Someone told me recently that Paul is the same age as me and was also born in October.) Leighton James, a player from Burnley FC, deputised for Paul on a couple of occasions.

I did manage to get on stage, performing my Frank Spencer at the Redcoat show during the end-of-season party. It was the 'Goodbye Campers' show, for Redcoats to show off their skills. I also made an attempt at Larry Grayson ("Look at the muck on here") and Eddie Waring, the rugby league commentator.

Butlin's was 20 weeks of unadulterated fun, and I intentionally avoided all news and information from the outside world – no TV, no newspapers etc. It was one heck of an experience – I learnt so much about people, organisation, entertainment and, most importantly, about life. I am sure Sheila also benefited and came back with more confidence, and of course a wonderful story to tell.

What happened at the end of 20 weeks? Well, if you were lucky, if they liked you, they might offer you a job at head office in Bognor Regis; you might get to take apart and replace the bearings of 10,000 pairs of roller skates, or paint the inside of the swimming pools … people that they didn't want to lose and wanted there next season were kept on through the winter. However, not wanting to repair roller skates or paint swimming pools for £16 a week, we came home.

In the meantime, I was keen to stay in entertainment and utilise the experience I had gained at Butlin's, so I went to see someone at the Batley Variety Club and Wakefield Theatre Club, but these large entertainment venues were struggling and certainly not taking on new people. An entertainment person at the council told me that they would love to employ someone with my expertise and experience at putting on shows, but that they had to employ from within (in fact, someone who didn't even have my knowledge). They were sorry, they couldn't give me a job. I knew I wasn't a comedy act or a singer, but I knew that I could be a compère, entertaining people and making them laugh.

After having no success getting into entertainment locally, Sheila and I should have moved to London, got a bed-sit and I should have gone knocking on the doors of the BBC, ITV, West End theatres … who knows where I might have been now. However, Sheila didn't want to move to London, and I obviously didn't want it enough. Memorable Maxim – "The very successful, do want it enough." Nevertheless, I have absolutely no regrets. I am not sure I would have really enjoyed the 'luvvy life' which is rife with insecurity. Very few make it successfully and it's rare to be employed all the time.

Meanwhile, Sheila and I had started seeing all our friends again and regaling them with our stories. The directors of BT&G heard that I was back from Butlin's and offered me a job managing a new department. In the absence of a job in entertainment, and needing to earn a living and pay the mortgage (which was my responsibility after having bought Jeanne out), I accepted their offer and very reluctantly went back to factory life. The noise, the grease and grime … I didn't wear my suit – it was back to overalls! Sheila got a job in Cleckheaton working in the computer department at the head office of Hillards, a local supermarket (later bought by Tesco).

I did enjoy one aspect of this new role. I accompanied the director Bill King down to Gloucestershire to learn how to operate a new machine. I remember we stopped for breakfast at the Hilton Park services on the M6, the one with the large tower on top. This was a new experience for me, and the company who we were buying from took us out for lunch to a beautiful country inn. I thought I could get used to this, but alas, that was the last of my business lunches – instead it was back to the factory making sure the machine earned its keep and paid for itself. I wasn't so much a manager as a well-paid machine operator, and I was the only person in the department.

After experiencing and enjoying the world of entertainment and fun, walking round in a suit, having a little bit of respect, feeling just a little bit important, I realised I couldn't come back to factory life. I knew this wasn't what I wanted to be doing all my life. I missed the happiness and laughter.

Then another of those coincidences turned up. I said in an earlier chapter that I have always felt God's hand on my shoulder, and here it was again. My friend Geoff Lister was a salesman at Sulzer Pumps in Leeds. He said to me, "You should get a job as a salesman, you have 'the gift of the gab'." So I took his advice and got a job selling ... although I have to say it took me quite some time to learn that 'the gift of the gab' certainly isn't the way to success in selling. Much to my joy and delight, what I did very soon discover about selling I will share in my next chapter ... and what a chain of events this would set off.

Are You Interested?

In a career and future advancement with a reputable well established Company.

If so, we are looking for a **SALES REPRESENTA-TIVE**, in the age group 22-45, experienced or inexperienced in sales, to join our home sales division to sell and promote our products through our various dealer outlets, centred on the city of Leeds.

Our business is the manufacture of the most comprehensive range of typewriters and business machine supplies in the U.K. Full training will be given, plus realistic salary, commission, company car and expenses to the successful applicant.

Appointment for local interview, phone
**Mr. J. S. Broadbent,
Dragonara Hotel,
Leeds 442000,
from 2 p.m. to 7 p.m.,
Wednesday, March 3, 1976**

THE COLUMBIA RIBBON & CARBON MANUFACTURING CO. LTD.,
Kangley Ridge Road, Lower Sydenham, London SE26 5AW.

In 1976 I saw this advert in the *Yorkshire Post*. Columbia International manufactured typewriter ribbons and carbon paper at their factory in Lower Sydenham, London. I had no idea about typewriters or what carbon paper was, but I liked the sound of the advert. The interview was at the Dragonara Hotel in Leeds, and back then I was able to park my green van right outside (you couldn't do that now!).

John Broadbent, the sales director, and John Lennon, sales manager, interviewed me. We were chatting away and they were asking me about myself. I told them about selling encyclopaedias, it was all going well, and then they said, "Do you have any questions, Barry?" Looking them both in the eye, I said, "Yes, just the one. Is there any reason you won't give me the job?" Since then I've used that in all my training, in all my closing of sales, when people were thinking of booking me. If they do say that they are concerned about something, then I can answer it directly and don't come out thinking that I should have said something. Anyway, the two from Columbia looked at each other and went, "No, I don't think there is Barry," and so I asked, "When shall I start?"

The job paid a small salary plus commission, but I realised that to make a good living I needed to get good at selling quickly. Geoff, who had suggested to me the idea of becoming a salesman, very kindly (and most importantly) gave me a little black book entitled *Effective Salesmanship* by Joe Windsor. This was to prove invaluable, and was the first of the many other books on selling I now own. Just like John Spencer's book that had improved my snooker and helped me win that trophy, this little book certainly gave me the knowledge and skills to put me on the correct path to becoming a successful salesman. Memorable Maxim – "Learn to Earn ... if you learn about things, you'll earn money doing it."

What I did quickly learn was that success in sales is just like show business. You have to look the part, act the part, learn your lines and also the importance of managing your time. Lessons learnt from the *Encyclopaedia Britannica* experience would serve me well. I had spent a week there learning the spiel and how to sell the books. The 'funny money' closing gambit I had learnt back then (it only cost a shilling a week) was something I regularly used over the years, proving very successful.

I didn't know it then, but getting this job was to set off a series of factors and events that were to have a huge impact on my life and give direction to what would happen over the next 20 years. As the words of the 1939 song said, "T'ain't what you do it's the way that you do it, that's what gets results."

So once again I handed in my notice at BT&G. I had to buy some business attire — suits etc — and kipper ties were in fashion, but Sheila made me a beautiful one on elastic, so I had no Windsor knots to tie when I wore that one!

I spent a week training at Lower Sydenham in London. We were selling ribbons not only for typewriters but also for computer printers which used 15-inch-wide ribbons. The computer paper went through the machines at a huge rate of knots, and the hammers had to fire ever so fast to strike the letters. I learnt all about record cards, postcard-sized cards kept in plastic record-card boxes on which would be listed who you were talking to, what you were discussing, all the whens, hows, whys, dates etc of sales appointments and contacts.

I had gone down to London on Sunday on the train and, along with the other new budding salesmen, stayed at a hotel in Crystal Palace. After a week's training I drove back home in my company car, a blue Ford Cortina with a black vinyl roof. It wasn't new, but it was a real upgrade from my green Bedford van. I thought, "I have arrived."

On the Monday, John Lennon the manager showed me the ropes and introduced me to my area and my customers. They were trade dealers, typically office stationery companies who then sold on to the end users (companies, business offices etc). I covered the West Yorkshire area and would call on these dealers weekly, fortnightly and monthly, according to their requirements or revenue.

A tremendous record at the time and big favourite of mine was 'Music' by John Miles, which hit No 3 in 1976. This was the perfect record to play in my Cortina as I drove round my area like a king. Although it was that very hot summer, I didn't care. I was having a great time in my new job. Had I at last found my perfect vocation? I thought I might have, although this would be just one of the many steps and stages to that vocation.

Like many other dealers, Dennis Sidebottom, the owner of McColl's in Horsforth, became a friend. This would always be useful when there was a sales competition, as friends would try to help you win by ordering more product than they needed, or maybe taking advantage of a special deal they didn't really want.

Selling to the trade was an easier sell, as they had to buy someone's products to have something to sell. Billy Wood from Office Supplies, Manor Row, Bradford, said to me that if I wanted him to place an order I would have to get some sales for him for a new type of carbon paper. It was like a film, much better and cleaner than other carbon papers – it wouldn't come off all over your fingers. Billy said to me, "I'll give you a box of this and, if you go and get some orders in offices in Bradford, then I'll give you a good order." So I went into this large building in Bradford, started at the top and worked down. There was a typing pool and I showed them this bit of carbon paper, wiping it down my face to show how clean it was … but it all came off on my face! These girls were wetting themselves with laughter, and I came out without an order (and stopped being so extravagant in my demonstrations).

I won many sales competitions over the coming years, with rewards of electrical appliances, money, hampers, vouchers etc. Of course I would repay these dealers by helping out whenever I could and doing them favours. My efforts were also rewarded with a brand-new yellow (my choice) Cortina Mark 3. Oh wow, this was something to park on the drive. I ought to mention I kept my Bedford van up on chocks in the garage, just in case I didn't like the sales job (or they didn't like me). That might sound a little negative, but it is always a very good idea to have a fall-back plan. Memorable Maxim – "Always have a fall-back plan, whatever it is you are doing." I needn't have worried, and I went from strength to strength (although, as we shall see, keeping the van was a very sensible move).

In 1977 Derek Bird joined the company as marketing director, coming from another large company within the office stationery trade. He certainly came in with a tough reputation and a big new broom. I understood that as I was last in I could be first out, so that van might come in useful sooner than I thought. Fortunately John Lennon spoke up for me and I survived the new broom.

Derek Bird had growth in mind, so a competition was launched where the winner would be the salesman with most new accounts opened. Unlike a lot of salespeople, I enjoyed the thrill of cold calling. Perhaps this was due to all that moving about, going to new places, new schools and meeting new people in my early life? Anyway, I won the competition and used the money to buy two new bicycles (more about these later).

COLUMBIA RIBBON & CARBON MFG. CO. LIMITED
Registered Office & Factory: Kangley Bridge Road · Lower Sydenham · London SE26 5AW
Telephone: 01-778 6011 (14 Lines) Telegraphic & Cable Address: Classicism, London, SE26 Code· Western Union 5 Letter

Registered in London   Number 182936
Telex: 262619

COLUMBIA   INTERNATIONAL

DATA SUPPLIES DIVISION

"MAY   MONEY   MAKER"

Congratulations to Barry Young who has won the "May Money Maker" competition and with it a prize worth £50.

Barry, who opened new accounts at a rate greater than one per day, has set the standard for all members of the Division to aim for. The opening of new accounts and the resulting account development is the very life-blood of a successful retail sales team, and a minimum of one new account per day must be the objective of every salesman wishing to be a part of that successful team.

Our congratulations also go to Brain Edge, who although having only recently joined us, was only just beaten into second place.

S. G. FASSNIDGE

5-6-78.

SGF/BA

Directors: F. Brandenberg, U.S.A. Chairman G. S. Burnett, Managing G. H. Kapralos, U.S.A. J. H. Winfield
V. W. Tennant, F.C.A. P. C. Jefferies, F.C.A., F.C.M.A. D. C. Bird

I won the competition!

Columbia sales team with Derek Bird on the far right

Derek Bird also had other grand plans. The new computer age was upon us in 1977, so he set up the 'Computer Products Division' and a new role for me, selling computer printer ribbons direct to users. Unfortunately the trade dealers were not happy. It was a bit like Cadbury's saying, "We are now going direct to the consumer, we don't need sweet shops anymore." However, the reason for going direct was that many of these stationery dealers were dyed-in-the-wool and not open to this new computer age. Derek Bird argued that we couldn't wait for them. The computer ribbons were £20 each, and companies might use 20 or more a month, so it was big business. I was responsible for the North East, Yorkshire, Nottinghamshire and Lincolnshire.

Like many new top people who tend to bring their good people with them, Derek Bird brought along Richard Whitehead as national sales manager and marketing manager Stuart Fassnidge. Mike Shove joined the company to cover the London area and lived with his girlfriend, Rachel, in Kingston upon Thames. Rachel's parents lived in Kildwick, near Bingley, about ten miles from where we lived. One time Mike brought an urgent order of computer ribbons up for me and we went out for the evening, which was the start of a wonderful friendship. Later Mike and Rachel asked me to be their best man when we were in a Dales pub in Appletreewick. I'd always wanted to be a best man and thought I could do a good job, and I cried in the pub when they asked me! It was a complete surprise. (During my speech I asked how this Canadian had met this beautiful Yorkshire lass, and then brought out a 'Jim'll Fix It' badge.)

Mike was a great salesman and we were often in competition for the top slot for salesperson of the month. He was also fantastic at making macramé items. He went on to great things after leaving Columbia, becoming CEO of CSC and moving all over the world, including Vancouver, Toronto, Melbourne, Sydney and Singapore. Sheila and I visited them in Toronto (more about this fabulous holiday later). Mike is retired now, but you can see him on YouTube: 'Mike Shove, CSC'. Recently I managed to contact him via LinkedIn, and at the moment he is living with his second wife Kerstin in Whistler, Canada.

My geographical knowledge of the north grew with each week. Next door, Ken's son, a teacher in Sunderland, drew me a fantastic map of the Sunderland area, detailing the companies that I planned to visit.

It was very important to plan and make appointments with the computer operations manager, the person responsible for purchasing within the department. Unlike the office dealers who would be happy to see you at almost any time with a cup of tea and a chat, these people were running vital operations within businesses.

In addition, travelling all the way to Sunderland, Newcastle, Nottingham or Newark and not seeing anyone was out of the question, so I made every effort to see at least seven prospects in each town. This involved a lot of research, identifying the large companies which had a computer department, locating them on a map, organising my route to minimise travelling time between them, obtaining the correct contact name and then ringing them to make an appointment. I would take a packed lunch with me on these long days out, and I also bought a water boiler to plug into the cigar lighter to make tea and coffee with. It was brilliant fun exploring all these new towns.

I vividly remember making an appointment with the AA in Newcastle at 9.00 am. This was 1976, when the traffic was nothing like it is today, but I did not want to be late so was sat ready outside at 8.00 am. (I have only ever been late for an appointment once, with the MD at a company in Wakefield, who refused to see me then or ever since. Memorable Maxim – "Better 30 mins early than 5 minutes late.")

On some occasions I would stay overnight in a hotel in Whitley Bay. This was another new experience for me, and I enjoyed walking along the sea front and looking round the fun fair. A lot of people think it must be great to be a salesperson, staying overnight in smart hotels, but not many salespeople actually enjoy it, as you don't get paid for this extra time and most would rather be at home.

Having met Sheila's dad and Joyce, as well as other family and friends, it was time to meet her two brothers. Alan, the elder of the two, lived with wife Jeannie in Chalford Hill, near Stroud in the Cotswolds. Now that I had my Ford Cortina we went down to visit them. They had a new garden so a rotavating party was organised. Sheila's other brother, Peter, and his wife Trish also came, but someone cut through the water mains pipe, causing consternations and a good laugh. I was just glad it wasn't my fault, as that wouldn't have got me off to a good start! We visited a lovely local pub and had the most marvellous ploughman's lunch. Alan worked as parts manager for Lex Motor Group in Gloucester and Peter worked for British Steel in Corby. Jeannie was a photographer and Trish was in education.

We made many trips, both to Chalford and Corby, and also reciprocated by entertaining them in Yorkshire. Jeannie was a great cook and it was here I was introduced to rogan josh, dinner parties with wine and classical music … crumbs, I was going up in the world! A favourite track they played a lot was Rodrigo's 'Guitar Concerto'. A whole new world opened up for us, and I wondered what my mum and dad would be saying.

That year we bought some extra land at the back of the house from the farmer who owned the field. We only had five yards at the time, but all the neighbours bought an extra ten yards – the width of their gardens. The stipulations were that we had to move the dry stone wall and erect a concrete post and rail fence to ensure that cows or sheep couldn't get out of the field and into our gardens. We all got together to erect the new fence and did our own wall-moving. Sheila and I arranged a wall-building party. Alan and Jennie came up to reciprocate the help we had given in their garden. We roped in another three couples to participate. The wall was dismantled, the stone moved and rebuilt, and Sheila and Jeannie fed and watered the workers at regular intervals, although we were careful to not get them too drunk too early in the building of the new wall. I kept moving them to a new position on the wall to ensure random building. The wall still stands today and is looking just as good over four decades later.

It was about this time that Alan and Jeannie moved back to Yorkshire. Alan ran a parts department in Rochdale, but I remember there was a large snowfall one year and the M62 and all other roads were closed, so Alan ended up walking back from Rochdale. That prompted him into starting his own business, Motorbits, selling all the bits that people wanted for working on their cars. He found a nice niche market and Jeannie would go out selling to trade garages. If you were a local repair garage, Jeannie would supply.

1977 was memorable as the country celebrated the Queen's Jubilee and we had a street party, for which I made some stilts and provided the music.

Jeanne and I had visited my ex-landlady, Mrs C, when she lived down in Dymchurch, near Folkestone in Kent. Now with our new Cortina we went over to Great Yarmouth to visit her and her daughter Pauline (who lived nearby with husband Ray) and son Michael (who by coincidence was having an engagement party that weekend). I remember disco-dancing the night away to the *Saturday Night Fever* songs by The Bee Gees. 'Night Fever' was a No 1 in 1978, and I still boogie round the house very well to that record, as well as many others ... such as my favourite disco record, 'Love Train' by The O'Jays. It's a super exercise for mind and body alike. Another great record is 'Don't Forget to Dance' by The Kinks, but the title is most important (it is also mentioned in Baz Lurhmann's record 'Everybody's Free (To Wear Sunscreen'). Memorable Maxim – "Don't forget to dance and to laugh together."

On the way home we called in at Feltwell to see the airmen's married quarters where I had lived with Barbara and Peter when Mum died. Very sadly this visit was the last time we saw Mrs C. Pauline and Ray moved to Tasmania in 1978 and, although Mrs C went to live out there, she couldn't settle and came back to England. She sadly died with dementia some time later. I have visited Ray and Pauline several times ... more about that later.

The late 1970s were a great time for us. We had a terrific social life, enjoyed our jobs and our new-found activity of walking and exploring the Yorkshire Dales with a pub lunch. In 1978 we made our first of many visits to Burnsall Feast Sports, very much a Yorkshire thing. Held in Burnsall, the event includes a 32-mile cycle race round the Dales, clay pigeon shooting, children's races and fancy dress, ten-mile road race, the classic fell race, fly-casting, a silver band on the green etc. The fell race is a mile up and a mile down (I did do it one year). It was very much a northern thing, and the whole event would end with an egg-throwing competition and the mass singing of a hymn – a marvellous day out.

We had visits down south to family and friends who also came up to see us. On one occasion we took Mike and Rachel walking over the Pennine moors with a promise of a pub lunch at a lovely old remote inn. After several miles and hours we were horrified to find it closed. However, I had a backup plan – just a mile away was my reserve hostelry, so all was forgiven (although not forgotten). This was just one of the many walking adventures we have had over the years. (I will elaborate on some more of them later.)

I was doing so well I was promoted to northern area sales manager in 1979. This new role meant that, as well as looking after my own area, I was responsible for overseeing the salesman who covered the Liverpool, Manchester and Hull areas. The company thought that I was such a good salesman that they should make me a manager, but they lost their best salesman and got their worst manager – they never trained me to be a

COLUMBIA INTERNATIONAL

Columbia International
Contracts Division

Supplies for Data and Word Processing,
Reprographic and Business Machines.

Barry Young
Northern Area Manager

COLUMBIA RIBBON & CARBON MFG. CO., LTD.
Kangley Bridge Road, Lower Sydenham
London SE26 5AW Tel: 01-778 6011 Telex No. 262819

manager! "If you promote someone you must train them to do the job" –
Memorable Maxim.

My 'little black book' came in useful when I had to make my first
presentation to the sales team. I used Joe's pre-approach planning chapter,
calling my presentation 'The Five Knows': know where to go – how to get
there – who to see – when to go – what to say and do.

I worked over in Hull with John Wright; I really liked the place and
there were some impressive companies with large computer departments,
such as BP, Reckitt & Colman, Smith & Nephew, Ideal Standard, British
Aerospace at Brough and many more, including F Smales, a leading
seafood supplier and a good place (no pun intended) to finish the day –
they had a factory shop so I would come home with some delicious and
very fresh fish.

When I was selling in Leeds, I would time my calls on the clothing
manufacturers like Burtons, Hepworth's and John Collier for midday,
which meant that I could take advantage of having lunch in the works'
canteen. Leeds was a massive clothing manufacturing centre – Colin
Welland's 1970s Play for Today, *Leeds – United!*, is all about the women
striking for equal pay. In a similar vein, a favourite film of mine, *Made in
Dagenham*, is about the same subject, and amongst the stars is the very
talented and beautiful Rosamund Pike. There is also a brilliant CD of the
same name, with a terrific title track written by Billy Bragg and sung by
Sandie Shaw.

Bradford also had some well-known names, such as the catalogue
companies Empire Stores and Grattan Warehouse, along with the
engineering companies Mintex, Crofts and Hepworth & Grandage.
Sheffield was the home of British Steel and the large steel manufacturers,
and was a great selling area for me. I always remember that at ICI in
Middlesbrough they had a 'Paternoster Lift', a brilliant idea which
probably would not be allowed now due to health and safety.

In case you weren't working or not involved in computers back in the
1970s, I should tell you about these computer departments. The brains of
the computer were the Central Processing Unit (CPU) which used a fixed
disk on which to store the data. The CPU was linked to a disk or tape drive
to produce a removable copy of the data, just like today's memory

143

stick/flash drive. Huge air-conditioned rooms with dust-free environments housed these computers. To give you some idea of how critical it all was, the data on the disk was written and read by the head that was flying above the surface of the disc; if the head touched the disc, it would result in a 'head crash', which was a major catastrophe, with critical data lost and damage to both the head and disk. The distance between the flying head and disk was so small a human hair or even a smoke particle would cause a head crash. The printers were also linked to the CPU but, because of paper dust, these were in a separate room. The two most popular printers were the IBM 1403 and ICL TP 1500. More information online if you're interested!

Bill Symonds, the salesman over in Liverpool, was great – we had some marvellous times together calling on the large companies in his area: John Moores, BICC, Littlewoods and ICI, and most of the councils now had computer departments. If we had a bit of spare time, Bill would show me some of the local area, including the Pier Head and Liver Building, and the museum in Salford (with its lower floor like an old Victorian street and also its LS Lowry Gallery). We had calls over the border into Wales, and he took me to see the Great Orme at Llandudno.

It was all wonderfully exciting, and of course challenging, trying to get a sale of computer ribbons, especially from a company they perhaps were not familiar with. Our job was to convince them of our quality, reliability and delivery, and so Derek Bird's 'new baby' was to become a big success.

Do remember that I could hardly spell, and so my English had to improve. I bought a dictionary and a thesaurus and read books on selling. I had a determination to be the best and win the competitions and prizes. In selling it seemed important for me to know what all these buzzwords meant. I was constantly told or reading about the importance of 'enthusiasm'. "What does it mean?" I thought. The dictionary definition was "keen and eager interest" and, of course, if you don't have a keen and eager interest in what you are selling, your company or indeed yourself, why would anyone else? Memorable Maxim – "Enthusiasm" I'm sorry this is a well hackneyed cliché but the last four letters IASM say it all "I Am Sold Myself".

It was about this time that I became aware of the Institute of Sales and Marketing Management (ISMM), and the book *The A–Z of Industrial*

Salesmanship. I bought a copy for the princely sum of £3.95, and with that was introduced to its author, John Fenton, a man who has probably had more influence on my life and inspired me more than anyone else. John Fenton was the first of the motivational speakers in this country.

I was working hard at being successful at Columbia and it was paying off – I remember getting my first £1,000 for the month. Now I did have some worth and felt valued. I was loving this!

Sheila was putting her personality into our home, and we were buying new things together. As I had finished working at the nightclub and stopped playing snooker, I was now occupied with DIY and gardening and spending time with the girl I loved. Our cat Beano used a couple of his nine lives. The first was to climb under the bonnet and onto the engine of our neighbours, Ken and Renee's, car. Renee drove off with Beano, and some four miles later in Wyke he jumped out whilst the car was moving. A wonder he wasn't killed then, but Renee had seen him and rang Ken, so we set off to find him and indeed spent the next three days searching. We made notices to put through letterboxes etc, and on the Monday evening someone rang – Beano was in their garden. Much to our relief we recovered him. A visit to the vet followed. The pads on his feet were injured due to the landing when he tried to grip the road, but otherwise he was fine.

I mentioned earlier that Alan and Jeannie had moved back to the area and now had their Motorbits business. We spent quite a bit of time with them. In a pub one evening Alan said, "Do you fancy starting your own business? You are obviously an excellent salesperson, I am good with finance and administration. That would make for a good partnership. I have premises, we don't need any capital outlay, we can go into business selling computer ribbons which you know all about – you have the contacts. Sheila is working, so can support you whilst we get established. We can get your green van out to get us going, I can run the business alongside my Motorbits company … what do you think?"

What did I think? I needed to discuss it with Sheila and we both needed to give it careful consideration. Was this providence and an occurrence presenting an opportunity or, as I would rather see it, another example of 'Consequences and Circumstances'? What should we do? What would you do? What did we do?

Chapter 11: The Enterprising Eighties

This is what we did do – in 1980 we started Alba Data Supplies. I came up with the name, with the 'Al' from Alan and 'ba' from Barry.

Columbia insisted on me having one month 'gardening leave', a month when I couldn't work with Alba. I've mentioned that when I was at school in Wales I enjoyed woodwork and made a kitchen stool for Barbara and Peter – well, I used my time off to make four more exactly the same for our new kitchen, complete with breakfast bar, an island etc. I built all the units, the cabinet doors, and the unit top was made from Formica – the glue made me high! Having a whole month like that was ideal as I was able to leave all my tools out. Sheila did the tiling above the worktops, and we were both very proud of this accomplishment, which lasted over 20 years until I had the whole house renovated. The kitchen had a Tricity cooker in it when I bought the house with Jeanne, which was still there in 2010!

For Alba, Alan sorted all the legal side with the solicitors and arranged that he would have 51% and me 49%. He financed it and supplied the premises, so I didn't have a problem with that. We struggled to get help from the banks with finance, as we were a new start-up, and after Alan's bank NatWest refused to open an account for us, we went to my bank, Lloyds.

We took the green van that had been up on chocks in my garage since 1967 out of retirement. Geoff, a neighbour opposite, was a rally driver, so we used his trailer and towed it to Alan's premises in Eccleshill near Bradford where he and a mechanic had to hit the rusted pistons with a large hammer to release them. So with some effort we brought the Bedford Viva van back to life. I mentioned earlier that it was a good idea to keep it, and it certainly provided a company car for me to get started with.

A small regret from this time – Geoff competed in the RAC Rally and often invited me to go along as a driver of one of the support vehicles, but I had to decline; having just started a new business, my focus had to be on that.

Alan was excellent at administration, finance, computers and stock control, and his existing Motorbits business provided him and Jeannie with an income. Sheila was working to pay our mortgage, so all I had to do now was walk the streets begging for money – well, you know what I mean, *selling*!

My Columbia contacts were very useful when we started. We wrote to them advising them about the new business and then I started to visit them with our offering. I made out some new record cards for them, and began lots and lots of cold calling on the telephone and face to face as I went round my area. It's amazing what you can find when you search hard enough. A verse from the Bible is my Memorable Maxim here – Matthew 7:7, "Ask, and it shall be given you; seek, and ye shall find; knock, and it shall be opened unto you." Changing the order of the words perfectly describes the selling process: Seek out new prospects, Knock on their door, Ask for the order and turn them into customers. Remember the letters: SKA – Seek, Knock, Ask – also a music genre, fashionable with mods in the sixties.

We spent the early days sourcing suppliers. Prior to handing in my notice, I had tentatively approached one of Columbia's competitors, Caribonum. I had a meeting with them but they weren't interested and instead informed Columbia of my plans. Columbia rang me to ask whether I was thinking of leaving, so I came clean, told the truth and suggested a business idea to them – that they make Alba their northern distributor. They would save on my salary, my car and expenses and sell to us at trade prices. I would then be selling their products for them. It seemed a very sensible business proposition. It may have been a bit of sour grapes, but they were short-sighted, very silly and refused. Following Columbia's decision not to supply us, we needed a computer ribbon manufacturer. I had a lovely couple of days in Glasgow with the company Farquharson, who were interested in our business, and this trip introduced me to what is one of the loveliest train journeys in the country, the Settle–Carlisle line. Anyway, we eventually settled on a ribbon manufacturer and we were off.

This is how we operated in these early days: Alan had a warehouse area at the rear of his premises where we stored our products. The upper floor provided offices which Sheila and Jeannie helped us decorate and furnish. Our friend Angie designed our logo. I would go out selling in my green van, give the orders to Alan, who would then purchase the products. I would then revisit the area, perhaps a week later, deliver the orders and repeat the process by getting more orders.

As I went round speaking to computer department managers and selling printer ribbons, it became very apparent that purchasing the supplies that these departments required to keep these all-important machines running was time-consuming, a hindrance and an interruption to their work. We needed to make it easy for them by offering a complete range of products.

At the time a satsuma cost about the same amount of money as an orange, but the satsuma is half the size of an orange – so why would people pay twice as much for the satsuma? The answer is that it's easier to peel. A satsuma I could peel in my suit, but with an orange I'd have to stand naked in a bath. Memorable Maxim – "Become the satsuma (make it easy for people to give you money)."

We would become the satsuma of our industry by offering all the things they needed, not just ribbons. So instead of an assortment of salespeople to see and lots of purchase orders and invoices they would have just one supplier to deal with, Alba Data Supplies. However, my enthusiasm to always please the customer sometimes would frustrate Alan, like the occasion when I came back with an order for a stepladder that a customer wanted for his department – but we did supply it!

We began to look for suppliers for these other products – data storage items such as reel-to-reel magnetic tape (£20 each), data cartridges (£100), computer disks (£200–£300), computer listing paper (that green-lined, fan-folded paper with sprocket holes down the sides), printout binders to file the paper in, the cupboards to put the binders in, huge fire safes to store and protect the data storage devices like the tapes and disks (which could cost anything from £1,000 up to £10,000) etc. I made up a ring binder with plastic pockets and produced a visual portfolio of our product range that grew with each new supplier's literature.

Obviously, we started to sell locally and focused on the major cities – Bradford, Leeds, Huddersfield, Dewsbury and Wakefield. As the business grew, I explored further afield into the Sheffield and Chesterfield area, and then into Lancashire, always aware of the need to deliver to these areas (although over the years some manufactures did start to offer to deliver direct to our customers).

Alan quickly saw the Alba business becoming much more lucrative than his Motorbits shop. He told me that in the first couple of months we sold more than his business had in a year, and they had been working seven days a week. It was important for them to be open at the weekend for all the DIY car mechanics that were desperate for parts when they found they needed new spark plugs, brake shoes or a cylinder head gasket. Alba would offer them a five-day week and a greater return for their efforts, so they sold their business and rented the shop to the buyer. Jeannie worked with the new owner to help them become familiar with the running of the business, but Alan could now concentrate on Alba.

Six months later Jeannie joined us as a salesperson and used her Citroën Dyane 6 to get her going. It wallowed along and was quite an experience to ride in – it could almost bring on seasickness! I produced another of the ring binder visual portfolios for her, and used this to teach her all the product range. To give her a good start I passed on my Bradford, Keighley, Huddersfield, Wakefield and Halifax customers, so I now concentrated on Leeds, York, Harrogate, South Yorkshire and Lancashire.

Some time later I recall speaking to one of the customers I had passed on and was shocked when they told me, "Yes, Jeannie comes to see us. She never sells us anything, but we always buy something." Jeannie sold in a very different way to me. She had the ability to go in and talk about their dog or their wife's bad leg, and talking about all those things would result in an order. I would make 20 calls a day, Jeanne would make ten, but be just as productive.

Rosalind Bates was our first employee and joined us in February 1981 as bookkeeper. She was excellent at her job and a lovely person, and certainly contributed to our success – so much so that we gave her a company car for her birthday in October later that year, and she stayed with us for 15 years.

As my South Yorkshire area became lucrative, we decided to take another big step and employ a salesperson to take over the area. I produced another ring binder visual portfolio and we began another stage of the Alba success story, although this was to also be one of the most challenging that I will always remember. I was opening up areas, making it viable for someone to earn a living on commission, so we advertised in the local Sheffield paper, hired a room in a pub and ran interviews all day Saturday. Some people just didn't turn up, but we employed Brian as our first salesperson in Sheffield. He was an ex-computer operator, so he knew the products, and I just had to train him in sales skills.

This was to be the start of a bit of a nightmare. Once you start employing people, you also employ their problems. We made the mistake of choosing the best of a bad lot and expecting too much too soon. Alan said to me, "Barry, you are always going to be disappointed. Not everyone is going to do the job like you." I had too high standards. It could take several failed attempts to find some very good and even some very average salespeople, and it took a lot of time and energy. A salesperson would have to send me in a sheet with all their calls and appointments, so I would go to their first call and be waiting outside to see them on their appointment. If they were late, I would sack them. They were on a small salary, a good commission if they sold and did the job well, plus a Ford Fiesta, and they received all our excellent sales and product training. By the end we probably had about half a dozen (covering the north of England).

Alan and I joined the ISMM and attended their road shows, which is when I first saw John Fenton in action, producing a tiny spark in me. John Fenton was the Billy Graham of selling, the first person like him to appear in the UK. An ordinary Brummie bloke, but an excellent showman, in 1983 he hired the Albert Hall with Henry Cooper as a guest. There were many American motivational speakers such as Earl Nightingale, Zig Ziglar, Dale Carnegie and others, but John was the first in the UK and was to play a very large part in my life!

As Alba's success grew over the years, suppliers would be beating a path to our door and potential suppliers entertained us. Alan and Jeannie and Sheila and I enjoyed some lovely corporate entertaining and dealer conferences. We attended a large conference in Stratford-upon-Avon, and while Sheila and I were out on the Sunday she saw some gorgeous earrings in a jeweller's window. The shop was closed, so I made a note, came home and the next week I drove all the way down there and bought them for her as a surprise – she was very pleased.

We were coming back from the pub one night when Sheila suggested that if I taught her to drive she would be able to drive me home so I could have a drink. I couldn't miss such an offer, so we started the next day … I thought it was a great idea to take her to a car park somewhere with a slope to teach throttle and clutch control – if she could hold the car without using the handbrake, she would learn how to control the car. So that's how we started, in a supermarket car park. It should be said that I might not make the best instructor – I was a very impatient driver myself. Coming through a village called Priestley Green, Sheila nearly hit a large rock on the verge and I went mad. She pulled up and got out. I asked, "Where are you going?" She said, "I'm walking home." Having said that, Sheila did pass her driving test first time!

We had a day out with a supplier at York Races. It was a corporate day, with our own box, champagne cocktails as we arrived, strawberries and a large lunch with lots of alcohol all day, resulting in me becoming very drunk. Sheila was driving and I suggested that we all went into York, to a pub on the river. We sat round an outside table and I said, "If you put £50 on the table, I'll go up to the bridge, strip naked and jump into the river." So there was money pouring onto the table, but fortunately for me Sheila got very angry with me and banned me from doing it! We never knew who put what in the pot, but I became sulky and angry. Sheila drove home and had saved me from a very dangerous jump. Coming out of York she asked, "Which way?" and I said, "You're the ruddy boss!" – which summed up my attitude at the time. What an arse I was!

Some of the suppliers' names I remember include American Clip Company (ACCO to you and me), Twinlock, CDC (Control Data), RPS (Rhône-Poulenc), Wabash, 3M, Lampertz and Chubb Fire Safes. There were many more I cannot remember now.

Our first order for computer listing paper from the manufacturer Standard Cheque Company was something like 20 boxes, but it wasn't long before a huge articulated lorry was delivering 20 pallets of the stuff.

*Loading the green van outside Alan's Motorbits shop
and (left) the sign for Alba Data Supplies*

We were certainly in the right place at the right time, although I remember people saying 1980 was not a good time to start a business – it was the time that interest rates were at 15%. When we started we were only the third company selling this type of product range. I mentioned that when I was at Columbia Derek Bird was concerned that the office stationery industry had been reluctant to enter this new market. Well, much to our benefit, they still were, giving us a clear field to take advantage of this growing and lucrative market. Alan was also aware of the difficulties of finding a good supplier of these products from his experience at Lex and Lookers.

One day I went into Leeds where I had made an appointment with this chap. I sat down in his office and gave him my card, and when he looked at it he said, "You're not from round here, are you?" It was a large engineering works, so perhaps he knew me from one of the factories. "Do you know me from somewhere?" I asked. "No," he said, "I know someone you know and I would like you to leave." I said, "You can't do that without a reason." I thought that my only skeleton in the cupboard was Jeanne, so I asked whether he knew her, and he said, "Yes, I married her." He stood up, came across the room, and I thought he was going to hit me, but he pulled out a photo from the drawer of two children and said, "She's happy now." I did what any good salesperson would and stayed and chatted and asked about her parents ... and we ended up getting on ok! Talk about coincidences ... but I didn't get an order!

I had an appointment at Waddingtons in Leeds, and I was in reception waiting for my appointment. There was a large queue of people, so I asked what they were all waiting for. There was a brand-new Monopoly game coming out based on Leeds, so I asked to buy one when I met my contact, and I still have it – unopened.

In 1986 we bought a copy of *Who's Who in Computing*, an alphabetical listing of companies in the UK with a computer department – bingo! Now we could identify our target market all over the UK. Alan's computer knowledge was invaluable – he set up systems to manage sales, stock and finance, all to make us more efficient, effective and most importantly profitable. Who was the guru that said, "Turnover is vanity, profit is sanity"?

Alan was good with money – in fact, in our very successful years, Alan would invest our spare money, just overnight, in the Channel Islands to get a better interest rate. As partners we took drawings (we never took a wage). We bought shares in all the privatisations that were happening at the time, such as BT, Rolls-Royce, water, electric, gas, building societies etc. As a result we all became 'carpet baggers'! We used a company called Manor Finance, an investment company, and our contact Patrick Wilkinson got us to invest in PEPs and MIPs. These were tax free and I did ever so well at the time. A year or two ago I rang Patrick at home and thanked him – he's retired now, but he said in all the years he had been in business, no one had ever phoned him up to say thank you for his advice. Memorable Maxim – "Remember to say 'thank you', they are two very underutilised words."

As a thank you to Jeannie for all her hard work we made her a partner. She took on the role of sales manager while I concentrated on training and marketing. One of the first promotional aids I had made were drip mats, just like a beer mat, but for your tea or coffee on your desk. I found a

Alba drip mats

manufacturer of beer mats in Huddersfield, and Angie who designed the Alba logo helped with the design of the drip mat, which proved to be very useful and successful. I would leave the mats all over the place, including pubs, to advertise our brand. Another popular marketing aid was the plastic pocket calendar, and I put character spacing down one edge and line spacing on the other as a tool for computer programmers.

We invested in a new Fiesta Ghia for me, but it was a nightmare – I had to take it to the garage 30 times, with problem after problem, and I even wrote to Ford. We replaced it with a Volvo 340 Variomatic, a lovely smooth and safe car.

In 1983 we engaged the services of Chris Kendal, a freelance advertising and PR expert who came two or three times a month. One of the first projects he implemented was a company magazine which profiled the people and the products. We sent these out with invoices, or as a follow up to a phone call with the sales team. Yearly calendars were always popular and of course stayed on show for 12 months. The first issue of *Albadata* featured Alan on the front cover, me inside and our sales team at the time – Jeannie, Madeline (who now looked after the Leeds/York area), Barry (who had joined us in 1982 and covered South Yorkshire), Terri (looking after Manchester City) and Julie (responsible for Greater Manchester) on the back cover. I also now had an assistant to help me (I apologise for not remembering her name; it was 40 years ago, although some names from those days have stuck: Brian, Amanda, Kate, Julia, Dallas and Stuart).

Chris helped us produce all sorts of marketing and publicity material which we would send out with mail, including postcards with prepaid return for more details. He also started to do press releases and helped us when we took a stand at a business show in Bradford. We hired a vintage barrow from Golden Acre Park in Leeds, I dressed as a barrow boy (or

Barrow boy Barry

albadata

Issue 2

The newspaper of Alba Data Supplies, 26 Stony Lane, Bradford BD2 2HN

ALBA OPEN NEW OFFICES

Alba's busy new Sales Office

Alba launch new NC catalogue!

Designed specifically with the NC user in mind, this brand new 8 page catalogue contains everything you could ever need... paper tape, splicing units, storage boxes, spoolers, cabinets - it's got them all!

If you're in NC, don't delay!
Get your FREE copy now. . .

**Ring the Alba Dataline
(0274) 633218** (65)

* A huge choice of consumables and accessories

* Only top quality products at competitive prices

* Quick, efficient and personal service

* Fast, no-fuss deliveries

Alba Data Supplies

* Friendly and knowledgeable advice from local representatives

* 'Dataline' number for tele-sales enquiries

Increased demand for computer consumables and accessories results in need for 100% more office space!

The growth and use of computers in the last 3 years has created an unprecedented demand for high quality data processing consumables, accessories and computer room furniture. Nowhere has this increased demand been felt more than at Alba Data Supplies, the Bradford based specialists formed by Alan Gibson and his brother-in-law Barry Young in 1980.

A fast-growing order book has meant that Alba has had to recruit and train more staff to maintain a quick, efficient and personal service - the sort of service that has made it one of the leading companies in its field in the North of England. And, naturally, more staff has meant more space.

The enlarged office block was opened in August. It consists of a new reception/sitting area and sales office at ground floor level, and a spacious demonstration room at first floor level adjacent to the executive offices.

As Alan Gibson explains, 'It was essential that we had more space, but we were determined to get that

Alba's partners, Alan Gibson and Barry Young, in the new Reception Area

space in a planned, organised way. Not only did we want to cater for our immediate requirements, but for what might be needed in say 2 or 3 years time. We think we've got it right now, but only time will tell!'

There was no mistaking Alba Data Supplies stand at the recent 'Computer Open Day' held at the Dragonara Hotel, Leeds.
IT WAS THE BUSIEST ONE THERE!
Barry and Madeline spent all day showing visitors just how quickly and efficiently PAPER HANDLING's advanced range of bursters and decollators will deal with computer print-out.
A 'guess how much paper' competition was won by Mrs Hazel Blackburn of Control Data, Leeds, with a guess of 562. There were in fact 563 sheets, and for such accuracy Mrs Blackburn won first prize!

Alba magazine

should that be 'bara boy' – another bit of show business?) and did my, "Roll up, roll up" to attract attention to our stand and we also sponsored a show at the Leeds Grand Theatre. We were working hard to promote the company in all manner of ways to continue our success.

All those business books and tapes I was reading and listening to made me aware and gave me an appreciation of the importance of training everyone in the business, so that is what I did. It is no good having great salespeople selling the product, only to have the van driver ruin everything by being offhand or rude when they deliver the goods. I also encouraged the drivers to prospect for new customers. I do love to see initiative, people who make an effort, go out and make things happen, like the guy with sandwich board on the side of road that read, "I want a job." Alan and I were always impressed when someone knocked on our door, looking for a job – it demonstrated enterprise and initiative. Remember the Memorable Maxim – just ten two-letter words – "If it is to be it is up to me."

Promoting the company… this photo appeared in a local newspaper, when I took some Care Bears into a Children's Hospital to cheer up the young patients

Jeannie also assumed the role of social secretary and did all the organising of activities, always interested in people's welfare issues. She ensured we were a very inclusive, caring and sharing company. She was brilliant at it – if someone didn't come to work, she would go round to their homes (sometimes to their annoyance or embarrassment). Alan decided to refurbish the premises to make more office space and install a new roof. It was a Yorkshire stone building, and because I went running at lunchtime, Alan kindly installed a shower for me (I was running on average about 35 miles a week).

We had all sorts of parties and events, including water-skiing with BBQs on the shore of Windermere. Whole families were invited, and Jeannie sorted all the food and drink. Alan would take people out sailing and water-skiing, a great way to build and boost company morale and loyalty. He would take a van full of us up to Windermere on Wednesday evenings to water-ski, and we even had water-skiing practise at Eccleshill Swimming Pool after work. There they had a winch at one end of the swimming pool so that you could sit at the other end with your skis, and then suddenly the winch would pull you off to teach you how to stand up! I also organised Alba's rambles, which were great fun and engendered a team spirit.

By this time Alan also had a yacht moored at Bowness-on-Windermere where Sheila and I enjoyed weekend visits, able to use the yacht to stay overnight if they were not using it. Sheila loved the sailing, but we couldn't move it from the mooring of course. They had also invested in a beautiful log cabin at the Langdale Timeshare in the Langdale Valley, not far from Ambleside. A few years later we used this as a venue for a company get-together. Jeannie had booked a motivational speaker, but I didn't think much of him and thought that I could have done better! I didn't realise at the time, but this was to produce another little spark in me.

There were many parties at Alan and Jeannie's home, Hawkscliffe, up in the Pennines above Sowerby Bridge. It was a lovely large, detached stone-built mill owner's house. In fact, we went with them on a viewing and offered to go halves and share it. It was a delightful home and setting, with extensive views over the Calder Valley, and we have had some wonderful times there. Almost every week we went up there for Jeannie's wonderful Sunday roast which inevitably also became something of a board meeting.

159

This seems a good moment to relate the dog story. We were going to Alan and Jeannie's for Sunday lunch, but I decided to go for a run beforehand. Running across the fields near where we lived, I gave a group of ramblers with a dog a wide berth. Coming back round, they were sat down on an embankment having coffee, having tied their dog by the stile, but they made no attempt to move the dog. When I got to the stile, the dog was in the way, so I climbed on top of the stile and leapt onto the embankment to avoid the dog. However, he shot up and bit me in the b******s and I fell to the floor clutching myself. One of the walkers asked if I wanted a coffee. "No," I said, "I want your name and address!" My trackies were soaked with blood and, clutching my testicles, I ran to the road, waved down a car and explained that I had been bitten by a dog in the groin! Luckily this guy took me home.

There was a doctor living opposite us who was cleaning his car at the time, so he came to our house and examined me as I was sat on the toilet. I got in the shower – it was like something from *Psycho* – and he told Sheila I needed stitches, so we went to the Halifax Infirmary. The A&E receptionist didn't look up, pulled a form over, asked for my name, address, age and what had happened. I said I had been bitten by a dog. "Where?" she asked. "In the testicles," I replied, and then she looked up! She got a nurse (thankfully a male nurse) and when I saw the doctor I was put in a large room on a trolley, completely naked, with four paper towels surrounding my exposed private parts as everyone came in to have a look and a laugh!

The nurse asked, "How should we dress it?" She came back with a suspender-belt type of device with a cup and a hole … my manhood had shrivelled away in fright; the poor nurse struggled to fish it out through the hole! I said, "Don't worry, leave it in there with my balls!" I eventually hired a solicitor to obtain compensation, but the walker's solicitor said that I had startled the dog. I received a £50 out-of-court settlement. In the meantime I went to the small claims court (excuse the pun!) where a young girl at the desk asked for the details. "How much does it cost to sue someone?" I asked. "The fee depends on the claim," she replied, so I had to explain what happened, and she could barely control herself – she went back behind the screen and I could hear everyone laughing, so I thought to myself there was no way I was going to court with this claim!

Alba Data Systems was our next enterprise. Graham Thompson came to see if we wanted to be dealers to sell hardware as well as consumables, as smaller computers were starting to appear on the market. After some discussion, the three of us became partners in Alba Data Systems. We later started another business, ABC Trade Print (with Alan, Barry and Chris), because we were buying a lot of print for ourselves. Alan suggested we buy our own printing press, do our own work and also offer it to others, which meant that we could handle all our own printing requirements. Our first machine was a Heidelberg, and then we had a continuous stationery printing press for producing invoices, delivery notes etc (those with sprocket holes down the side and fan-folded). We also started CCCC (Computer Consumables Cash and Carry) for trade dealers to buy everything they needed. At the same time we purchased a new warehouse on the other side of Bradford, on the Manchester Road, closer to the motorway. Alba Data Systems never really got going, and I dropped out of it, although they carried it on … and then the same happened with ABC Trade Print.

I remarked to Alan one day that we had all these businesses, but I knew nothing about business itself – I was a salesman. I had seen a free six-week course advertised which involved one day a week in Leeds. If I went I would learn about all aspects of the business – accounts, insurance etc – and Alan thought it was a good idea. Alan Stopford owned Strategic Consultants and led the sales training on the course, using other experts to train on other subjects. I mentioned to him that if he ever needed a sales trainer (if he didn't always want to do it himself), would he consider me – and he did, and started giving me bookings! They were running courses down in Sheffield, so he booked me for an evening to do a sales training course for new start-ups etc. As a result I was going down to Sheffield and working for him in the evenings. I had very positive comments from Eileen (who worked at ABC Trade Print), who said how good I was at training, and also Graham, who complimented me on an evening presentation I did for everyone in the businesses.

We made another advance in the company when we introduced telesales and began recruiting for this. We invested in 'TeleMagic', a computer programme designed to manage the records of the customer/orders/call-back date etc. This would replace hand-written record cards and diaries and also monitored the productivity of the telesales team. There were no visual ring binders to produce this time for the new recruits, but an awful lot of training for me, which I loved. If the successful applicant had some knowledge of the products or computers, it was an advantage and made things somewhat easier. I could concentrate on the selling aspect of the job. The *Who's Who in Computing* also proved to be invaluable in expanding our geographical coverage, and we assembled a wonderful assortment of people and gradually increased our spread, including Birmingham.

Again, I cannot remember all the people in our telesales team, although I do remember Ian, who was an excellent salesperson, dedicated to his job and a hard-working and enthusiastic individual. He was also a drummer in the band Terrorvision – I just knew he would be successful, he had the right attitude. It was disappointing but no big surprise when he left us to go professional with the band, and he later married our telesales supervisor Julie. Other names that have stayed with me are Chris, Keith, Cathy and Charles. Charles was another young man I admired – he struggled at times and would disappear for days, but with Jeannie's help and encouragement he also became a successful member of the team, selling into Birmingham for us. He ran a chess club in Bradford and I suspect that the game contributed to his character. I spent some lunchtimes with Charles discussing the future and I am still in touch with him – he now runs a pub in Cumbria.

Eileen from ABC was involved in a charity rowing race on Windermere, so Sheila and I entered with Maggie and Graham, staying at a B&B in Ambleside. It was exhausting but a very entertaining weekend.

Sheila's ideal walk was five or six miles to a nice pub lunch with a pleasant three or four miles back to the car, but walking had become more of a sport for me and I wanted to go further and higher. This was when I persuaded her to walk the Dales Way, an 80-mile walk from Ilkley to Windermere through the beautiful Dales over the Pennines, through the Howgills and into the Lake District, culminating on the shores of Windermere at Bowness. We had driven round the route, planning and booking our B&B accommodation. I had dangled a carrot by arranging for us to stay at Skelwith Bridge Hotel (one of our favourite hotels) for the weekend when we finished.

It was challenging, both emotionally and physically, but a fantastic experience. We walked it in five and a half days, averaging 15 miles a day. We finished in Windermere at lunchtime on Friday and took the boat along the lake to Ambleside to get to our hotel. I had gone up the previous week and left my car at the hotel containing all our posh clothes. I think Sheila enjoyed the couple of nights here more than the walk – in fact, I'm sure she did!

I mentioned earlier that when I worked at Columbia I had won two bicycles … well, a couple of years later I coaxed and cajoled Sheila into cycling the Cumbria Cycle Way. This is a 260-mile cycle route around the perimeter of Cumbria (perhaps 300 miles for the number of times I got us lost). On our third day on the way to St Bees it was pouring with rain and so windy that Sheila was absolutely cheesed off – we had all the wrong gear, including tracksuit bottoms that were soaking wet. There was a station, so I said, "Let's go in the pub, get a drink and food and I'll go and check the trains." I found a train to Carlisle in 1½ hours, so I went back to Sheila and said, "Here's £30, you catch the train, find somewhere to stay in Carlisle and then tomorrow you can get the train from Carlisle back to Bradford and go home. I want to finish the cycle ride."

She agreed, we went to the station, walked to shelter on the platform and I started talking about continuing the journey. She picked me off the ground by the lapels and was smashing me against the glass shouting, "You can't cycle in this," and a couple near us walked away! I got on the train, and in the end I agreed to go with her to Carlisle. We bought two tickets, but after 30 minutes the sun came out and the weather looked beautiful, so I talked her into getting off at Maryport and continuing the cycle ride. I got a refund for the rest of the tickets, left the train at Maryport and cycled to Allonby. The next day we went to Brampton via Carlisle, then down to Castle Carrock, to Kirkby Stephen and then from there to High Bentham where we caught the train home. So we did five days, with about 60 miles a day. Sheila didn't do any more cycling.

In the meantime things were going extremely well at Alba and Alan suggested we each buy a Porsche. I thought he said a 'porch' each, so I built one on the front of the house using those DIY woodworking skills I learnt at school. Later he drove up in his Porsche 944! The porch was a great addition to our home).

One time he wanted to travel to a house he had hired in Port Grimaud in the South of France for a holiday. He wanted to take his boat, so he asked to swap cars with me. The first day I got in his Porsche, I forgot about the long bonnet and drove it into a wall. I worried myself sick about that, about what he'd say to me when he returned home! He was very good about it, and I eventually bought a Mercedes Benz 190E, a real treat for me (which was to save my life a few years later).

I was reminded recently by Maggie and Graham of some of the mail I received addressed to 'Alberts Tata Supplies' and 'Mr Barney Yang' – barmy, perhaps, but not Barney. Richard Whitehead had been my boss at Columbia who had turned us down when we started Alba. Later in life he left Columbia and became sales director with a Singaporean manufacturer of ribbons. He very much wanted our business then and invited us to visit the factory, so I took another chap with me from telesales to Singapore for a fabulous few days as Richard's guests, when we visited the famous Raffles Hotel and sat at the bar with our Singapore Slings.

Sheila worked at Alba for a short period but, as many people will tell you, working with relations is not always a very good idea. There she had her brother, sister-in-law and husband. It was not good for our home life either, spending the evening discussing work. After her brief time at Alba, we decided she would stay at home to look after all the domestic side of things, leaving me to concentrate on the business. It also meant that when I came home we could spend all our time together. She was amazing, doing all the decorating, even outside the house, and would ask a passing neighbour or the postman to move her ladder along a few feet so that she could paint the next bit of the house. I had lots of men jealous of me! When we bought the extra land, we started growing our own vegetables, so she also looked after that.

Having had the life-changing and illuminating experience with Don and Joyce on the fells, we were now enjoying exploring and walking the Yorkshire Dales at weekends. We also enjoyed shopping trips to York, Harrogate and Chester. We had trips up to The Tan Hill Inn, and we arrived there on one Sunday when they and their guests had just ended being snowed in for three weeks. The Bowes Museum was also a favourite destination.

Apart from her two brothers, Sheila had an extended family of stepbrothers and sisters, all of whom made me very welcome and, along with Don and Joyce, they made me feel part of the family. With any family of mine down in the south, this was truly wonderful for me. We had some great times together – nights out, parties and family get-togethers, with weddings, anniversaries etc. One of my abiding memories was when we all went to The Craven Arms in Appletreewick for Christmas lunch, when there was even snow on the ground to add to the atmosphere.

The fields at the back of the house used to be home to a microlight club, using large metal containers to store the craft. One Saturday I saw them out and went over, thinking to myself that I wanted a ride. They told me I should have come over in the morning, as they had been over to Scarborough! Anyway, we went for a quick ride over the area and I thought about joining the club, but sadly someone later stole their machines and it never happened.

We came home from holiday one year to find the peas in our garden had dried out and been ruined, so this prompted us to landscape the garden. We invited six landscapers to quote for us who all promised the world; three replied, and the one we chose put a badly spelt note through the door: "I dont wan your job". So we hired skips and did it ourselves, doing a lovely job using Yorkshire stone for a wall – Sheila would get the stones and cement ready for when I came home. It was a lovely joint effort, including a patio and summer house.

I would go to see presentation lectures by speakers such as Chris Bonington, and I still use the advice he gave back then, "Always keep three points of contact with the mountain." His brilliant book, *Quest for Adventure*, enthrals with a brilliant variety of stories of adventure.

I saw Hugh Symonds, a very well-known fell runner, speaking in Huddersfield on *Running High*, the story of his epic 2,000-mile run in 97 days, half a million feet of ascent, including 277 Scottish Munros, 4 English tops, 15 Welsh peaks and 7 Irish summits. His was the first continuous traverse of the 3,000-foot mountains of Britain and Ireland,

and his video sections were accompanied by the fantastic music from the CD *Into the Light* by Chris de Burgh.

The second visit to Gaping Gill (after the attempt with Henry when his car broke down), this time with Sheila, was successful. We went with Graham and Judi, and a winch lowered us down in all our caving gear. On the way home we called at a pizza place in Shipley, where I bought my first ever calzone … but I ate all the crust first, so was full up and couldn't eat the filling, so Graham ate that part! Now I eat the best part first.

During the 1990s I compiled pop quizzes using a cassette tape-to-tape machine and recording from 45s, LPs and the radio. I would go into a venue and play a piece of music (an intro, or part of it). I would then ask what the group's first LP was, the name of the lead singer etc, and this would go on for four or five rounds, with classical music, easy listening, Christmas hits and more. The landlord would provide a prize for the winners. I used to fill the pub, people were sat on the floor, and I loved doing this and spent hours and hours making these tapes – I think it was that frustrated performer raising its head again. Unfortunately, I eventually had to give up, due to the cigarette smoke and the need to concentrate on the business. I visited pubs such as The Pear Tree, run by Ron and Pauline (Sheila worked behind the bar there a few years later), and The Friendly Inn, run by landlords John and Christine, friends from Sheila's work at the university.

We bought a lot more LPs, including the Mamas & the Papas, Neil Diamond, Simon & Garfunkel, Christopher Cross, Barry Manilow, Stevie Nicks, Duran Duran, Thompson Twins, ABBA, Laura Branigan, REO Speedwagon, Shalamar, Shakatak, Lamont Dozier, Gerard Kenny, Luther Ingram, The Stylistics, Paul Young and Tanita Tikaram. It would be a little while before I fully embraced CDs, as I thought the sound was too clinical and preferred the sound of vinyl (as many do now, with vinyl making a resurgence).

As well as home music, we made home brew using a Boots wine kit and Tom Caxton beer, buying demijohns, plastic barrels and hydrometers etc. It was just about drinkable!

We loved Christmas. I would make a large Santa sack for Sheila and fill it with those polystyrene quavers and add 20 or more presents, like a lucky dip. One year we nearly threw away a pair of leather gloves she hadn't found, but luckily the dustbin men hadn't been! We did lots of entertaining and, to go with the home-made wine, I used my bottle chopper to make six wine glasses from beer bottles (see details online). Unfortunately, and much to everyone's amusement, they fell apart, leaving the stem and the wine all over the table! I think we received wine glasses from our friends the following Christmas.

A thing Sheila didn't love was my insistence on standing on chairs in restaurants to announce people's birthdays – I'd stand up, clap and shout, "Ladies and gentlemen, your attention please." It would be all dead quiet and then I'd say, "It's my lovely wife's birthday today, would you sing happy birthday?" So she would have to stand up as everyone sang happy birthday to her. This was quite a regular thing I did to friends for the next 40 years – to Terry Brooks on the train on the way back from Twickenham, full of supporters, and to Maggie in the Three Shires Inn in the Lake District. Sheila would sometimes be presented with a cake or bottle of wine on the house, even when it wasn't her birthday!

Holiday reading included authors like Harold Robbins and Jeffrey Archer in those days but, as I drove round in my car, I would listen to motivational business speakers like Earl Nightingale, Brian Tracy, Zig Ziglar, Norman Vincent Peale and Dale Carnegie. I also had a Dictaphone to make notes with, so I would write them down later and compile a manual for success.

We enjoyed having trips to see my family down in Kent and looked forward to showing visitors the beauty of the Dales. We took Austin and Rita on a tour of Wharfedale and over the tops to Malham. I have a lovely picture of them at Gordale Scar, complete in waterproofs that we had lent them. There's a sunnier picture at Shibden Hall, the location for the BBC drama *Gentleman Jack*. My niece, Linda, who is very interested in social history, also enjoyed a visit here. We had lovely weekends away to places like Warwick and Shrewsbury, and we walked on the Stiperstones. Teresa and Rita came up on a visit and, as we enjoyed showing them the Dales, we saw a red squirrel – a first for me.

In 1984 we celebrated my 40th birthday at the Lane Head Hotel in Brighouse, attended by friends and family.

With Austin and Rita at Gordale Scar

Austin and Rita at Shibden Hall

We missed the first National Garden Festival in Liverpool in 1984, but we went to Stoke-on-Trent in 1986, Glasgow in 1988, Gateshead in 1990 and I went to Ebbw Vale in 1992. They were all such brilliant events where we had a marvellous time, and it is sad now to see the festival sites fall into neglect as they have. When I went to Ebbw Vale I was able to visit my friends in South Wales, including the sisters who looked after myself and my dad for many years. It was lovely to see them again. Dad had moved back to Kent in the 1970s.

Sheila was always a very keen dressmaker and decided to go back to college for a City & Guilds in dressmaking. She was brilliant – the long coat she made for her exam was stunning, and this and other fabulous items she made secured her City & Guilds qualification. Stuart was our salesperson in Manchester and, in line with our inclusive, caring, sharing, friendly company, Sheila made his wife's wedding dress – it was wonderful and greatly admired on their big day, and we all went to the wedding. Amongst other items she made a couple of sweatshirts, which I still have.

I bought Sheila a lovely book all about the fashion industry called *Sultans of Style: Thirty Years of Fashion and Passion, 1960–1990* by Georgina Howell. It discussed the careers of Ossie Clark, Vivienne Westwood, Karl Largerfeld, Giorgio Armani and Christian Lacroix, amongst many others. Sheila and I were both interested in fashion and fans of Kaffe Fassett, a renowned knitwear designer. We watched *The Clothes Show* regularly on TV and went to the show at the NEC in Birmingham, where we saw Jeff Banks, who we were also fans of.

I encouraged Sheila to go to a similar show in Harrogate. It was a large exhibition with people selling machines and wares, and she visited the PFAFF sewing machines stand and ended up getting a job with them as a demonstrator for sewing machines! Later she joined Husqvarna sewing machines.

I loved going shopping with Sheila and enjoyed helping her buy clothes, unlike lots of men you see sat outside the changing rooms looking bored and being unhelpful. When the women ask, "What do you think?" they usually look away embarrassed and say something like, "Get it if you like it." We also bought a lot of gold jewellery from a small shop opposite the Grand Theatre in Leeds or from Dyson's on Lower Briggate (their clock is quite a landmark in Leeds). Amongst other items we bought a beautiful string of Mikimoto pearls from there.

In 1986 I organised a surprise party for Sheila's 33rd. If you have ever organised a surprise birthday party, you'll understand how difficult it is! I hired a large room in a hotel and got our friends Judi and Graham to call Sheila to ask what she was doing for her birthday. They arranged for the four of us to go out for a meal, so we all dressed up to go to this hotel, walked in and Sheila was surprised by 60 friends and family!

Alan came to me about this time and said that we were doing so well, and because there were 'no pockets in shrouds', we were going to take three months' holiday a year, going away at different times.

English Wanderer

Because I had all this time on my hands, and Sheila was away with her job quite a bit, in 1993 I applied in response to an advert for guides to take guests on walking holidays. The interview was at the Hotel Commodore, in Llandrindod Wells, Powys. They had described all that I would need to know, so I spent three months learning about birds, wild flowers, trees, history, geology and geography. I researched so much and even went up and walked the routes up at Whitby where I left hidden notes in churches to add touch of entertainment. Sheila wondered why I was going to this extent, especially as I didn't even get paid. (although I did get a free holiday). For me it was about personal pride in doing my best – I had a responsibility to do a brilliant job for the guests, the company and myself.

I nearly didn't get the job as, during the interview (which was more like an audition with applicants using a map and their knowledge to lead the walk in turns), the owners called me to one side to comment on my exuberant behaviour. The two owners said I'd done an excellent job, but they thought I was too much of an entertainer and joker. I replied that I'd know whether the guests were up for that or not, so I did get the job in the end.

They explained that the guides buy everyone a drink on the first day, but assured me that for the rest of the week the guests would then be buying me drinks … but no one ever did, and we weren't even allowed to take tips! However, a guy from Australia said rubbish to that and gave me £20!

The first trip was to Whitby. We were sat in a pub one time, when I asked why the guests had chosen this walk – was it due to Bram Stoker, Captain Cook, or what? However, it was the only week they could make! The second trip was to Swaledale, where I learnt about lead mines etc. Two American couples on that trip treated me more like a nurse maid than a guide – "Will it be steep?", "Should I wear this?" – and I had to help the two women over stiles. I didn't do any more trips after that.

Afterwards I did receive two wonderful complimentary letters, one from Australia and one from the UK, as well as a phone call from New York. The Australian customer wrote, "You impressed us by putting your heart and soul into your job."

Cats

At about this time our cat Beano was to use the second of his nine lives. He was a very outdoors animal and would go off hunting and then bring us home his trophies, sometimes still alive. We have often had to rescue a small, terrified rabbit from our lounge. Beano would often stay out all night but was usually back by the morning, but due to this roaming we had put a name tag on his collar. One morning he didn't turn up ... and then neither on the second day. We began another search and delivering notes again. After three months we began to consider the horrible idea that he wasn't coming back. Perhaps he had found a new home or, although we didn't want to believe it, died. Any animal lovers, especially those without children, will tell you how your pet becomes like your child. I always said that if our house was on fire and I could either rescue my neighbours or my cat, I think you know my answer!

We got a new cat, a beautiful white kitten called Misty. We found out later that she was deaf, apparently common in white cats, which provided some challenges. Then one evening we got a call from the wood yard owner, just round the corner – our cat that we had lost was in their garden. We recovered Beano but they wouldn't accept the reward. He had a bit of a wild look about him, but otherwise looked fit and healthy and had obviously been eating plenty of rabbits. Across the road from the wood yard was a large manor house surrounded by woodland, probably where he had been living. When we took him home, he wasn't very pleased to find another cat in his house, and she wasn't too happy about this big black interloper, but after a few altercations they managed to tolerate each other. Sadly, all of Beano's lives came to an end one day and Misty also passed away. We missed them tremendously, but thought they would understand if we got another cat. In fact we got two – Harry from Bradford RSPCA, and Honey from Halifax RSPCA. Both lived happily to a good old age of 15-plus years.

Social Life

Many people I know have a large circle of friends from school days, college, university, playing or watching sports, their children's lives, work etc. Envy is not a good word, but I had always watched *Four Weddings and a Funeral* with a hint of jealousy, where the characters had such a fantastic and eclectic group of friends. Although Sheila and I had missed those opportunities for friends, the 1980s were to be a wonderful time for us, and amazingly we were to meet almost all of our wonderful friends on holidays.

We met Terry and Debbie at Appletreewick, who introduced us to bird spotting. Debbie was playing Mozart's clarinet concerto when we visited them in Mansfield, and I became a Mozart fan after this (Terry was also in a blues band called Old School). We had many, many marvellous times together, with weekend visits at each other's houses, lots of walking and we met their friends Mel and Janet. Janet remembers all the quizzes I used to do.

Sheila worked with Lyn and, on our first night out together with her and husband Neil, Neil and I were trying to out-do each other with impressions, like the programme *The Trip*. Neil played rugby league for Halifax.

Sheila met Hilary at Halifax College when she was doing her City & Guilds course and with Adrian they became good, wonderful friends. We went to a party at their Tranmere Park home and were also invited to a party by a member of the group Smokie, a local band who had a number of hits in the eighties. The four of us had brilliant weekends at a cottage belonging to a friend of theirs, right on the edge of the cliff at Kettleness, near Whitby. It was a delightful one-storey timber structure, painted white and pale blue, with an outside toilet which (if you left the door open) had a fabulous sea view.

This was to start another passion for me, collecting books on Yorkshire topography. It began with some lovely old books that I found on the bookcase at the cottage, including *Broad Acres* by Alfred J Brown (1948), *The Striding Dales* by Halliwell Sutcliffe (1929) and a beautiful book, *Yorkshire, Painted and Described* by Gordon Home (1908). These wonderful books describe a special bit of English life as it was, and as I scoured the antique and second-hand book shops to find my own copies of these gorgeous books, I discovered many other wondrous delights. I now have those first three books among my fabulous collection on Yorkshire topography.

Carol was the daughter of a neighbour and, along with her boyfriend Malcolm, we had some great times together, including staying in Scarborough on New Year's Eve. We'd been introduced to bird spotting by Terry and Debbie and had got Malcolm and Carol hooked as well. All of us had started hunting for a kingfisher and they were down at Yorkshire Sculpture Park when they saw the kingfisher first (we saw it the next weekend).

Apart from being annoying and sometimes embarrassing with my Frank Spencer impersonation, my friends also had to tolerate and often endure my penchant for streaking. 'The Streak' by Ray Stevens was a No 1 hit in 1974 and, although I am not sure if I started then, I do recall my first streak was at a party at our house when I ran round the close, with a policeman (who was a neighbour) sounding a hunting horn to encourage me! I haven't looked back since, although I have had some tricky moments, like when our friends over in Marple locked me out on a winter evening. I was so drunk I set off to walk home, naked, the 30-odd miles to Yorkshire. Graham came and rescued me (not Sheila you notice!). He also almost got into a fight in a pub over there, defending me during a dominoes game. I realised I was stuck with my double six and dropped it into my pint of beer, upsetting the locals!

Judi arranged a surprise party for Graham's 50th where I was the strip-o-gram. The girls lent me the clothes, did my makeup and found me a wig. I wore my large walking boots with stockings and suspenders and, after my striptease act to the music of 'The Stripper' by David Rose, Graham's mum commented that she thought the strip-o-gram was a bit ugly!

This fantastic group of friends that Sheila and I discovered were just like the folk from *Four Weddings*, and for the next ten years or so, these were 'halcyon days' for Sheila and I (dictionary definition: a time, usually in the past, of greatest happiness or success). This was now, and it was fantastic.

Barry the strip-o-gram!

Holidays

One of the first holidays I took with Sheila was camping in the green Bedford van (a very small camper van) to Devon. I remember parking overlooking the sea at Babbacombe, near Torquay, and then we stayed on a farm near Prawle Point – although the toilets were eight miles away in Kingsbridge, a very long journey in the morning … and sometimes a very close thing! One moonlit night we were returning from Dartmouth when I pulled onto the sand and promptly became stuck at Slapton Sands. I had to walk a few miles to a farm and find a friendly farmer with a tractor to pull us out.

We went back to Prawle Point two years later, staying at Maelcombe House B&B on the beach. I was introduced to Bach by a fellow guest and, as with Mozart, became a fan, especially of his Brandenburg Concertos. We had barbecues on the beach, and the owner was a fabulous character. One of the guests asked him, "Is the bathroom ensuite?" to which he replied, "No, oncorridor." This is where we first saw glow worms.

Following our decision to take three months' holiday, Alan and Jeannie's choice of destination was Port Grimaud in France, which took a few days to get to, but he couldn't unwind for the first week, so he stayed for a month. We went down there on one occasion and called in at Chamonix, which is when I fell in love with the Alps.

We met our friends Kath and Dave when we stayed at the Hotel Dolomiti at Malcesine on Lake Garda. When we first went, there were very few British people, although it was very popular with the Germans. Dave helped me with some Italian as the locals didn't speak any English and thought that I was German because I have a fair complexion. Dave and I got better by helping each other. We visited the beautiful little harbour in the evenings, where a small orchestra with piano and violin was playing 'Ballade pour Adeline', which had been a massive success for Richard Clayderman, selling over 20 million copies. This beautiful melody became 'our tune' for Sheila and I. We drank small bottles of wine or ordered a carafe, and took boat trips up and down the lake.

Monte Baldo, behind Malcesine, is 1,760 metres (5,000 feet) high. It has a cable car, but I said I didn't want to take that, we should walk up instead. So some three hours later we reached the top, both exhausted, Sheila more than I (remember, I was a keen walker). She made us go down in the cable car, but it would have been better to do it the other way! Kath and Dave lived in Wakefield and we remained good friends with them. Sheila and I loved Lake Garda and returned, staying in Limone on the other side of the lake at the Leonardo da Vinci Hotel and took a trip to Venice.

We met Tina and Tony from St Helens in Sorrento and had day trips together. Along the Amalfi Coast road, past Positano and up to Ravello. We also went to Pompeii and Herculaneum, which is a smaller and quieter place than Pompeii, with a real atmosphere. I remember we were stood on the coastline on the Amalfi Coast when a great big wave came and soaked me. I had no other clothes with me, but Tina had a little pink one-piece swimming outfit in her bag, so I wore that on the coach! When we first met them, when we finished our meal we went to the square in Sorrento for a drink and they asked if they could come with us. My Italian was much better by then, so I ordered a bottle of wine and three glasses

My pink one-piece swim suit

for them, and a beer for me, in what I thought was beautiful Italian. The waiter replied, "Do you want a pint or a half mate?"

We called Richard and Barbara 'the Carpenters' when we met them in Spain. We took a boat trip to a desert island, I found some driftwood and other items on the beach and dressed up as a Zulu warrior. We drank Sangria for the first time in a bar on that holiday and we all drank a lot that night! I kept saying to Barbara, "It's a killer this stuff," as we staggered back across the beach to our hotel.

Sheila and I went swimming in the sea when Sheila suddenly said, "Look there's jellyfish." I said, "Don't panic, swim gently back," then one stung me and I went out like a jet ski! One night we went out to a BBQ serving cheap beer and wine. There was a band playing, and during the interval we went to the toilet. As always the queue for the women's was huge, so I went into the men's, looked round, took Sheila back in to a spare cubicle, leading her past all these blokes whistling, before I took her back out!

Maggie and Graham (my partner at Alba Data Systems) became close friends and we were to have some brilliant, fun times together. They introduced us to their wonderful circle of friends: Sue and Tony, Sue and Vic, and Dick and Leslie. We enjoyed everything from fancy dress at Christmas in their local pub, 5th November fireworks in their garden (where I sat on top of the lit bonfire), and the Great Yorkshire Show (where Graham was exhibiting his skills as a wood carver and they gave me a beautiful carved otter as a birthday present). Graham amazed us all with this sudden talent of wood carving and over the years has created some wonderful work.

We also had many trips away together to Scotland, including Mull, Gairloch (where we climbed the Horns of Alligin), An Teallach and many more. On a Yorkshire walk from Kettlewell to Lofthouse in Nidderdale, as we set off it started snowing. We couldn't see where we were going and, although I had a compass, we were going a bit off road and, walking for over an hour on the bearing, I couldn't find the track. Then we saw a track with footprints, so someone else had obviously gone that way and we started following them. Sheila eventually said, "They're ours you silly sod!" We had walked round in a circle in the snow! That day I'd promised we were going to get there in time for afternoon tea, but we just about got there in daylight and in time for dinner! Luckily we were staying overnight.

In September 1980 we met Graham and Judi and Ann and Martin at the Hotel Pink in Sicily. When I took a shower the tap came off in my hand and water flooded out of the hole. Sheila ran downstairs to reception, asking the clerk to come to our room, and reluctantly he came up. I had my hand over this hole and, when I took my hand off, water shot out across the floor and sent the clerk into a panic. On the first night, Graham heard the waiter threatening to kill the chef with a carving knife, so the chef left and the food was abysmal! We called the hotel the Spanish Fawlty Towers!

We all went out that night to a bar and got plastered. Graham came up to me with a large mug of beer and said, "It's not Tetley's, but it's a big 'un!" Graham had grown up about half a mile away on Scholes Lane (his parents still lived there), and Ann and Martin lived in Marple, so we all swapped addresses. The four of us went to surprise them one Sunday, me dressed up as Frank Spencer, but there was no reply and a neighbour told me that they had gone to visit friends in Yorkshire. However, we did get together many, many times and had the most fantastic adventures.

I remember Graham and I standing Martin on his head in the snow and Graham falling into a stream after trying to walk across a pipe that went across it. Sheila and I went to Starbotton village in the Dales for a New Year's Eve when, as we were lying down on our bed resting and waiting for dinner, Judi and Graham burst in to surprise me! Mike Harding was also there and we met him out walking the next day. I have a couple of Mike's coffee table books about the Yorkshire Dales and the Pennines. I met him again a few years ago at a folk festival weekend at the Old Dungeon Ghyll Hotel in Langdale.

Judi and Graham had booked into a hotel in Carlisle so we also booked in there – we were going to surprise them at breakfast. However, during the night the fire alarm went off. Graham's mum was with them, and they had to wake her up, but as they were standing outside we crept up and surprised them!

The four of us went skiing in Italy, and like a typical stupid person I hid my money under the mattress. We were halfway back to the airport when I went, "Oh shit, I left the money under the mattress." We contacted the holiday company, they found the money and thankfully they sent me a cheque (with a bit missing) … but a lesson learnt.

Thanks to Judi and Graham giving us some vouchers, Sheila and I had a great holiday in Ullapool, from where we drove up to Durness to visit Smoo Cave. I also dragged Sheila up Stac Pollaidh, along with a few thousand midges. This was one of the many touring holidays of Scotland we enjoyed.

We had many weekends away with Don and Joyce and their two very good friends, Ann and Dennis. The first was also my first Lakeland fell climb, Harter Fell, and then on to Skelwith Bridge to stay at the quintessential English Lake District country inn, complete with outside veranda, beautiful oak-lined reception area, big log fire, smart bar, luxurious rooms with large baths … etc. At the end of a meal they would come out with a whole Stilton and a spoon – a world away from my normal lump of cheddar!

Dennis was an executive at a beautiful wool mill near Bradford, but I used to hide under bridges pretending to be a Zulu warrior – it was so wonderful to see an executive join in with silly things! We stayed at The Lord Crewe Arms, Blanchland, which was one of those pubs often seen on place mats, and The Bridge Hotel, Buttermere. I absolutely loved these weekends. Dennis had a beautiful guidebook to the hills and fells by WA Poucher and, just like I had done with Yorkshire topography, I started collecting Lakeland guidebooks, such as my treasured *The English Lakes* by WT Palmer, with glorious watercolour illustrations by A Heaton Cooper (published 1905). At this time I was introduced to Alfred Wainwright (or

AW as he is known), someone who along with John Fenton was to become a significant, inspiring and influential part of my life. His books have become integral and invaluable to my love for the hills, moors, fells and mountains. More about AW later.

After this introduction to the high life in beautiful country inn hotels, Sheila and I enjoyed walking the fells combined with a bit of luxury. There were two occasions when a weekend trip and one of these guidebooks was to get me into trouble with Sheila and both of us into danger. We arrived at the Sawrey Hotel, Sawrey, on a Friday afternoon; Sheila wanted to relax, but I wanted to go for a walk. However, we became absolutely lost in this wood, so we scrambled down to the lakeshore in the dark. We had to walk along the lake, then back up the hotel, just in time for dinner!

On the same holiday we were going to walk the 'Helvellyn Horseshoe', parking in Glenridding. The guidebook describes a 3 -hour walk, but I hadn't turned over the page where it described the second part – another 3½ hours, and so we scrambled back down again in darkness – that poor girl!

Tordoffs, an outdoor shop in Pontefract, ran skiing trips to Aviemore, although on that trip, on the return journey, the coach became stuck for five hours due to a landslip. We then went to Austria with the same people, and on the horrendous overnight return coach journey I ran some of my pop quizzes to entertain the passengers and pass some time. Before we went, I read the book *Learn How to Ski*, so that when we arrived I knew what to do and I didn't need to spend so much time in the ski school.

Memorable Maxim – "Read a book on your subject objective to give yourself a better chance of success and enjoyment."

Our neighbours Chris and Moyra had recommended the Isles of Scilly. There are various ways to travel there – you can fly from Land's End, or sail from Penzance – we've done both. Some go out by boat but fly back (due to it being a rough journey by sea). There are five islands which you can visit by boat. I remember we walked into the Atlantic hotel bar where the 1984 *American Heartbeat* album was playing. When I bought a drink I mentioned that it was a fabulous album, "I think I would call it soft rock, but I understand the new name for this genre is 'yacht rock'." On this first trip, we had two nights at the top hotel, the Star Castle.

We visited the Isles of Scilly four more times in the 1980s, staying at the Boat House B&B on St Mary's, with the same bedroom each visit. It is such a tiny B&B that you can't but help other guests becoming friends. I remember explaining to some that I thought I was in utopia – I had a beautiful wife, a great business and a good life … although Sheila was not so keen on the phrase. Don and Joyce came with us one year and we met Joy and Richard from Kent, with whom we became good friends and we visited each other many times over the years. From St Mary's we took boat trips to the other islands – Bryher, Tresco, St Martin's and St Agnes. We also used to run around St Mary's (about ten miles); by this time Sheila was also into running and would join me on this stunning run.

We were sat on the beach one morning on St Mary's watching a helicopter fly backwards and forwards carrying sand, water and bricks for building work on the other islands. I asked Sheila what she wanted to do in the afternoon. She fancied a sailing lesson, and asked if I wanted to join her, but I said I'd give it a miss and go to the airport to ask for a ride in the helicopter. "Don't be daft," she said, but I could only ask, especially as I'd always wanted to ride in a helicopter.

At the airport I saw two chaps standing, waiting for the helicopter; when the aircraft came to land, one man who had a large metal stake attached to a wire would touch the helicopter in order to earth it. Once landed, the bag was filled with building materials. So I said to them, "On a scale of 1–10, what's the chance of a ride in that helicopter?" He replied, "Nil … not while we are undertowing." Anyway, I persisted, so they asked me to wait until they had finished when they had a word with the pilot and I was given all the relevant safety drill (and when they said, "If we ditch in the sea" I became a little worried).

Halfway between Land's End and the Isles of Scilly is Bishop Rock Lighthouse. Sheila had often suggested a boat trip there, and I always said no. Anyway, the helicopter took off, and in the distance I could see this finger sticking up … and we only went and landed on top of the lighthouse – I couldn't believe it! We flew back to the airport and I was very grateful to the men. Sheila and I had arranged to meet at the bar for a drink when we had finished our different trips. She had all the gossip from the sailing, and then she asked me, "How did you get on?" So I told her I got a ride to Bishop Rock Lighthouse! I can't tell you what she called me! Just to make up, the next day we took a boat trip to the lighthouse!

Unbeknown to us, we were to have another helicopter adventure … We had started to hire cottages with Don and Joyce for a week in the Lake District, in both March and October, which would of course coincide with my birthday. On one of these October trips we hired a cottage at Buttermere and met for a pub lunch at the Bridge Hotel. After lunch, as it was a beautiful day, I suggested a walk to Joyce, who was the more adventurous of the group. We hadn't even gone into our cottage yet. Nevertheless, we set off up Red Pike (2,150 feet of ascent).

After a short while, Don became less keen, but by the time we had reached the top it was too late. We walked down the ridge, onto High Stile and then High Crag, intending to head down to the lake and back to the cottage. I stopped to watch some climbers at High Stile while the others went on. When I reached High Crag the others were not there. Dusk was coming, I was getting worried and I looked over the edge to see them climbing down an edge which wasn't the right path. So I had to go down and help them back up, but Don was showing signs of tiredness. As we were going back up, Don collapsed. We let him have a rest … but then he stopped again.

Fortunately Joyce is a nurse. She said that I had to go for help – it might have been a heart attack. We had nothing with us – no food, drink, torch – nothing. I thought to myself, "Oh no, I've killed my father-in-law and it's all my fault." I rushed down to Gatesgarth Farm, which was a Mountain Rescue call point, and called the police, who called Mountain Rescue. I told them exactly where our group was, and luckily there was a rescue team on the other side of the mountain on a training exercise who could go up to get them.

By now it was pitch black. I went outside to look at the mountain and suddenly fell into a blooming hole – just like the railways situation all those years ago! Thankfully I scrambled out. The rescue team reached the top of High Crag, but they couldn't find them. Eventually coming down the valley I heard the sound of a large Sea King helicopter, thinking to myself, "How much is this going to cost?!" The helicopter hovered using a search light, then landed so that there could be quiet and the rescuers could shout in the silence, but they still couldn't find them. Then the phone rang again – the party were safe and sound, back in Buttermere. They had come off the mountain when Don had come round and walked back to Buttermere! The doctor examined him, we donated to the Mountain Rescue team and the helicopter team from RAF Boulmer, and Don never went up a mountain again – although he continued to enjoy lower-level walking.

In 1994 I took a trip to the Scottish islands. I bought a 'Scotch Hopper' with Caledonian MacBrayne ferries, starting off on the Isle of Arran, known as 'Scotland in miniature'. Arran has beautiful sweeping glens, with lovely mountains and coastline. I camped in Glen Rosa and climbed Goat Fell. I stayed there for about a week, then caught a ferry across to Islay, then over to Jura where across the road from the distillery is the only hotel, which lets you camp in their garden and get a shower for £1. I went to climb the Paps of Jura route (a famous fell race), which has 2,300 metres of ascent and covers 28 km. I completed it in 12 hours, boasting to the locals, who commented that the fell runners do it in less than four hours!

Running

Burnsall Feast Sports was now a fixture of our leisure calendar. We would stay in the work's transit van, but The Red Lion was open all day during the event and I would get very drunk and ill. To avoid this I decided to enter the fell race in 1986. It is a mile straight up and a mile back down. I thought I had trained hard, but when the race started the climb I realised I had not trained enough. Neighbours Malc and Chris also entered and so we had trained together – I was already doing quite a bit of training, but needed to do more hill work. The path going up the fell is very narrow, making it very difficult to overtake, but fortunately I was right behind a girl with a nice bottom and because of the angle it was right in my face, so I just concentrated on that to forget about the pain! When I got to the top the winner was just finishing back down at the bottom!

The ten-mile road race goes through one of my favourite villages, Linton, with the superb Fountaine Inn which still has a traditional 'Bull Ring' game (if you visit Yorkshire, do not miss Linton). The author Halliwell Sutcliffe also had a beautiful home here. On the Sunday following the sports day, a gang of us would gather at the Fountaine and take our drinks onto the village green. Ever the entertainer, I would borrow some Wellington boots from the landlord and organise a 'Wellie Wanging' competition. Oh, we had such a brilliant time, life was glorious, it really was a fabulous *Four Weddings* gang.

Following the fell race I started to do a bit of fell running when we were away with Don and Joyce. My biggest claim to fame is that I completed the Fairfield Horseshoe, 11 miles over eight summits, four of them over 2,500 feet. I joined the East Pennine Orienteering Club (EPOC), bought a book on how to improve my navigation skills and began entering orienteering events (and even won a few in my age category class). It was a perfect sport for me, involving map reading and decision making, and so combined physical and mental exercise. The other great thing about it is that when you are competing, you cannot think about anything thing else – you need total concentration. Memorable Maxim – "To do things well you need to focus and concentrate your mind".

Burnsall Sports fell race

I entered 'The Karrimor' with Ray Stone, a two-day orienteering event over the Lake District northern fells, during which it snowed. We set off with tent, food etc, and had to visit locations on the map where our card would be punched to prove that we had been there. At the end of day one everyone camps overnight at a designated site where there are two large holes for ablutions, surrounded with canvas for modesty. In the morning I went outside and wasn't sure I could hang over a hole, but the canvas had blown away anyway, and toilet paper was flying everywhere as people were crouching! I decided to give it a miss and set off on day two!

About this time some members of the club invited me to join them climbing Monte Rosa, the second highest mountain in the Alps. I wasn't sure, as I'm not a mountaineer, but they said it was flagged all the way to show you the route. I told Sheila, who said I was mad, but I explained that the route was flagged – as a Yorkshire person, she thought 'flagged' meant paved.

Following the Dales Way adventure, I wanted more of the same. The Pennine Way came onto my radar, and of course Alfred Wainwright had written a guidebook – *Pennine Way Companion* – who better, I thought, to be my companion? It certainly wouldn't be Sheila, and she made that very clear! More of the Pennine Way in my 'Adventures' chapter.

The End of Alba

When we started Alba in 1980, we were only the third company in the north to specialise in computer supplies. We had found a niche market and were incredibly successful. However, by 1994 there were 3,000 or more such companies and the market had changed radically, as the large computer departments had all but disappeared. PCs had replaced them, and data storage was no longer a £300 disk, but a £2 diskette. The office stationery trade got into the market, which meant the purchasing department were now involved. Those two facts brought large discounting and an end to a relationship with the computer manager who had done his own buying. The big sheds such as Staples and Viking Direct were opening, and every man and his dog was now selling computer consumables.

We were losing money and decided to sell the business. Jeannie and I went back on the road to boost sales. In late 1994 Alan said that in order to sell the business we should become a limited company. The accountant explained that Alan took 51% of the company, and Barry and Jeannie a quarter … so by this time I had gone from owning a half, to a third, to now a quarter. Little did I know that at this stage Alan and Jeannie's marriage was also on the rocks. Was this all connected, symptomatic of family working together?

It took a while to find a buyer for the business. In the meantime I had to decide what I would do. I could go freelance and offer training for sales and customer service people, or another idea I had was to approach John Fenton (the man who had influenced and inspired me so much). John had sold the ISMM for £13 million, a large proportion of which came from the sale of the properties, large mansions which had been ideal for residential training courses. With some of the proceeds he had bought Kissing Tree House for £1 million. He set up John Fenton Stratagems PLC, accommodating 16 delegates on his day 'Master Classes' courses, at £300 + VAT per delegate, with usually two courses a week.

At home one morning Sheila was surprised to see me dressed in my suit, collar and tie and smart shoes. "What are you doing?" she asked. I replied, "I am just about to make a potential life-changing telephone call to John Fenton." I was amazed and delighted when I was put through to him. After thanking him for taking my call and introducing myself, I put forward my idea of working with him. He asked me if I was married, and when I confirmed that I was, he suggested that Sheila and I went to stay with him for the weekend to discuss the idea.

A week later we arrived on a Friday morning at Kissing Tree House (KTH), a home previously owned by the Bradford author JB Priestley. It was a stunning property, which apparently cost £40,000 a year to run. John's wife Julie worked with him in the business. I had taken an easel and flip-chart so that I could give a presentation.

John's idea was that I would run his training courses in the north, which of course meant doing them word-for-word, using none of my own ideas. I made several trips to KTH, I sat in as a delegate on one of his Master Classes to get an idea of how I would present them and we also went to another lovely house he owned, which had been a rectory, where it was suggested Sheila and I might live there and run courses.

I was at work one day when Sheila rang me in a panic: John Fenton was on his way to see us. I hurried home and Sheila rushed round the house tidying up. We went out for a meal to The Duke of York at Shelf, just a few miles away. He had come up to have a look at the Hilton Hotel at Ainley Top, just off the M62, as a possible venue for me to run his Master Classes. In fact, I'm not sure that he hadn't already booked it. As I sat in the pub with my guru, I was looking round wanting to say to everyone, "Look who I'm with" – talk about star-struck! I also became concerned that he might be a bit of an autocrat and that my life would not be my own. I had worked for the last 15 years with an autocrat and certainly wasn't going to do so again. I suppose it could be argued that many successful people are autocrats and want control over their own destiny, and perhaps that is really what I wanted. Anyway, Teresa's husband Colin and I had a long chat about my options and we agreed I should plough my own furrow.

The eventual purchaser of Alba was a competitor of ours, Contrac, based in Hull, who I used to sell Columbia ribbons to years ago. I knew Mike well from those days and remember he rang me at home one evening to say that one of the reasons they were interested in buying Alba was me. "I'm sorry Mike," I explained, "I have to disappoint you – you won't get me, I have other plans for my future." In the event, Jeannie and I did some work with Contrac for the first six months to ensure a smooth handover, and I also did some training for their telesales team over in Beverley.

I was sorry to sell, but in truth it was amazing that we had stayed together so long – we were such different characters, although perhaps this had also contributed to our success. We had a good run and a lot of fun, and it had given us a good lifestyle and helped us make some good investments for the future.

Marriage Problems

Meanwhile, as all this was going on, Sheila and I were having our own personal troubles. We hadn't been getting on as well as we had done. I buried my head in the sand, but we should have sat down and discussed things – we never did. I am sure the business played a part in this. I would come home moaning about her brother, which must have been difficult for Sheila, and like many couples we had drifted apart.

I was going away on all these walking holidays on my own. Sheila had a new-found confidence and competence with her job, was loved by everyone and her company and customers thought the world of her. She was travelling all over the country, staying in fine hotels and earning good money. I remember I went with her on a wonderful trip to Elgin in Scotland where I was able to go walking while she worked with her customers, training them and their customers how to use and get the best from their sewing machines. She really was in her element, and all of this would play a big part in both our futures.

It amazes me how couples stay together – some people have told me, "If it wasn't for the kids we wouldn't be together." Maybe Sheila and I should have read *Men are from Mars, Women are from Venus* by John Gray. It sold 15 million copies and I am confident I could have learnt a lot from it – after all, what did I know about women and marriage?

Were we really compatible ... but then, is any couple? She was an evening person, I was a morning person, so we had to meet at lunchtime to have sex. (To explain this, I have to tell you, writing this biography is so tiring for me – I try to work from 7.00 am to 12.30 pm, have something to eat, and then I am in bed for 3.30 pm... but I am 76.)

Sheila liked lying on a beach: I had very fair skin and I burnt easily (remember the Broadstairs incident in the 1960s). I also get fidgety and could not just lie or sit, I had to be doing something. We did compromise and Sheila went away to the sun with the girls whilst I hiked up mountains. I always thought this was very healthy for a marriage, but what do I know?

Sometimes at late-night dinner parties I was so tired I had to lie down while Sheila would still be going strong. I'd say to Sheila as she was still at the table, "I'm going to the toilet, when I come down, we're going home." I look back now and realise how awful this was, but I obviously didn't at the time, or I wouldn't have treated the girl I loved so much so badly. Why was I like that, I wonder? The awful thing is, back then I thought I was a Christian. I realise now that this was not the behaviour of a Christian, but no one told me at the time. I did what I wanted to do and didn't do anything I didn't want to do. One time when we were in Amsterdam, I wanted a beer while the rest of the group wanted a coffee, so I went and sat somewhere else for a beer while Sheila and the other two had a coffee together.

We were up at Alan and Jeannie's on a Sunday evening with some other people; another occasion when I was tired and Sheila was still in full swing. After a bit of discussion, I said I would go home and come back for her in the morning. That was a Sunday, and on Tuesday Sheila told me she had been in Harrogate with a friend all day and she wanted to talk to me. Then she gave me the news ... she didn't love me anymore and was leaving me. I broke down and pleaded; she was very kind and said she wouldn't leave until she thought I would be OK. I said I would stop doing my Frank Spencer impression if that might help. Sheila said, "Baz, I don't want you to stop doing your Frank Spencer impression, you give a lot of people a lot of enjoyment."

We had been together for over 20 years; it must have been unbelievably hard for her, leaving her home that she had worked so hard in, leaving our cats, our friends. Indeed, friends have told me they were shocked at the news. I expect there are many couples who, like us, hide the truth.

I have found recalling all this very difficult and I am struggling emotionally. I have cried an awful lot – even now, after 25 years, it is so painful. I found a piece of paper the other day with the hand-written notes that Sheila had made in Radio Butlin on the procedure for making baby-crying announcements. I broke down in tears again, just seeing her handwriting. I did get an awful lot of solace and boost to my morale the other day, when a friend of ours reminded me of how much I adored Sheila, which also made me cry all afternoon! I have to say all this crying is helping me ... I am wondering if this is some kind of delayed grieving process.

I had to move on then ... and I have to move on now to the next chapter in my life. My circumstances changed dramatically yet again. What would the consequences be of all this?

CHAPTER 12: PLOUGHING MY OWN FURROW

Sheila and I had our 20th and what was to be our last Christmas together. My diary entry for 3rd January 1995 reads,

Sheila and I opened a bottle of wine and had a good long natter about our future. We cleared up a lot of things and both agreed to keep things amicable and avoid paying solicitors. I felt very saddened by it all but Sheila thinks being apart will be better for both of us. We both felt a lot better after a chat (I expect the wine helped). Now it would be the task of telling friends and family.

Sheila rented a house close to her very good friend Debbie in Mansfield – I was pleased she had such a wonderful friend to care for her. Fortunately, I had plenty to keep me busy. The sale of the business was progressing, I had some bookings for training at various companies, my work at Alba and the evening pop quizzes, along with putting together the agendas for my training courses, delivering the evening training courses at Strategic down in Sheffield and of course most importantly 'selling' the idea of training to likely suspects. Memorable Maxim – "Nothing happens until someone sells something."

On 2nd February I had a meeting with Alan and Jeannie at the Guide Post Hotel in Bradford to discuss the sale of the business. We then had a meeting with the buyer at our accountants, Haines Watts – the sale was moving and looking promising. I wanted it sold and to move on with my life.

The next big hurdle for that to happen was on 14th February, the day that Sheila was actually moving out. We had arranged it so that I would not be there to see her go. I had secured a booking for two days of sales training at Ingersoll Rand, over near Bolton. My diary on that Tuesday reads, "Got upset saying goodbye to Sheila as I set off to Horwich at 6.35 am." This must have also been a difficult day for Sheila, leaving the home she had lived in for 22 years, and also leaving her beloved cats. Alan used the firm's van to help her move. It certainly was a challenging day for me, but perhaps a blessing to have something else to focus and concentrate on. As the saying goes, 'The show must go on.' However, I will never forget coming home on the Thursday and seeing the indentations in the carpet where the bed had been.

This is all very difficult to write about now – it must have been absolutely awful back then, after over 20 years together, and although it was not all happiness and bliss, nevertheless we were together all that time. I sincerely hope Sheila did get something from our years together to add to life's rich journey and provide her with many happy memories. The Butlin's experience, which was unique, the Dales Way and the Cumbria Cycle Way must have strengthened her resolve and resilience and hopefully given her some pride in accomplishing what were demanding experiences. I still have the Christmas greetings, birthday cards and love letters she sent me during all our wonderful years together.

We agreed to have the house valued and split the proceeds, and we also decided on how we would share items of furniture and belongings, such as CDs, video tapes, ornaments and other household items. Sheila took the Black & Decker jigsaw – yes, and she knew how to use it! She was a very talented individual! I kept the three-piece suite, Sheila got the bed, I kept the Hi-Fi, she got the TV I think (it was 25 years ago). We would deal with the financial side of things as soon as the business was sold.

Developing My Business

I came up with the name of Training for Business Success (TFBS) as I felt it aptly described exactly what I did – providing training for business success. If you want more success, then here I am ... now all I had to do was demonstrate that to lots of businesses and prove myself. To achieve that I had to devise, design and develop my training courses. The content would be based around everything I had learnt from the hours of listening and making notes from those audio tapes and the many, many books I had read on the subject. I had of course already garnered a lot of material from all the training I had done at Alba, as well as my work with Strategic Consultants.

I learnt early on in my sales career not to be a product pusher, but to be a problem solver. In order to do this, I had to find out what problems the client might have. No one wants to buy sales training, but they may well want to increase sales, improve profits and reduce their costs. So my first training solution was SET – 'Sales Efficiency Training' – for internal or external salespeople, providing them with the necessary skills to achieve those ends.

My second solution was CAT – 'Customer Awareness Training' – which does what it says on the tin (thank you Ronseal for that), highlighting the importance of providing exceptional customer care and explaining how to ensure customers are delighted to buy from you.

My third solution was TELEX – 'Telephone Expertise Training' – designed for anyone using a telephone to help improve their professionalism. It was very obvious to me that many companies needed a lot of help, which I could tell when I rang them up. As part of my solution, some companies employed me to mystery-shop their telephone manners.

Customer Awareness Training
Training for Business Success are delighted to certify that those pictured below have Endured & Enjoyed the Distinctive Delights of Barry Young's Training Course
Training for Business Success - Tele / Fax - 01274 - 874302

When I called and asked for a certain person, I would hear phrases like, "He's actually on his lunch at the moment," or, "She's gone to the toilet, would you like to hold?" which always made me want to say, "Why couldn't she?" If I was told, "He's wandering around the warehouse," I wondered if the person was drunk! "I'm sorry, I'm getting no reply," so I'd ask, "Can I hold?" "No, you're clogging up my lines." A lot of these phrases were accompanied by sniffing or conversations with other people or, worse, shouting across the office – I don't think anyone had told them about the mute button! I thought I was on to a winner and composed a training handout entitled, 'Bloopers and Boosters', including the lines just mentioned, as well as many more examples. The 'boosters' were to help with diction and pronunciation, along with a list of the NATO phonetic alphabet, which should hopefully stop people saying, "A for apple and B for banana." All this was to promote a more proficient and professional image to the customer.

I had to decide on how much to charge for my services. I knew John Fenton was charging £285 + VAT per delegate per day. I decided to create a niche market for myself by targeting businesses like Alba, companies who could not afford to send perhaps three or four people at £300 each – it was also not practical for them to take people out of the businesses for a whole day. I had a plan, a USP ('Unique Selling Proposition'). I would offer to do the training at their premises in the evenings, at weekends or for one group in the morning and another in the afternoon. I would tailor my training to suit their situation and, for just £585 a day plus travelling expenses (the AA and RAC had a recommended mileage charge, whereas John Fenton charged £1 per mile for his Rolls-Royce), I would train up to 12 delegates, which would work out at a fee of just £48.75 per person: a gift! Memorable Maxim – "Offer your prospects a USP with something different to your competitors."

I set myself a target of 50 bookings a year, which would give me about £25,000 a year, less expenses. There were no products, no people, no premises: just me, plus low overheads – perfect. Another thing I was keen not to have was bad debts or overdue accounts. I did not want to spend my valuable time chasing payments. I decided I would have two terms and conditions: No 1, clients would pay me at the end of the day's training;

secondly, if they or any of the delegates were unhappy, they did not pay me. Even if anyone said it was just 'ok', they could keep the money – I did not do 'ok', I only did, "Wow, that was great!"

If I was to secure these 50 bookings, I had to have a plan and clear objectives. I used the dictum that objectives should be out of reach but within stretch. At Columbia and Alba, the aim had been to book at least eight appointments a day and then achieve my daily sales target. Now the goal was easier – to get a booking every week. I set a target of making 100 phone calls a day, but to do this I would need the contact details of at least 100 companies. I spent hours at the library researching, getting information on possibilities from trade journals, associations' listings, books, newspapers, job adverts, looking for companies expanding, employing new people, or moving to larger premises – all of this meant an opportunity for TFBS. I went home when I had a list of at least 100 potential clients.

I also had a Dictaphone in the car to record what I saw when I was out and about, looking for telephone numbers on lorries and buildings. If I had a bit of spare time, I could do some cold calling. I would be happy if I came away with a compliments slip and a name, and if I got to see someone it was a real bonus and a chance to impress. Finding 'suspects' became a way of life – suspects were anyone who might have a use for my training solution. When I spoke to them on the phone and they confirmed that they possibly had a need, they became a prospect; and when they gave me a booking, they became a customer.

The prospect might not have an immediate need, so I would record the information, then contact them in a week, a month or a year. Gradually I built up a portfolio of prospects that were going to pay my mortgage in the future – happy days! Good record keeping came into play, and at first I used the good old record cards and my diary, but it wasn't long before I bought myself a PC – an Elonex PC-486SX with 1MB of RAM, 260MB hard disk drive, 1.44MB floppy disk drive, MS-DOS 6.2, Windows and Microsoft Works package, with keyboard and mouse, all for £1,163.25. Now we were talking!

I soon learnt the critical importance of my calls-to-bookings ratio. I knew that if I made 100 calls, I would speak to about 40 people (the other 60 were not in, not interested or a whole lot of other excuses). Of the 40

I spoke to, I would have ten meaningful conversations with suspects. Now my task was to turn these suspects into prospects and get at least one of them every week to give me a booking. Securing the booking would normally involve writing to them, a personal visit or both, and on some occasions another phone call.

I mentioned before the 'Five Knows' from my little black book: know where to go – how to get there – who to see – when to go – what to say and do. The other maxim I mentioned earlier is, "Better to be 30 minutes early than 5 minutes late." The other reason that I would arrive early was to change into my presentation clothes – after all, this was similar to walking onto stage to perform. I drove in an old pair of shoes and changed into my shiny clean shoes and non-creased jacket in the car park. It was not unusual for me to have all my clothes in a suit carrier and change in supermarket or hotel toilets. I always remember being told, "You don't get a second chance to make a first impression" – Memorable Maxim.

It really was all about attention to detail, which included knowing clearly what my objectives and fall-back objectives were for each interview. My objectives were to secure a booking or the promise of a booking, or at worst to make contact again in an agreed time scale, but I had to come out with a commitment of some kind. I remember the question that I asked at my interview with Columbia that secured me the job, "Is there any reason why you won't give me the job?" I used this same question before I left an interview with a prospective client, "Is there any reason you won't go ahead with the training?" It was horrible to come out and not know how well I had done or what my future prospects were. It takes courage and confidence to ask the question, but I didn't want to sit in my car saying to myself, "What if" or, "If only." *What if* I had asked that, *if only* I had mentioned that. I didn't like to use words I did not know the meaning of and enjoyed using my dictionary and thesaurus. There are two definitions for commitment – "dedication to a cause or principle," and "an obligation, responsibility or promise." Understanding these meanings helped me tremendously. So it was important to give and get commitment.

The interview was the critical part of the process for me, as I was going to be the person delivering the training. My first objective was to build rapport (the definition of rapport is "harmonious relationship"). The prospect had to warm to me and feel that they and their team could get on and work with me. I read that 84% of decisions are emotional, so I needed to put 'emotional deposits' into their bank account. I used the MMFI phrase – 'Make Me Feel Important'. I know that when I am buying something, I don't want people to be subservient, but if I am giving them my hard-earned money, I do like to know it is appreciated. The very simple dictum, 'customers pay our wages', was the thrust of all my training. Remembering and using people's names was critical and helped me make a good impression, as did the art of using my two ears and only one mouth.

It took a lot of time and a lot of reading to understand the benefits of 'Mirror and Matching' – Memorable Maxim. This involved mirroring the speed and volume of a person's voice, their choice of words, being very aware and careful with the use of jargon and colloquialisms, observing their body language and then mirroring and matching all these characteristics. It is a fascinating subject and very beneficial in personal intercourse and interaction. I found that people like you more if you are like them; you have to be a bit of a chameleon, which took me years to learn, and in fact I am still learning the art of rapport even now.

Communicating by telephone is different – there is no visual body language (which I read is 53% of communication), but nevertheless you can still mirror and match the voice. If I put a smile into my voice it conveyed so much to the listener. I used what I call 'positive power words', in the same way that great sport commentators do, "What a brilliant goal!" "What a superb routine." "Marvellous shot!" The great commentators like Murray Walker and Bill McLaren would make everything so much more exciting and exhilarating with their positive power words.

If you ask some people, "How are you?" you often receive answers such as, "Not bad," "Could be better," and "Mustn't grumble." To avoid the risk of answers like that, I filled my head with positives and used the first letter of the days of the week – so on Monday I was, and everything about my training was, "Marvellous"; on Tuesday "Terrific"; Wednesday "Wonderful"; Thursday "Tremendous"; Friday "Fantastic"; and there are plenty for the weekend. I learnt it is not just what you say, it is how you say it – conversing with a smile in your voice engaged and excited the prospect.

I used a female sheep as my mnemonic: EWE ('Enunciate with Enthusiasm'). 'Enunciate' was another word I had to look up, but the dictionary definition is "utter articulate sounds." I listened to BBC announcers and newscasters to help me improve my diction and pronunciation; I used my dictionary and learnt new and different words. I also read about the importance of the handshake. Many of us have shaken hands with a wet, sweaty palm, a cold, limp fish or had our fingers crushed at some time! The brilliant thing about all these insights was that they worked for me, which meant I could share it with the delegates on my training courses with confidence. Selling is all about discussing with a view of mutual agreement. Selling is not telling, it is creative, colourful, coherent, cohesive, constructive, confident and convincing conversations with prospects.

I wrote earlier about how the key to great communication skills was using the gifts that God has given us – two ears and one mouth, in that ratio. Rudyard Kipling wrote, "I keep six honest serving-men / (They taught me all I knew); / Their names are What and Why and When / And How and Where and Who." This is beautiful, probably one of the best pieces of education you could ever receive, which certainly contributed to my success and ultimately my happiness. To ensure I asked the correct but also 'leading' questions, I devised a list of questions that would result in a booking, using Rudyard Kipling's six honest men to great effect. I made use of a fabulous mnemonic: AIDA – Attention, Interest, Desire, Action – cheesy, but effective.

My contrived, conversational closing questions to secure the booking included, "When will we do the training?" – note the presumption that we were going ahead with the training and it was just about when it would happen. My classic booking securing question was, "Where will we do the training?" If they answered this question with the name of a hotel or other venue or, as often happened, showed me where it would take place, the booking was mine. If they took me to see the training room or canteen or the warehouse, I would start moving things around to facilitate the delegates, ask where the plug socket was, where and at what time the delegates would have coffee … anything that got the prospect to visualise the training taking place. It was poetry in motion, salesmanship as an art form and a joy to see. Even better, when on the training day I taught the sales team this technique, the sales director would say, "That is exactly what Barry did to me" – fantastic! I had used this technique when I was selling bursters, decollators and paper shredders at Alba.

My Early Customers

I had a bit of a kickstart for TFBS with some of my customers from Alba and, although my contacts weren't responsible for training, they were happy to introduce me or suggest who I should speak to, which got me some of my early bookings. I cringe now and wonder how I got away with it, as when I started it was all very amateurish, with just a plain sheet of paper and a typed letter heading. I remember Greg Tunesi and Bob Old at Rocom telling me that I was lucky they saw me after seeing my poor letter. It was obvious that my telephone manner got me through the door and a case of the proof of the pudding, because interestingly I worked with Rocom on seven occasions over the following year. I can't remember even having any business cards! How on earth did I get away with it?

It would seem companies loved the idea of my flexibility and very reasonable cost. Early takers of my offering included: Wallace Arnold, William G Search, Sulzer Pumps, Brooks Textiles, Rocom, Nickerson Chemicals, RL Insurance, Britannia Rescue, Rentair, Andrew Page, Charles Birch, Rema Tip Top and Ingersoll Rand, all well-respected companies. The MD at Rema Tip Top was Terry Brooks, with whom I had a rapport straight away. His business was of a similar size to Alba and Terry was a firm believer in investing in his team, so wanted the benefits my training offered. Terry booked me many times at Rema and also secured me bookings with his business associates, becoming a very good friend. Another like-minded man was Phil Hutchinson at RL Insurance in Bradford. I know he had to work really hard to get his bosses to invest the money, but he succeeded, and our first training took place on a Sunday in June. I used the word INSURANCE as a mnemonic to leave with them. More about the adventures of Terry, Phil, me and others later.

I learnt a great phrase from John Fenton, "The best-selling word in selling is sold." He was passionate about testimonials, letters from happy customers, so that is exactly what I set about obtaining from these early customers so that I could then show them to prospects. It worked brilliantly because, when another well-known company said I had done an excellent job, it gave the prospect confidence in my ability and reputation.

I had to make a concerted effort to get these letters, but it was well worth it, providing me with a huge sales team extolling my virtues. I started a ring binder to hold these testimonial letters that I could take to appointments, which was to prove invaluable. I would show the prospect the letters during the meeting, always trying to use a company they knew or that might be in their industry. I would then use a technique to maximise the effect of these testimonials by asking to use the toilet and leaving the binder with them to look through, giving them more time to absorb and register the benefits I had brought to other companies. Quotes such as:

Dragging people from their homes on a Sunday and have them plead to be included on the next course whether it be a weekend or not is a major achievement in itself!
I have never had so much positive feedback about a course as I have for this one.
Money well spent.
Barry oozes enthusiasm.
I have attended similar courses before, but they have rarely been delivered with such aplomb, style and commitment.

Memorable Maxim – "Get other people to say how good you are."

In late February I had a booking at Despec in London, run by Richard Whitehead (who had been my sales manager at Columbia). It's not always what you know but who you know, and I made a habit of networking and keeping in touch with anyone who might be able to give me money or knew someone who could. I combined this trip to London with a family visit, staying with Kevin and Maggie in Rainham. On the Saturday Kevin and I cycled to South Darenth to visit my sister Barbara. It was always nice to see some of my family and as usual Maggie's cooking and hospitality were wonderful.

I secured fabulous multi-bookings from Andrew Page in Leeds. The MD at Andrew Page warmed to me because I had owned and run my own similar-sized business which, although a different product, used the same principles. Like Terry Brooks, he was keen to invest in his growing business, and we shared the same passion for increasing the skills of his team and ultimately improving the whole customer experience. Rapport and enthusiasm at its best again.

I suddenly realised that I had a real USP — me and my previous 20 years' selling experience and business expertise — and that I really appreciated that customers pay our wages. I was going to maximise my USP to benefit my potential for success. I was on my way, paddling my own canoe and ploughing my own furrow. As the record title of that No 1 for Starship in 1987 declared, "Nothing's Gonna Stop Us Now." The bookings with Andrew Page took me to their depots all over the country, and in March 1995 I visited Newcastle. I used this opportunity to go up to Bamburgh Castle, where I remember walking on the beautiful beach just as Sheila and I had done a few years earlier — sadly, this time I was crying my eyes out and shouting out in anguish at my pain inside. I would be doing this sort of thing for years to come.

Our friends Graham and Martin both obtained me introductions to their companies. Martin was instrumental in my working extensively with Ingersoll Rand, introducing me to Roy Heyes, their field sales manager. We hit it off straight away — we spoke the same language regarding sales training, had the same enthusiasm for improving sales skills and it was rapport working again. Paul Moody was Roy's boss, and it was obvious straight away they had a great relationship. I had some brilliant times with them and their sales team. They introduced me to Dave Thompson, divisional manager for the Air Compressor Group, and I worked with his team several times, including a booking at the fabulous Last Drop Village, not far from Bolton (a wonderful venue and lovely place to stay, highly recommended). Both teams sold their products to plant hire companies, and so I would also enjoy a great number of bookings to work with them, as well as the internal people at Horwich — it was a rich seam of business for me. Roy and I are still very good friends, and I have stayed with him for weekends over in Southport. He plays guitar and sings in local pubs and we've had some great times together. In selling situations Roy used a wonderful phrase which I later copied. When the customer asked about cost, Roy would say, "We're not going to be vulgar and talk about price are we?" I love that phrase … thank you Roy.

Graham did the same for me at Croda Paints. I worked with them many times at Hull, Liverpool, Huthwaite and Erith. John Darcy, the commercial director who booked me, also became a long-term friend, and with his wife Angie (who also worked at Croda) we had some wonderful times together. I was to enjoy this wonderful partnership experience of work and pleasure for many years to come. I will be writing about the BBBW in a later chapter. It wasn't really like work, I loved it so much, and it felt like show business with me on stage entertaining people. It also helped me cope with the split from Sheila, and I am sure it helped with the healing process … although I am not sure I will ever heal completely.

My weekend training idea was proving very popular. Some company bosses struggled with getting their people to work on a Saturday and Sunday, so I suggested that they give them a day off in lieu because some people would enjoy having a day off in the week, especially for Christmas shopping! They also had to ask the question, "If our people will not give up just one day to improve themselves and the company, then maybe we have the wrong people?" It is critical to have team players who contribute to the success of the company. If two people have the same skills, what usually sets them apart is their attitude – these are the people who will make a difference. It can also provide an awful lot of job satisfaction.

Securing Bookings

To help me secure bookings, I had produced a list of 26 "Objectives and Benefits of Barry Young's Training". Everything from "Boosting Morale, Motivation and Mentality" to "Developing Internal Understanding, Co-operation and Teamwork". I was certainly in the right place at the right time and benefited from the ISO 9001 certification quality management principles, which encouraged companies to be customer-focused and strive to exceed customer expectations. That was exactly the basis of all my training, as my primary principle; my No 1 Memorable Maxim, was, "Customers pay our wages". They pay for our holidays, buy our clothes, pay our mortgage – just consider that, and you are on the way to providing exceptional customer care. A principle I preached (yes, preached) was that everybody is a sales body and contributes to the customer experience. I call it 'customer concentration'.

Cold calling on the telephone is very demanding, needing all the tenacity and perseverance I could muster. Luckily, I also found it wonderfully challenging and rewarding. The first obstacle was to get past what I call 'the gatekeeper' with their remit to shield the person I wanted to speak to. They could provide quite an obstacle, but it was satisfying when I got past them. The other benefit was, if I did get through to the sales director or managing director, they usually admired my persistence and tenacity, and hopefully thought that this guy could teach our sales team a thing or two – it might be a good idea speaking with him.

To boost my chances of success, and because I couldn't ring people at weekends, I would also send fax messages. (Depending on your age, you may have to ask an older person what a fax machine was!) These were a fabulous way of keeping me in the suspect's mind, and gave me an opportunity to send my latest testimonial letters. I was constantly asking myself, "What am I doing now to get an order?" Like those early gold prospectors, finding new suspects and prospects had to be consistent and persistent. An excellent quote by Calvin Coolidge declared,

Nothing in the world can take the place of perseverance. Talent will not; nothing is more common than unsuccessful men with talent. Genius will not; nothing is more common than unsuccessful men with talent. Education will not; the world is full of educated derelicts. Perseverance and determination alone are omnipotent.
(I had to look up what omnipotent meant.)

I settled into a routine of making my 100 cold calls each day. Many salespeople have doubted the possibility of doing this. I have the evidence

*Training for
business success*

Training for
business success

and would show them my BT telephone bills to prove that it's easily achievable, *if* you concentrate on the task and objective. The point was that if I didn't get bookings, I didn't eat, which focused my mind. Many salespeople receive a salary, so the necessity and hunger might not be there. If they were on commission-only, they would make their 100 calls!

Of course, over time these were not all cold calls – they would be what I call 'warm calls', that is, someone I had spoken to in the past and had agreed that a further conversation would take place. This call may have resulted in an appointment to meet, a further phone call, maybe a week, a month, or even a year later. The call might have followed a meeting to confirm my booking.

All this information had to be meticulously recorded and carefully diarised. When I started in sales with Columbia I was told that it was a good idea to record personal information and use it on future visits. Personally I found this idea fraught with danger. Firstly, I didn't think a busy manager, director or business owner always had the time or the inclination to discuss their health, holidays or hobbies. Secondly, if they did tell me they are going to Bournemouth for two weeks, if, when I spoke to them next time, I thought it was clever and rapport-building to ask them about their holiday (when in fact their partner died in the sea when they were there), would that be such a great start to our conversation?! If they brought up the subject, I would join in. Remember – two ears, one mouth – used to talk about the prospect. (I am sure you have met those people who ask you where you have been, you answer, "Bournemouth," and that is the last thing you say on the subject as they proceed to bore you stupid with their holiday stories … not a great way to build rapport!)

To deal with these follow-up calls I needed all of my dogged determination, tenacity and persistence. As a salesperson it is sometimes difficult to judge the situation and when to make another contact with the suspect. If you ring too soon you may annoy them, but if you leave it too long this may be seen as a lack of interest. It's a thin line to walk, and it is quite an art to get it right. It was important for me to have a very good reason for contacting them again. I refer to this as being 'pleasantly persistent'. Unfortunately, sometimes I was like a dog with a bone and wasted too much time chasing wrong suspects, not realising when to give up. Again, I learnt by experience.

We all get 86,400 seconds or 1,440 minutes a day, and they are finite. There is an adage, "The difference between high and low achievers is how well they use their time." I have been reading my diary for 1995 and I certainly don't seem to have wasted a minute – it is amazing how much I did. Of course, now I was on my own I had everything to do. I did my days at Alba, my 100 TFBS telephone calls at home, visited prospects, prepared for the training days, travelled all over the place delivering the training and the usual paperwork and bookwork associated with running your own business. There were also my pop quiz evenings which I loved – that ego again enjoying the limelight. Not to mention shopping, cooking, housework, washing, ironing, paying bills, changing the bed, mowing the lawn and going for runs over the moors. I was still managing to run regularly – I loved running over the wild, remote Pennines, as the spongy ground was kind on the legs and the peace was wonderful. I was still suffering, crying and missing Sheila so much, so these exerting excursions over the moors were good therapy for my mind.

A benefit of working with Strategic Consultants was that they had many of the Video Arts training films, a company founded by John Cleese, Sir Antony Jay and a group of television professionals. These humorous training films on selling and customer service etc featured many well-known actors and were a good addition to an evening's session, and I took some great ideas from them.

A Busy Schedule

My diary entry for Wednesday 9th August 1995 listed the following: dentist; some good phoning including afternoon appointment on Monday with Cox Hire Services in Leatherhead and Career Track in Milton Keynes; called at Dennis Williams in Bradford re training course arrangements; called in at Alba; went for petrol; drove to Braunston Marina near Daventry to buy the book, permit and key for my Grand Union Canal ride (see chapter on 'Adventures'); had a look at Towcester Racecourse; great meeting with Jackie at Career Track (an American company that delivered a range of training courses all over the UK and were looking for people to deliver them … once again I decided to continue paddling my own canoe, but it is always useful to have a backup); arrived at Ariel Hotel at Heathrow 5.45 pm ready for the two days' training for Rentair Plant Hire; went out for a walk before watching some TV and getting to sleep despite the aeroplanes (I eventually left the hotel on Friday evening at 6.30 pm and had an horrendous two and a quarter hours on the M25 to get to Maggie and Kevin's at Rainham).

On the Saturday Kevin and I cycled to the Isle of Sheppey, where my mum and I had lived in a caravan all those years ago. The sea was lovely and warm, so I went in for a swim several times, and as always Maggie fed me wonderfully with her great cooking. On Sunday we cycled to see Barbara at South Darenth, which was the second time Kevin got me to do this – it was 25 miles each way, and boy was that tough, especially along the A2 with the traffic hurtling past just a few feet away. Teresa was there, so it was great to see her again, especially with her brother and mother. Barbara was sadly in the early stages of dementia, but we had a lovely afternoon, before the challenging ride back home. On the Monday I had a very good meeting with Cox at Leatherhead, securing a booking, and then I went on to meet Richard Whithead in Epsom and secured another booking before driving home, returning at 6.30 pm. All in all a very satisfying six days' use of my 1,440 minutes a day!

Training Philosophy and Style

I mentioned the stages of the sales process earlier: suspects, prospects and customers. My training warned companies not to start taking customers for granted or forget how important they are (just as I had done with Sheila). I prefer the term 'customers with a history', which keeps the focus on them and their future potential to the business. A very good way to do this was to develop a habit of always asking satisfied customers for referrals – did they know anyone else who could potentially benefit from my training? If they did recommend someone, I always sent a thank you letter … it is the last impression that makes the lasting expression. These two words, "Thank you," featured highly in my training; I am often disappointed by the lack of their usage in general society and especially by business managers. Saying thank you, especially with a letter to the home of a team member that has done something well, costs so little, yet can mean so much.

I believe people learn more if it is fun and they enjoy the process. I decided early on that my training would be educational, entertaining, inclusive and engaging. This meant including the managing director, sales director, managers etc. This was important to me because, if they were not there and nothing changed, I might have received the blame, but if they were involved, they would know what areas of the business could be and should be improved. A lovely quote from David Batchelor, the quality and development manager at Saga, summed it up well, "Your presentation was likened to an annual service for a vehicle – you don't really notice anything is wrong until it has been properly tuned."

Every time I stood in front of a new group it was a challenge, but a challenge I relished. There would be the unbelievers, and I could immediately see the person who did not want to be there, who thought that they should not be there and so were going to let me know it. They would sit back from the table, trying to distance themselves with their arms folded, classic body language for 'my mind is closed', not open to what I was going to say. This was an early lesson I had learnt, identifying a buyer who is not interested in what you are trying to sell. The salesperson's job is to get those arms and then the mind 'open', and this was now my job. My literature stated that all courses were presented in a very practical, effective and enthusiastic manner, encouraging delegate involvement. I had to engage and encourage the non-believers to open their minds.

I started the day playing music on my 'ghetto-blaster', so when the delegates arrived they would be greeted with the soothing sounds of Mozart or similar (another favourite was 'Adiemus' by Karl Jenkins). They would be wondering what the music and all my props were about – the table would be full of an assortment of items, including a huge yellow alarm clock with a big smile on the face, a plastic Viking helmet and sword, a rugby ball, a Teletubby, fishing net, large white sheep, golf-putter, policeman's helmet, safety hat, a bowler and a jester's hat, an orange and a satsuma. There would be mutterings, so immediately I had created some interest and involvement.

When I first started these training courses I would go round the table and ask delegates to tell me what they wanted to get out of the day. This made people feel embarrassed and uncomfortable, so I dropped that idea very quickly and replaced it with something much more involving and enjoyable.

I thought if people were investing in this training, then they should attend with their own pads and pen. At my booking with a large building society, I hid all the pens and paper before I asked them, "Write this down." They looked around. "Haven't you got a pad and a pen?" I asked, and suggested they go to reception to beg, borrow and steal something! However, I had to stop doing this, because it started the day off in a bad way and set the tone wrong. I had to accept that not everyone was going to be like me.

To open the day, I would introduce myself to the record 'Young at Heart' by The Bluebells. "My name is Barry Young," I said, "but you can call me Baz. Good morning everyone." After their replies of, "Good morning Baz," I continued, "Today will be a day for the young at heart and a lot of fun. Anyone of a nervous disposition will be frightened to death … Only joking, no one will be embarrassed or asked to do anything silly, the only one being silly today is me." Then I would add, "Here's a chance to earn a bonus point. Hands up if you can tell me who is singing this record." Afterwards I would ask them to make a name plate for themselves with a smiley face on the back to remind them to have fun.

I asked them to arrange themselves into teams of three, mixing the teams with people from other departments – sometimes these people had never met each other – and choosing a team name. As soon as I announced a pop quiz, the unbelievers moved their chairs up to the table and in doing so had to unfold their arms. "The winning team wins this packet of Liquorice Allsorts," at which they all went, "Ooooh!" I would then mention the woman who said, "I don't like Liquorice Allsorts," to whom I almost said, "P@*s off then!" There was nearly always the negative one! I remember being at Manchester Airport where everyone was complaining and moaning about how cold, wet and miserable it was. We arrived in Spain and they were immediately moaning about how hot it was!

As I played the 20-second clips from ten different records, the person in the middle of the group wrote down the answers under the team name, before they all swapped answers and I read out the names of the artists. The teams would clap and cheer when they had the right answer, and then we all celebrated the winners with their packet of Liquorice Allsorts. (By the way, how many would you have recognised? The answers were Heather Small, Chris Rea, David Gray, Dusty Springfield, The Walker Brothers, Kylie Minogue, The O'Jays, The Corrs, Ronan Keating and Ken Dodd singing (what else?) 'Happiness'.)

During a review of the quiz, I would ask how they might have got on if they had been on their own, and whether they did better in a TEAM (Together Everyone Achieves More) – that is, how they would do better at work. We discussed the importance of everyone taking responsibility and ownership, having understanding and consideration for others and why communication and co-operation help teamwork.

Next I would say, "I know there will be those of you who are sitting there saying in your mind, 'Teach me something you little ginger nit'," which always got a laugh. "Well, I am not going to tell you anything, I would not presume to tell you how to do your job, or how to run your lives. You seem to be doing very well without Barry Young. I cannot teach you anything, unless you want to learn something. All I am going to do is just talk out loud, **very loud**, as you can hear, and then you decide what you like about what I say. I love to see success and happiness. I will share ideas and ideals to remind, reinstate and rekindle those things you already know." Later one MD said to me, "I had forgotten I knew that, Barry."

I would ask the delegates to write down one word which is meant by these three definitions: a rule of conduct, a principle and a general truth. The word is 'maxim', and then I introduced the challenge that they had to put their hands up when they heard anything they thought should be a company maxim. At the end of the day everyone wrote down their maxims, and ended up with a list that provided a guide for everyone in the company – and I meant everyone. So when a new person would join the company, they could show them the list of maxims so that they understood the company guidelines regarding conduct and behaviour. We nearly always ended up with a couple of classics such as, "Wash your own cup up," "Put the milk back in the fridge" and "Make customers feel important and welcome." People would also want to add the importance of teamwork and many of the words I used as maxims. They would often finish the day with over 30 maxims, a clear list of concrete ideas and ideals to enhance their future happiness and success. As well as serving as guidelines for how everyone should contribute to the company's success, it also meant I left a meaningful and practical reminder of my training day, demonstrating how the company's investment in me had been worthwhile and money well spent.

After these opening sessions, everyone began to relax and realise this was going to be fun. The more astute realised that these ideas and ideals were transferable and could increase their personal career success in the future. We were off and running and by the end of the day ... the little ginger nit wasn't so bad after all. So the day finished on a high, with us all (well almost all) great friends. It gave me a great deal of satisfaction and joy.

The next day, I had the wonderful challenge of doing it all over again with a different company. Sometimes I did two groups from one company, one in the morning and one in the afternoon. This could be interesting because, as one happy group went out, the nervous, sceptical and perhaps non-believers came in. It was wonderful to see, and I would have to start all over again. I was in my element and loving it.

Outcomes

My training day had to deliver on many fronts. I had promised the person who booked me that my training would increase sales, improve profits and reduce costs. My personal objectives for the day were to inspire and invigorate the delegates to greater and better things for themselves and the company, to enhance their success and happiness. I also wanted to improve the reputation of the salesperson. At one time, if you went to a party and were asked what your job was and you answered, "I'm a salesperson," you were often greeted with, "Why, couldn't you get a proper job?" Yet sales is such an important part of any business and deserves much greater respect. In America, salespeople are much better respected and appreciated for the important job they do. In a large manufacturing plant there, if a salesperson walks past the workers, they all cheer and clap, especially if you'd secured a large order ... whereas here in the UK they might complain about you generating all this work!

My props served as prompts, memory aids for me, and also as visual reminders of important messages for the delegates. I am sure if a previous delegate was asked today what the significance of the big yellow smiling alarm clock was, they would reply, "It's not an alarm clock, it's an opportunity clock – an opportunity to be joyful, full of gratitude and to enjoy those 86,400 seconds we have today." If you go to bed with your objectives for tomorrow and how you will take advantage of those precious seconds (which can never be retrieved), instead of waking 'alarmed' you will wake 'armed'. I am sure some people are quite surprised when they do wake up and then waste those valuable seconds wondering what to do with themselves. I use a to-do list to ensure good use of my time and would get great satisfaction as I crossed items on the list out. (Although I recall one of the items I crossed out that didn't give me any happiness was selling Sheila's bike – although it did remind me of that epic bike ride we did together!)

Some of the comments I received from delegates after a training day included:

"Factual and practical"; "refreshing"; "educational"; "motivational"; "inspirational and effective"; "everyone present enjoyed and benefited from your unique and entertaining presentation skills"; "highly recommended"; "lifts the spirits, your impact has been significant, worth every penny"; "Barry was very approachable if something needed clarifying; "Barry we love you coming to our organisation, you make us feel uncomfortable."

People left the day feeling more positive about themselves and their work. This was all very rewarding for me and reassuring that I was delivering what I had promised.

Over the years I have met people who are not happy in their job and are waiting for the job to prove itself ... but the job could not care less, we have to prove ourselves to the job, so we have to get hold of it and make it happen for ourselves. Remember those ten two-letter words, "If it is to be, it is up to me." That is certainly what my dad taught me. If you are not enjoying your job, do something else, because you spend a third of your life at work. Some people complain that they couldn't change jobs, they had a mortgage to pay for, they didn't have any opportunities. Yet I know people with no legs who have won Olympic medals – nothing is out of reach.

Pushing Onward

In March 1995 I drove down to the Wembley Conference Centre to John Fenton's National Sales Convention. It was a five-hour show with seven speakers, including John of course. Had I joined him, I would have also been on the stage that day. The whole atmosphere and excitement of the venue did ignite another spark inside me and put thoughts in my mind, "One day."

During this period I was going through a roller coaster of emotions. The training was a great success, I was having a marvellous time wallowing in the praise and my ego was being seriously massaged. I was hitting my bookings target. Yet my heart was very unhappy. In March my new bed arrived, when I wrote in my diary, "Spent an entire hour crying; I am missing Sheila so much it's tearing me apart."

Sheila and I did see each other occasionally and had some lovely evenings. Sometimes if she was travelling up this way she would stay overnight, when I slept on the sofa bed and she had the new bed. She sent me a postcard from America that made me cry, calling me "Baz" and writing, "Love Cherry X." Reading my diary, it would seem I cried my way through all of 1995. Telling friends and family was also not something I enjoyed and would upset me – they were surprised and saddened, although didn't take sides, which was good. They were all wonderful to me, and I shall be eternally grateful for their friendship and kindness over the years. I was invited to parties, weekends, Christmas dinners and a whole manner of fun and festivities, which all helped me through this awful and difficult period of my life.

On 11th June the England Rugby Union player Rob Andrew kicked a drop goal in the last minutes of a Rugby World Cup match to win the game against Australia and keep us in the competition. He of course got the glory and the accolades, but I introduced this to my training days as a perfect example of teamwork. In the build-up to the actual kick, many other players were involved in the move, giving Rob the opportunity to kick the goal. Sometimes in our businesses it takes many individuals to win, and everyone must play their part to give you the best chance of success. I also used *Riverdance* as another excellent illustration of teamwork, with the whole troupe of dancers working together in perfect unison. It is so important that we take responsibility for our actions and do our own bit brilliantly.

In June I did another music quiz at The Pear Tree, although during a Gene Kelly dancing impression I fell off a bar stool, much to the audience's amusement. There was never a dull moment at my quizzes, and I loved these evenings of music and merriment (although some of the participants took it very seriously, so I always had my *Guinness Book of British Hit Singles* on hand to settle any disputes).

In July I received a good ego boost thanks to my first referral call from a company that had received a recommendation for my training. I followed up with a visit and secured a booking for two days training – brilliant.

Along with my work I had some very happy times with friends and my neighbours Pat and Mike over the road, who invited me over for Christmas Day and we had other evenings out together. Each year they hired a lovely bungalow that backed onto Windermere at Ambleside, where I was invited to join them – swimming from the end of the garden was a real treat. The hire included use of the leisure facilities and spa at Low Wood Bay Hotel, which was marvellous after a day on the fells as I could swim and have a sauna. Then we would all go out for a meal, perhaps at The Drunken Duck. It was Mike who helped set up my computer when I started TFBS. They are the longest residents of the close and they have been, and still are, very kind to me.

Life was at this stage exciting, hectic and exhilarating. I read or heard that the way to success was to mix with successful people, and so I read successful people's books. I had a fabulous collection of second-hand books and Hay-on-Wye was the perfect place to buy some more. If I asked the question, "How did I become successful?" – well, the content of these books made a massive contribution. When people were impressed with my knowledge of self-development and improvement, I would explain, "They hide all this stuff in books you know." I bought a new book that I felt would enhance my training: *20 Ways to Manage Better*, by Andrew Leigh, which is an excellent book and highly recommended for anyone in management – it was incredibly useful to me.

On 31st July Alan, Jeannie and I agreed the sale of Alba with Mike Goss at Contrac and signed away 15 years of the company. Alan was glad, Jeannie sad and I was somewhere in the middle. We went to a fabulous and favourite restaurant of ours, Over the Bridge at Ripponden, for a celebration meal – or should that be commiserating meal? I have always been grateful to Alan for suggesting the idea of going into business together back in 1979, and the consequences of that certainly contributed to the success I was currently benefiting from. The downside was the unhappiness of my circumstances at the time but, as I write this now, some 25 years later, I have no idea what I really felt then. Did the happiness I was enjoying delivering my training make up for the sadness in losing Sheila?

Anyway, we sold the business and I got my share. I gave Sheila half the money for the business, but then I had to buy her share of the house because she was leaving, so gave her the other half of that share. So in the end I had nothing ... but I did have the house, which I still own 50 years later after I first bought it ... with that view!

I think it was August when we shared out the money. Sheila bought a gorgeous quintessential English country cottage in a village just outside Mansfield, which had been renovated by a woman – it was beautiful, with roses round the door and wonderfully decorated inside. I often went for weekends, and we had some really good times when we still used our pet names for each other, 'Cherry' and 'Baz'. In fact, we seemed to get on better now than we had for some time. Perhaps this was because the business had been sold and Sheila and I were both enjoying our new-found individuality and success. Or maybe I had stopped taking her for granted and realised how precious she was. Probably a bit of both.

I do know my emotions were in turmoil. The words of 'Without You' by Harry Nilsson (a No 1 in 1972) were very, very poignant at this juncture. I had to constantly remind myself of the quote, "Don't be sad for what you've lost, be glad for what you have." I spent many happy weekends with Sheila at her cottage, so she couldn't have hated me too much. In fact, it was seven years before we got divorced, and we never wasted any money on solicitors as Sheila arranged it all at her local court for £120.

Part of the business sale agreement was that the three directors had to continue working three days a week for six months. On 7th September my bookings target received another boost when I spent the morning in Leeds selling for Alba. When I returned to the office, Chas, Sue and Cheryl explained that the new owner Mike Goss had been to see them, so they had sung my praises regarding training – so much so, that Rod, the sales director in Beverley, called to arrange a meeting to discuss the subject. I arranged to call him when I returned from my Grand Union Canal cycle ride, which I began that Saturday(see the Adventures Chapter for more on this). I later secured the first booking of what was to eventually be 15 days' training, right through to March 1996, so a big "thank you" to Chas, Sue and Cheryl!

Bookings, Bookings and More Bookings

I had been working with Interprint in Knaresborough and, following the training, I received a letter from the MD who explained, "The feedback from the 63 people that attended these courses has been fantastic, with the vast majority of them commenting on the uniqueness of your style, which makes the training something to be looked forward to rather than (as in many cases!) something to be dreaded or, at best, tolerated." This was closely followed by an offer of a six-month contract working for them full-time. This presented me with a dilemma, which I discussed with Sheila in a favourite pub of ours, Whitelock's in Leeds. She thought that I should accept the offer, but once again I decided to continue ploughing my own furrow, which was to prove to be a more correct decision than I could ever imagine.

I continued to work with Interprint and had a wonderful relationship with them for many years to come. Dougall the MD sent me a note in January 1996 which read, "Cheque enclosed even though you were crap! God knows why we keep using you. Seriously though a BIG THANKS – you were excellent." The 'excellent' was in very small writing, followed by, "hope you can't read this!" Dougall was a wonderful man with a great sense of humour, who moved on to work with Marshalls Group in Halifax

– no surprise that I also worked extensively with them over the coming years.

I was still presenting evening training courses for Strategic in Sheffield when in July I had a call from Alan Stopford to arrange a meeting with Kingfield, a stationery wholesalers in Sheffield, which sounded a promising prospect. I had no idea what an impact this meeting would have on my life and career. We were met by a lovely woman, Susan Browett. The meeting was to discuss training courses that they wanted to provide for their dealers all over the UK: selling skills, customer service, telephone skills and all the subjects I was successfully delivering. Who better to provide the training than someone who makes 100 cold calls a day, and who had been the sales director of his own very successful company for 15 years (in the same industry)? I came out of the meeting with bookings for Watford, Bristol, Barking, Nottingham and Sheffield. I was of course delighted, but still had no idea of what the tremendous consequences of that meeting would be.

Susan arranged everything – promotion, venues, hotels, agendas, delegate notes and the dealer bookings, who paid for the day's training at a subsidised rate. Susan was wonderful company, a delight to work with, who even did the driving. We stayed at some lovely hotels which had swimming pools and smart restaurants and we had some marvellous times together. All I had to do was what I love to do – enlighten and entertain. My Frank Spencer impression always received a great reception and I had some very positive feedback, "Very good course, I've been in the trade for two years and thought I knew a lot – how wrong I was!!"; "Excellent, I wish Barry was in our office." Susan was able to use these comments in her promotional material for future courses.

My diary for 20th September 1995 records that I was working with Rainbow Holidays in York for two days. After I finished the first day I went for a run along the River Ouse and around the racecourse. I did a lot of thinking and talking to myself. Who helped me to this success? Was it Dad who gave me values – he certainly made me aware of the importance of standing on my own two feet and being responsible for myself? I never really got to know my mum in our short ten years together, but it must have been her who taught me how to tie my shoelaces and wipe my bottom! I am not sure if she was a Christian, but I am sure she will have brought me up with Christian values, good table manners and all those other growing-up lessons. I have no idea what her favourite colour was, what music she liked, where she had been, although that is true of my dad as well – I don't know what he did at work or what his first job was, or anything about his childhood. I never sat down for a meal with both of them, but I was sure they were looking down, hopefully pleased with me. (Writing this book has made me think even more about them, and indeed all of my family – I encourage readers to talk to their family *now*, as you will be richer for it.)

1995 finished on a fantastic high. My bookings target had been 50, and I ended the year at 60, with 11 bookings already in my diary for January. The Music Quiz Christmas Special at The Pear Tree on 20th December had its largest number of players, 61, with people even sat on the floor. Pauline and Ron were delighted, I wore my brightly coloured clogs, and it was a brilliant night as all the Christmas music questions made the perfect start to the festive season. I went down to Kent on Christmas Eve to spend Christmas with Linda and Chris who gave me a very warm welcome. We had a wonderful time, with too much to eat and drink as usual on these occasions. Afterwards on 28th I caught the train home where the cats were pleased to see me. My neighbours Morag and John would come over to feed them when I was away.

As I prepared for the New Year, I looked back on 1995 with sadness and satisfaction. I had done pretty well on my own, both personally and in business. As businesses and as individuals it can be a good idea at that time of year to do a SWOT analysis (Strengths, Weaknesses, Opportunities and Threats). If we know our strengths, we can play to them and see where our opportunities will come from. Identifying weaknesses tells us what our threats might be. Now I could determine what I needed to address or take advantage of in the New Year, so I compiled a list of ways for myself personally, as well as to use in training. How could I improve my performance to increase revenue and profits? These were three of the 17: "Make more telephone calls to better prospects"; "Only call on people who are going to say *yes*"; "Increase my fee."

Two Ken Dodd records played a part in my life in 1995: 'Tears' (which I had shed a lot of this year), a track that had been a No 1 in 1965; but on a happier note, I began ending the training days with 'Happiness', a hit for Ken back in 1964. So we all sang this as we finished the day – it is still a favourite of mine, and I plan to have a lot more of it.

Working with a Kingfield group in Barking, 1997.
Susan seated on the right.

Chapter 13: Positive Prospects

Looking Forward

Something I had been taught ten years previously at Columbia, which is also the title of one of the most influential books I own, *The Power of Positive Thinking* (by Norman Vincent Peale). So that is exactly how I started the year. I had 11 days of training booked in January alone – what a start! I have heard people with all sorts of New Year's resolutions: give up smoking, lose weight, but these are more often than not just promises and abandoned before the end of the month. A friend of mine told how his wife had made a resolution to give up sex for a year, but he didn't find out until September!

Anyway, I found that it was better to make commitments: my first was to continue all the things I was doing that were bringing me success, and my second was to do more of them. I had a diary full of suspects and prospects waiting, so it was back on the telephone, utilising and maximising one my big 'strengths'. Following some research, I also took the decision to increase my fee. Spearhead Training were offering 'Customer Contact' and 'Selling Skills' training days at almost £400 + VAT per delegate per day, so it wasn't unreasonable for me to charge a little more for 12 people. Another big 'strength' for me (and great for the customer) was the convenience of evening or weekend training on their premises. Plus it was much more fun and better training! I used the 'price sandwich' technique – first, highlight some of the benefits of my training, tell them the price and, without hesitating, add more benefits. "Never finish the sentence with the price."

I constantly added new ideas to ensure my training continued to be exciting and engaging. I used my list of 17 ways to improve etc, and my new list of 16, "'How can I ensure customers are delighted they dealt with me?" My favourite from that list is, "Save them time, money and effort". It is all about making it easy for people to give you their hard-earned money (we all know who has become rich and famous by doing just that don't we – I'm delighted to say that Amazon's boss attended one of my presentations … only joking). I made new handouts, 'Why everyone in the company needs to care'; 'How can I improve my performance to increase revenue and profits?'; 'Dos and don'ts for success'; 'How much is a customer worth to you?'; 'How many new customers have you gained this month?'; and 'How many have you lost and why?' I told them that 50% of customers leave us because of 'indifference' – we stop demonstrating that we love them, a bit like I did with my wife, I admitted.

If I thought my life in 1995 was exciting, hectic and exhilarating, that was nothing compared to what 1996 was going to be. I was to have a whale of a time in the next 12 months, travelling all over the UK, working with all sorts of interesting companies and staying in some wonderful places. I did training for and stayed at the Sheraton Grand in Edinburgh, and on the way home I had a night at the famous Tibbie Shiels Inn at St Mary's Loch, halfway between Selkirk and Moffat. This gave me chance to walk along the Grey Mare's Tail waterfall. The Kingfield bookings took Susan and me to Darwen, Birmingham, Glasgow, Bristol, Sheffield and Norwich (where there was an extra dimension, as among the delegates were members of the Christian Brotherhood, so I had to watch my language).

I worked with Call Back, a business based in Southend where I walked along the famous pier and visited the Kursaal amusement park. I hadn't been there since my scooter-boy days, 30-odd years previous. I worked with an amazing variety of businesses, from Wiggins Teape in London to Treats Ice Cream in Leeds, Central Motor Auctions in Leeds to Jespers, a family stationer, in Harrogate. I also had repeat bookings with Cox in Derby and Cambridge.

Other bookings during the year included Hewden Plant Hire in Castleford and Cartwrights in Leeds. I also benefited from recommendations from ex-Alba employees – Chris found me three days' work at Hardy Printers in Castleford and Jackie used me for her telesales team at her new employer in Brighouse. Good old networking – I used my fishing net prop to reinforce and remind delegates of this beneficial activity.

I ended 1996 with bookings at Britannia Rescue, Kingfield and two days with Horsell, giving me a total for the year of 58. I was delighted and buoyed that my second year had again exceeded my 50 target. Some of the feedback from the year included:

The course was superb with plenty of humour mixed with serious notes.
Barry Young is very talented and it is obvious that the UK sales team has benefited from his programme.
Your enthusiasm and determination to communicate the key messages result-ed in a most enjoyable and informative afternoon.
Each and every one of the girls found the course extremely enlightening, not to mention enjoyable.

I had seven bookings for January, so things were looking bright and I was looking forward to another exciting year. I read a lovely quote in one of my books, "There are only two kinds of people who pay our mortgage … customers and rich relatives, and customers are easier to find." I am delighted and grateful that customers are very happy to pay my mortgage.

Perks of the Job

I always asked to be put up the night before to avoid any traffic problems on the day of the training, and so travelling down early the day before gave me a great chance for some tourism. Sometimes the companies also accommodated me the night afterwards, which was a real bonus, and the perfect occupation for me – getting my bed made, my food cooked and making a contribution to people's happiness and success. Keeping busy was also helping my head and my heart. Throwing myself into my work, I believe was also a large contributing factor to my success, along with my passion for the 'noble art of selling', to 'improve customer service' and a strong desire to invigorate and inspire others to better and greater things.

Visiting second-hand book shops was always a priority when I went to these towns and cities. On one such visit I found the most amazing and appropriate book, *The Knack of Selling*. It had no author name but had been printed in 1919 by AW Shaw Company Ltd. I own 20-odd books on selling, but this one is a classic. The language is beautiful, from another era, something akin to Wordsworth. The last paragraph reads,

> *If you will study what the successful salesman does, and think out the reasons for it — if you will work to utilise the motives that make people 'willing to buy' and learn the methods of the salesman to arouse them — you can do what he does. That is The Knack of Selling.*

Oh, pure poetry — music to my ears. I have introduced several passages from the book into my sales training day, as it really spells out what a wonderful art selling can be, if it is done properly and professionally.

Sheila and I saw each other periodically, usually when I went down to stay for the weekend. On one occasion Kingfield booked me into a hotel at Alfreton, so Sheila came across and joined me for a meal. We also met in Baslow, near Chatsworth, and had a walk along Froggatt Edge followed by a pleasant meal. It was always good to see her, but of course it also had that tinge of sadness. I was reminded of the phrase, "Yesterday will never come again, but you have today."

The medal for the 1996 London Marathon was inscribed on the reverse with the phrase, "Nothing great was ever achieved without enthusiasm." At the end of a day working with Rentair, Mick Burgess the MD asked me what pills I was on. "No pills," I said, "just adrenaline and enthusiasm." Remember the definition — keen and eager interest — exactly what I had in abundance, which was in no small way a major factor in my success.

I worked with Croda over in Hull again in June, and one of the attendees, Ian Moor, fed back, "This course was definitely made more interesting by the presenter himself, what a crazy guy! The world would be a far better place if there were more people like him around." Ian went on to win the 1999 *Stars in Their Eyes* Champion of Champions final, with his impersonation of Chris de Burgh, and I have his excellent CD, *Naturally*. My very good friend Graham, who was by then the commercial manager and introduced me to Croda, wrote, "Everyone who attended the seminar commented that learning was made into a fun experience."

Health and Social Life

For quite some time I had been experiencing problems with varicose veins in my lower legs and had been using calf compression sleeves. In September of that year I went for an operation to have them removed, and my neighbour John very kindly took me in and collected me from Dewsbury Hospital. As I was not allowed to be on my own after the operation, I had to stay overnight with Mary, another neighbour. Yorkshire folk have a reputation for their friendliness, and I am blessed with such folk in Moorfield Avenue.

I had met Paul Grieves back in 1966 and he was still a great friend, along with his wife Barbara. We had enjoyed many happy times together, and it was Paul who had repaired my VW Beetle. He and Barbara, along with their son Adrian, now ran WSC, a successful security and communications company in Skipton. Paul had become a councillor and, in 1995, the mayor of Skipton. He and Barbara used to come to my music quizzes at The Friendly Inn in Stanbury, and Paul had installed an alarm system for me many years ago. In October they invited me to a civic dinner in Skipton, a wonderful, grand affair, and I stayed overnight with them. I went to several more civic dinners and, because I worked alone, they very kindly used to invite me to their firm's Christmas dinner, which I enjoyed tremendously. They have retired now – Barbara is an excellent artist, and she even painted a portrait of me. We keep in touch and see each other for a pub lunch every now and again.

My diary doesn't record exactly what I did for Christmas that year, but it does mention Maggie and Graham and Angie and Dave, so I am sure I did spend some time with friends. I do remember that I used to beat myself up by doing things that Sheila and I had done together, such as going to The Pear Tree for a few beers on Christmas morning. I did this sort of thing for years, wherever I went – it might be Glasgow or Harrogate – and I would sit in the same place for coffee as Sheila and I had in the past. (Although one year this worked very well for me, as I met some neighbours from round the corner in the pub and they very kindly invited me to join them for Christmas dinner, so I had a much happier day than I anticipated.) I do always enjoy watching the 1951 film, *Scrooge*, with Alastair Sim – Barbara took me to see it all those years ago.

1997

My first booking of the year was on Saturday 4th January with Orchard in Manchester. A great day was topped off with a letter a week later from Nick Dykins that read, "Barry gets 10/10 for enthusiasm, course content and impact. He says, 'In sales you have to be memorable.' Well, he certainly is!" Imagine, I am getting paid to have nice things said about me – how did this happen? Well, whatever I was doing right, I decided I had better keep on doing and find ways to do it even better. I read that it is good to finish your price with a seven, so I did – apparently it seems less and is even better than the old £3.99 or £399, so instead, £3.87 or £437, for example. It certainly worked for me, as I never had any issues with my fee, and I still had my guarantee, "If I'm not exceptional, you don't pay me."

I posed the question earlier of why I was being successful, and I am sure a big contributing factor was my love of organising, preparation and planning. I enjoyed using maps to plan my journeys to ensure I didn't waste any time or wasn't late. I was always packed and prepared days before I was due to set off, and I am still the same with holidays. The old adage of 'fail to plan and plan to fail' must be instilled in my mind. I know it used to drive Sheila mad that we would arrive at the airport much too early, but I always wanted to err on the side of caution.

Content

The content of my training was growing and improving all the time. Personally I was fed up with mediocre, I wanted wow. How many times have you been let down by abysmal behaviour? All the awful customer service I experienced provided me with perfect examples that I could quote to the delegates and then explain how to really delight their customers and exceed their expectations. I was on a mission to improve customer experience. I used 'Dos and Don'ts – A Checklist for Success', with items such as "Don't pass the buck," "Take responsibility," "Don't make promises you can't keep," "Underpromise and overdeliver," "Give your customers something extra or add that little touch that will make them feel special."

I developed more sophisticated and advanced selling skills training, and taught salespeople to understand the definition of what selling really was and to know 'What and why people buy?' We all buy for just two reasons: 'Hope of Gain' or 'Fear of Loss'. That is why sales in shops are so successful, as we hope to gain because of the reduced prices and we also fear that we might miss out if we don't buy it now. I don't expect I am the only person to come home from town with something I didn't really need! I compiled a list of 40 ways to fail at selling, so now they knew what *not* to do.

Most customer service training courses teach people to smile, whereas I taught that it is not just about smiling; rather, we need to sparkle. This is much more than just smiling, it is a persona, a warmth that comes from within. It is about your body language, the words you use, the impression you portray, and the enthusiasm you demonstrate. The very strong message I conveyed during all of my training, which hopefully hit the nerves of the negative attendees, was that enthusiasm was contagious. In fact, there is only one thing more contagious, and that is the lack of enthusiasm. There are people whom I call the 'dream stealers', telling you, "You couldn't do that," or "That won't work." Science says the bumble bee shouldn't be able to fly with its little tiny wings and great big body, but the good news is that no one told the bumble bee!

I added a Phase Two of 'Successful Selling', another strength that would create opportunities for repeat business, which included a list from the entertaining book, *The Supersalesman's Handbook* by William Davis (he had been the editor of *Punch* and originated BBC Television's *The Money Programme*). The list was, "Why people say yes and why people say no," which provided me with an excellent structure for a training session.

Books

In amongst all of this I was still making my telephone suspecting calls, visiting prospects, securing bookings, organising the travelling trips, keeping up with the housework, gardening and running to keep fit. I did manage to find two more very useful books – firstly, *Making It Happen* by Sir John Harvey-Jones (who had a TV series, *Troubleshooter*, which I watched avidly). I used one of his quotes that I loved, "Most companies fail not in their attempts to be innovative or creative, in this country most of them fail because they underestimate the value and importance of

My passion for books

profesional selling." I wish I had said that, but it was an insight I wholeheartedly agreed with. The other book was written by Frank Dick who had been the British Athletics' director of coaching. His words I took advantage of and used for many years, "There are two kinds of people in my world, valley people and mountain people. Valley people seek the calm and comfortable ground of safety and security. Mountain people have decided that valley life is not for them, and seek to test ambition on the toughest climbs." Inspiring words and, when quoted along with the authors' names, added a certain amount of credibility to my presentations.

Occasionally I still entered local orienteering races. I mentioned earlier about the need for concentration during the event, but the other key to success is always knowing where on the map you are and where you want to go – just like life really, knowing where you are and where you want to be. *Wild Trails to Far Horizons* is a brilliant book by Mike Cudahy, who in 1984 became the first person to complete the Pennine Way in under three days (see how long it took me in my 'Adventures' chapter). Mike writes, "When I stand at the beginning of 100 miles of moor, mountain, valley and meadow I am standing on the threshold of a dream."

Later in the year I was back in Birmingham, working with Lansing again. As I was always extolling the merits of reading business books, one of the delegates lent me a superb book, *Grinding It Out* by Ray Kroc. The opening words of chapter one are, "I have always believed that each man makes his own happiness and is responsible for his own problems." This was captivating for me; I sent his book back to the delegate and bought my own copy. I had no idea who Ray Kroc was but, as it explained on the back cover, "Few entrepreneurs can claim to have actually changed the way we live." The film *The Founder* was released in 2016, although personally I prefer the book.

Samuel Smiles was editor of the *Leeds Times*, and his masterpiece *Self-Help* was published in 1859. I recently managed to acquire an 1880 edition. What a book: it must be one of the first self-help books of its kind (apart from the Bible, that is). In chapter four, 'Application and Perseverance', he writes, "As a bishop has said, temper is nine-tenths of Christianity; so are cheerfulness and diligence nine-tenths of practical wisdom. They are the life and soul of success, as well as of happiness; perhaps the very highest pleasure in life consisting in clear, brisk, conscious working; energy, confidence, and every other good quality depending upon it." Can't argue with that!

Busy, Busy, Busy ...

1997 would develop into another frenetic year; my travels would take me to new exciting places and involve working with different and interesting industries: Wessex Stationers in Christchurch; a forklift truck manufacturer in Chepstow; Horsell Anitec near Huddersfield; WABCO and Cearns & Brown in Leeds; Allied Floorcare in Bradford; Ingersoll Rand at Horwich; Lansing in Falkirk and Aberdeen; CEDA at the armouries in Leeds; Manor Finance in Bradford; COBRA in Aylesbury; Stanley Tools, the Accident Management Group (AMC) in Huddersfield; Allied, RL Insurance, Henderson, Kingfield in Hemel Hempstead and Glasgow; four days at Golden Rail in York; Dormy Stamps in Stockport; and Orchard over in Manchester ... to mention only a few.

The booking with the West Yorkshire Passenger Transport Executive was interesting to say the least. The training was for those who took calls from the public about buses and trains. I began with the usual music and merriment but was interrupted by a secretary with a message from the top man to either stop all the noise or get out – a great way to motivate your people! He really should have been in the meeting, keeping in touch with his people and his passengers.

I had volunteered to speak at a business event at Bradford University which was to prove very important and influential for my future. I made good use of this networking opportunity. Memorable Maxim – "The

Importance of Networking" – always look for a chance to meet someone new who can give you money or do you some good. I met some top people from Lloyds Bank at this event who enjoyed what I had to say and how I said it. That contact resulted in a booking to speak to about 30 of their staff at the Midland Hotel in Bradford, which was my chance to make a show reel, so I hired a video company to film my presentation. I am often asked what makes one person more successful than another. A rather glib but simple answer is, "They want to be more successful." We only have to look at successful sportspeople – the effort, hard work and dedication that they are prepared to invest is because they want success – and so did I. A great piece of advice from Olympic rower Ben Hunt-Davis is that, whenever the team were considering doing anything, whether it was going for a pint, changing their stroke style or training more often, they would always ask themselves, "Will it make the boat go faster?"

Earlier in the year Sheila and I had discussed the idea of a training course for the Husqvarna sewing machine dealers at her head office in Cheddar. So Sunday 31st August found me on my way to Somerset when I found myself shocked and saddened by the news of the death of Princess Diana. This made

Camera man in action at The Midland Hotel Bradford, making a show reel for me

the start to the day challenging, but nevertheless it was a success. I stayed overnight and had a pleasant evening with Sheila and her boss Michael. I was also booked to repeat the exercise in Nottingham on the Friday.

October included bookings with AMC, Croda, Lansing and Kingfield in Bristol and Manchester. Susan Browett had moved to a new job, so two new women were in charge of arrangements. Repeat bookings with companies was thanks to my range of training days, the Phase Two of Sales Efficiency Training, and my all-encompassing Customer Awareness Day that I had introduced that was perfect for *everyone* in the business. I believed everyone in the business had an important part to play in customer satisfaction. Remember *Riverdance* – although it is not just the dancers who put on a show like that, it is front of house, ticket sales, bar people, cleaners, the person at the stage door (if they are rude to autograph hunters, that could blight the memory of the fans), makeup and costume, lighting and sound engineers, directors, producers, writers, musicians … all contribute to the experience of that most critical person, the person who pays our wages, the customer.

ISMM

As a member of the ISMM, it meant that I could go to the regional sales seminars, ideal as a networking opportunity and for hearing ideas from other speakers. I would always ask the organiser Jennie Hardiman for a chance to speak at one of these evenings. After much pestering, she suggested I go down to St Albans to meet the chairman, Sheila Watson-Challis, which I duly did. Her advice was to send a video of me in action in front of a large audience, and if they liked what they saw and felt confident, I might be given an opportunity. This was my big chance – I was able to send my Lloyds Bank show reel. They then offered me the chance to speak at the regional seminars in 1998.

I always looked forward to October, not just because of my birthday, but more importantly it was the ISMM conference at the ICC in Birmingham. I had been going to the regional meetings, which always featured a speaker, but the annual conference usually included seven international speakers and an audience of 1,500 delegates. I would go down the night before and stay at the Britannia Hotel and have a great day out in Birmingham (it's a brilliant place). In the evening I used to sneak in round the back, where it would be bustling with a whole manner of people moving staging and sound equipment, so no one really took much notice of me. I would enter the conference hall and mingle with everyone who was setting up for the next day's event. Looking up to the stage I would say to myself, "One day I am going to be on that stage," in the same way that a football player views Wembley or a tennis player Wimbledon.

Next morning I would be one of the first in the queue, soaking up the atmosphere and excitement. A jazz band greeted us to the reception hall area where tea, coffee and biscuits were available, and around the walls of the room the speakers' stands were being set up. Speakers for the day included gold medal swimmer Duncan Goodhew, Allan Pease and Geoff Burch (I would cross paths with the latter two in the future). This is where they would sell their latest books, CDs, take enquiries or bookings and meet their audience – it was so intoxicating for me. Delegates would visit these stands at coffee and tea breaks and at lunch, so it was also a great day for networking. The conference leader, Adrian Gilpin, wound up the day with a presentation that involved us all standing up, closing our eyes and looking into the future to see what you would like to be doing this time next year. I saw myself on that stage.

Accident

I mentioned earlier that my Mercedes had saved my life – 22nd October was that day. I was out visiting potential clients in Leeds, driving down a hill which had one lane going down and two lanes coming up, with double white lines between them. A transit van was coming up the hill and being overtaken by another vehicle. Suddenly, right at that moment, another car came round these two vehicles, heading straight for me. I had to veer left as much as I could, as the overtaking car pushed these other two vehicles into each other, riding along side by side. There was nowhere for me to go and they hit me. I have no idea what the closing speed was, it could have been 60 or 70 mph, but the collision ripped off the side of their Renault, and they careered up the road for another 80 yards, narrowly missing some families on the pavement. The crash turned my car through 180 degrees, pushed all the engine of the Mercedes into the cab where I was sitting, and I ended up facing back up the way I'd come. All the glass had shattered and hit me in the face.

People stopped and came to help but they couldn't open the door, which was all crushed in. I couldn't get out and someone said I should not be moved, although another said that the engine might catch fire – so I said, "Move me!" They wrenched the door open, but my right foot was stuck under the pedal and I couldn't get out. Meanwhile someone had called the emergency services, and the paramedics managed to get my foot out of my shoe – my shoe was left behind, but they got me out! I was taken by ambulance to hospital where I had X-rays. My foot was badly crushed – the doctor explained it was a bit like a Crunchie bar which, if it has a clean break is cleanly split in two, but mine looked like someone had got a hammer to the Crunchie bar and smashed it to bits! So my whole leg was placed in plaster to keep it stable enough to heal.

Meanwhile the four men who had stolen the car, joyriders, had got out and run away. Whilst I had still been in the car, a police helicopter had come to search for them, but unfortunately they were never found. The families on the pavement had a narrow escape, as did I – the policeman said that if I had not been in a Mercedes, I might not still be alive. All the right wing and engine of the car were crushed, a write-off, and with no insurance from the joyriders the case was handled by the Motor Insurers' Bureau, who thankfully paid out.

Now on crutches with my leg in a plaster from the foot to the thigh, bookings in November were made possible with the help of others. Friends and neighbours took me to the railway station, and delegates sometimes picked me up. The two Kingfield women took me down to Hemel Hempstead, which was to be the end of a fantastic run with Kingfield, with whom I had been all over the country, delivering my various training courses (they now needed to offer their dealers something different). Bearing in mind that I had a huge suitcase on wheels with all my props, training manuals, clothes, shoes and overnight gear, I managed to use one crutch and the suitcase for mobility. The clients were duly impressed with my tenacity and delegates admired my resoluteness. I still did the bookings at AMC, GWS, Reliance, Amari Plastics and Wallace Arnold.

At the end of the month I went down to work with Guise in Milton Keynes, abandoning the crutch and using my suitcase to catch a couple of trains. The bridges over to other platforms were challenging, as was staying at the hotel. The owner of the business took me out for the evenings I was there and also took me to the coach pick-up point near the M1. This made the return journey much easier, and my neighbour John picked me up in Bradford.

My last booking of the year was on 22nd December at carpet wholesalers Mercado in Leeds, which was also to be the start of a long and fruitful relationship, both with them and their retailers who they introduced me to. So, all in all, a brilliant year – I didn't get killed, I had so much fun, visited new places, worked with wonderful companies, made a difference to hundreds of people's lives, and ended with 90 bookings and a healthy prospect list for the following year – plus the big one, a promise of a booking with the ISMM and the excitement of buying a new car. Considering that the policeman had said the Mercedes saved my life, the replacement was bound to be the same make!

Christmas was never the same for me after Sheila and I separated. Friends, family and neighbours were very kind, and I was invited to some lovely dinners and all sorts of festivities, but there was always that empty seat where Sheila would have been. However, I kept my spirits up, with walks on the moors and thoughts of an exciting 1998.

1998 and the Growth of Associations

Following the end of my Kingfield training days I looked for a replacement. I had heard of OSTA, the Office Stationery Trading Association, a buying group that enabled stationery companies to band together for greater buying power and therefore compete with the larger organisations. I arranged a meeting with MD Gareth Morgan and sales manager Brad Wilson at their head office in Barnsley. They had recognised the members' need for training and were organising "a varied, in-depth training programme for the first six months of 1999." Due to my background and the success at Kingfield, they were very receptive to my suggestions. We discussed the idea of copying what I had been doing with Kingfield for OSTA members and agreed to instigate the training. We set seven dates for 1998 and, just as with Kingfield, these would be all over the country. This was a wonderful boost to my bookings diary.

Associations offered a vertical market for me – I had already worked with the MIA and soon secured a booking with the BSA (Beverage Service Association) at Brafield-on-the-Green, Northampton. This booking was followed by a lovely letter from Ted Massey, MD of Cafe Marseille Ltd, "Using only one word to sum up Barry's effect on me and my staff, it would be 'Inspirational'. It is hard to see why we had to coax members to take advantage of this man's expertise when they really should have been queuing up for a place." The CSMA (Civil Service Motoring Association) gave me a booking at their conference in Northants, which led to me working with them at two of their holiday properties, Eaves Hall Country Club at Waddington near Clitheroe, and Whitemead Forest Park in the Forest of Dean. Both locations provided accommodation – what a way to earn a living – this was just getting better by the day!

1998 promised to be another brilliantly busy year with bookings from one end of the country to the other, including Croda, GWS, Lansing, Mechplant, Cearns & Brown, Reliance, CMA, Sulzer Pumps, Ring Lighting, Metro, Kernells, Charles Birch, Tyrolit, WABCO, Reliance, Ingersoll Rand, Wakefield Shirt Co, Halifax Building Society and of course my ISMM regional seminars bookings in Nottingham, Gateshead and Gloucester. I also secured the first of many bookings with GAP Tool and Plant Hire in Glasgow. I had been trying to work with them for some time, as it had been the plant hire vertical market that I had begun pursuing right from those early days of working with Ingersoll Rand – so all thanks to that introduction from Martin back in 1995. It was a great start to what was to become a long relationship and friendship with Ian and Douglas Anderson who ran the company and took it to fantastic success. In the meantime, my neighbour Robert was selling his Mercedes E estate car. I knew he looked after it very well, his father-in-law, Otto, was a Mercedes mechanic and, as the previous Mercedes had saved my life, I bought it.

Accounting and Selling

Our accountants at Alba had been doing my accounts but, as we entered 1998, I decided I needed to employ an accountant of my own and so interviewed two possibilities. I chose Jeffrey Dawson, a real down-to-earth Yorkshireman who told it like it was. I liked his manner. The accountant who was unsuccessful supplied me with a fabulous piece of training material. He wrote to me saying he was sorry he wasn't successful, but appreciated my reasons for choosing another, and that if I wasn't happy in the future he would be pleased to have a further conversation with me. I immediately put that idea into practice if I didn't get a booking, and used this in my presentations as a great demonstration of customer care. I began using Walter Dawson in Dewsbury in February of that year. Another very nice problem I had to deal with was that I had to register for VAT and, as I certainly did not want to spend any of my 1,440 minutes a day doing VAT returns, I also found myself a bookkeeper, a lovely woman called Jean Wrathal who worked from home in Meltham.

I once read a quote from Estée Lauder, "I have not worked a day in my life without selling. If I believe in something, I sell it and sell it hard." Prince Philip said, "It is a glaring glimpse of the obvious that no amount of production is of any use at all unless the goods are sold for cash." I have seen people with great ideas, services and products but unfortunately not the skills to sell. James Dyson demonstrated persistence and tenacity. He had over 5,000 prototypes of his bagless vacuum cleaner and once he got it right, he went out and sold it … and thank goodness he did, I love mine! His book, *Against the Odds*, is a great read. Anita Roddick said, "My passionate belief is that business can be fun, it can be conducted with love and a powerful force for good." Her wonderful, inspirational book is *Body and Soul*.

My thoughts are that selling is about helping people to buy, to make a decision. I am a Libran, which I believe makes me weigh things up too much and sometimes for too long. I need a salesperson to push me over the edge, to help make me take a decision. A perfect example of this happened in a men's clothes shop in Leeds. I was trying on a beautiful pure new wool and rather colourful jacket. It was expensive – in fact, I had bought complete suits for less – and I was procrastinating. A man appeared with the customary tape measure around his neck and said, "You look like a model in that sir." I couldn't get to the till fast enough! I have used this philosophy of helping people, making it easy in every way I can, for them to give me an order or a booking. It has proved to be very successful. I am reminded of the 1981 Eurovision winning song by Bucks Fizz, 'Making Your Mind Up'.

ISMM Chief Ex Patrick Joiner in the middle at front laughing

ISMM Regional Seminar and Eurotel

Tuesday 2nd. June 1998 would be another stepping stone, a pivotal date in Barry Young's life and ambitions. This was my first ISMM regional seminar with the title, 'Selling on the Telephone'. Only half an hour to an audience of about 50, but the good news about only 30 minutes is that you leave them wanting more. My new rather jazzy jacket that I thought would look good on stage would also have its first outing, making me be a bit different and a change from all the usual dark-coloured business suits. This half an hour prompted a letter from the ISMM chief executive, Patrick Joiner, with this observation, "The feedback from our members has been excellent and the ovation at the end of your presentation was the longest I have ever heard at an ISMM seminar." I can't tell you how important these few words were to my future.

That 30 minutes was also enough to get me a booking with Eurotel, a telephone communications company in Halifax owned by brothers Robert and Keith Lutener. I gave a three-hour presentation at their national sales conference and went on to work extensively with their telesales team.

The Institute of SALES & MARKETING MANAGEMENT

FREE Regional Sales Seminar

The Gables Inn, Bristol Road, Falfield, Gloucestershire

Thursday 17th September 1998

Tea/coffee served from 6.30pm. Seminar commences at 7.00pm

SELLING ON THE TELEPHONE
featuring Barry Young

C ... for Challenge
O ... for Organisation
M ... for Marketing
M ... for Management
U ... for Understanding
N ... for Networking
I ... for Inspiration
C ... for Communication
A ... for Achieve
T ... for Teamwork
E ... for Enthusiasm

With road traffic and parking problems growing daily, it is becoming increasingly difficult to make face-to-face selling effective and profitable. One way to overcome this is to use the telephone pro-actively to enhance the sale effort. Delivered with enthusiasm and humour, Barry Young's presentation will show how the telephone, when it is used properly for prospecting, qualifying and quantifying, reduces wasted time and effort and ensures that subsequent face-to-face calls are more effective. Barry's expertise in this area is based upon the knowledge and experience he has gained from more than 22 years as a salesman, sales manager, sales director (of his own telesales company) and as a successful trainer.

BOOK YOUR PLACE/S NOW! Complete the form below or call Jennie Harnaman on 01727 812500 for more details. And remember... you can bring a guest too!

- - - - - - - ✂ -

❏ Yes, please reserve me .... places at the Western Regional Seminar on 17th Sept 1998

Christian name ....

Daytime telephone number ....Surname ....(ME Invite)

Company name.. Fax number ....

Guest name(s) and company name..

Please fax to Jennie Harnaman on 01727 812525 or return to ISMM, FREEPOST ANG 0543, St Albans AL3 4BR

ISMM Regional Seminar advert

Robert and Keith had all sorts of terrific bonus schemes in place and, if there was a special football or tennis match, it was phones down to watch it on a big screen in the office. An amount of money would be paid for generating a lead for the sales team; if the salesperson secured an order, they would phone in with a special code that gave the telesales person another bonus. This would be relayed to the team and be greeted with applause, bells, whistles and hooters, creating the most tremendous atmosphere and motivating environment.

Like me, both brothers were well aware of the importance of the engineers who installed the equipment and were the final part of the process of happy customers. A 'Customer Awareness' session for these engineers was arranged for a Friday afternoon in October, the day before my birthday. As always Robert and Keith did things well, and a marvellous buffet lunch greeted delegates when they arrived. I recognised the "I don't want to be here," "I don't need to be told how to do my job" and all the other unbelievers. I started with my "teach me something you little ginger nit" and said to them, "What I know about installing telecommunications equipment could be written on the back of a postage stamp." We played the pop quiz, which they enjoyed.

Then I made them aware of the telesales team who sat in a room making cold calls all day so that they had the job of installation, and how important they were in the process. They began to warm to me, and soon it became an afternoon of laughing and learning with more buffet and bottles of beer served, and when we finished we followed the day with a night out in Halifax. I got very drunk, fell across the floor and into a girl's arms doing my John Travolta impression! When I was sent into the ladies instead of the gents, I decided I had better go home. I woke up feeling awful, wandered round for a while (as you do) and realised to my horror it was Sunday – I had lost a whole day, my birthday! I often wonder if one of my drinks was spiked!

Motivation

I was often asked how to motivate people. I don't believe we can motivate other people, because we are all motivated by different things. My aim is to inspire people and I believe that companies have to inspire their people to be self-motivated. One company had what I thought was a great idea – they paid a bonus if all the internal sales team came to work when they should and on time. If any one person didn't turn up or was late, no one received the bonus. This certainly encouraged teamwork and self-motivation. Another MD, when confronted with some of his people who did not want to come to a training session on a Saturday morning unless paid, announced that it would be voluntary – and then he did pay those who came voluntarily. This told him a lot about some of his people, revealing those who were self-motivated and interested in self-development. As I said earlier, it is not just aptitude, it's also attitude that demonstrates winners and makes a difference to businesses.

I am still trying to discover what motivates me. Is it because I love to see success? Was it my passion for my work? I wonder what you think … do you know what would be brilliant? When you finish the book, let me know your thoughts; you will make an old man very happy! My very good friend Damian argues that it is recognition that fuels my determination and enthusiasm.

A 'Territory Planning and Management' training day was added to my offering. As some salespeople's organisation and time management was sadly lacking, this resulted in repeat bookings for me. I was sometimes asked to spend a day with a salesperson to evaluate their planning, preparation and selling skills. I asked one such person, "What is the purpose of this call?" "Well, we won't get an order," they replied. "You have got to be more positive," I said. "Alright, we positively won't get an order," they replied. That's a joke by the way!

I saw in a book a list of "Ten Commandments to Success" that helped me and was added to my training days. Number two reads, "It takes 72 muscles to frown but only 14 to smile." A camera became part of my presentations, using it to take photos of the delegates, adding another dimension to my selling interviews. They say a picture tells a thousand words, and showing the prospect pictures of happy groups, large and small, backed by testimonial letters, added to my credibility. At Alba I had devised and developed my training using Alba as a mnemonic – listing the qualities of success as Attitude, Loyalty, Belief and Ambition. I ought to say that when I first heard the word mnemonic, I spent ages trying to find it in the dictionary! I began by searching under 'P' and then 'N'. In the end

I went round to the teachers next door for the spelling. Its usage has served me well and has become the mainstay of my presentations, especially if I can I customise the word to the customer's business name.

I was enjoying the wonderful benefit of repeat bookings and along with my marketing and telephone cold calling, networking and asking for referrals was also generating bookings with many new companies. One of these was five 'Customer Care' presentations to 180 people at Saga in Folkestone. I drove down the night before to have dinner with some of their top people. After checking into the hotel, I walked down to the seafront and was horrified to have the first symptoms of a migraine attack. It takes one hour before the actual pain starts, so I rushed back to take my tablets and tried to get some sleep. The pain usually lasts for about five hours, and it took a lot of resolve to get through dinner with a smile on my face. Fortunately the pain had subsided by the morning but, as migraine sufferers will tell you, they leave you absolutely drained. However, the show must go on, and it did. The journalist Alistair Cooke wrote, "A professional is someone who does their best work when they least feel like it." I received this from Saga, "A sincere thank you for a great two days, five presentations and no sign of flagging – what can I say?" … and what can I say?

All Over the Country

Itook a lot of Saturday bookings in 1998, including Belle Engineering in Buxton, Sunfield Printers in Bradford, Albert Haywood and Minorplanet Systems in Leeds, Andy Pear in Gloucester, Raaco in Witney near Oxford and Florco in Thatcham near Newbury (which gave me the chance to visit the remnants of the Greenham Common Women's Peace Camp). One of my other bookings was near Epping, so I took my Moulton bike and went cycling in the forest, a brilliant place to ride and relax with nature. I also visited Petits Hall where I had lived when I was eight years old (the hall has been converted into apartments now). I loved my bookings at Golden Rail and Superbreak and, staying overnight in York, I had some lovely meals at The Blue Bicycle (as a starter they baked miniature Hovis loaves with garlic butter). I saw the snooker player, John Higgins, in the hotel lobby one morning, who must have been playing at the Barbican.

Entertaining...

...and educating

In October it was back to Birmingham for the ISMM conference, where an impressive line-up of speakers included Allan Pease, Ian Botham OBE, Peter Thomson, Sandra Procter, yachtsman Pete Goss MBE and the hilarious American Larry Winget … but no Barry Young! Despite that, looking into the future those stepping stones were getting me closer to the dream of being on that stage myself. It was another great entertaining and invigorating day, and I heard some new material and increased my desire to be on the bill. All I had to do was keep finding those stepping stones. November and December were wonderfully busy with trips to Kent and Nuneaton, culminating with a booking in Blackpool for the Starline sales team (manufacturers and distributors of advertising calendars, diaries and business gifts). My presentation was filmed with the promise of a copy in the new year.

I read, "Do what you do so well that other people enthusiastically refer others to you," and this was definitely proving to be a big help to my success. John Fenton wrote that if you were having a tough time, feeling a bit down, then read your testimonial letters to give your spirits a lift. I wasn't feeling down or having a tough time – quite the contrary – but I still loved reading them … was this insecurity? I watched a docudrama about Barbara Windsor's life. She had a tough childhood and had struggled and worked hard to become recognised in show business. When she finally did get some plaudits, she was very emotional and explained it by saying that for the first time, "People were telling me I was doing alright." This was very much the same with me. People were telling me I was doing alright, so please forgive me for enjoying my little bit of success and a lot of happiness.

On Christmas Day my friends Kath and Dave had invited me to join them, their daughter Kristina and son Alex and stay overnight, which they very kindly did many times over the years. Although Sheila wasn't there, these were wonderful times for me and remain strong in my memory. I have no record of what I did on New Year's Eve for 1998, but I certainly was looking forward to the New Year with, like the title of the Dickens novel, "Great Expectations."

Robert Cheshire said, "In Britain the greatest problem is the poverty of ambition of its people." That certainly isn't true in my case. I had an ambition and 1999 would provide me with more stepping stones that would get me closer to my goal. I had the conviction that, "If it is to be, it is up to me."

CHAPTER 14:

1999, A DEFINING YEAR AND INTO THE MILLENNIUM

1999 brought a marvellous range of venues and businesses. In January I stayed at the gorgeous Ghyll Manor Hotel in Rusper, West Sussex. Maxxiom hired me to help them at an exhibition in the London Arena and put me up at the Britannia Hotel in the Docklands. I was up on the 17th floor overlooking Canary Wharf with the DLR trundling past – I didn't want to go to sleep it was so brilliant. I also worked with them at a hotel in Daventry. Then it was back to the lovely Eaves Hall in the Ribble Valley. I also worked with Anacomp, Eurotel, Lansing and Belle. Other lovely venues would include Ashdown Park, Stoke Rochford Hall Hotel and Golf Resort, Gloucester Cricket Club, and the Royal Theatre in Harrogate.

Spicing It Up

I will always remember the Dewsbury group. I made it clear that if you want to get on, read *The Telegraph* or *The Times*, not *The Sun*, and watch the business news on BBC1 at 5.00 am to keep abreast of what's going on in industry and commerce. I said to them, "If you sit there clicking your pen, I will tell you off, because if you do that in a meeting with buyers this will put them off." I told them to buy a beautiful pen and invest in themselves. Well, on the second day I went to get the training room ready, and some wag had put a copy of *The Sun* on every seat! So I quickly made a quiz, for which all the answers were from that edition of *The Sun* – 20 questions with a prize for whoever got the most questions right! (Questions like, who won the three o'clock at Haydock, what was on BBC at 7.00 pm that night.) All this got the day off to a great start and I thought it was a great gag.

Another new idea I had introduced was the 'grinder'. I would take individual delegates into an ante-room where I would be sat on a chair as the buyer and they played the salesman – a very one-to-one role play, sat knee-to-knee. "Thanks for coming to see me, what am I going to get out of this meeting?" I asked. I was encouraging them to think about 'WIIFY' – what's in it for you? So my second question would be, "What does your company do?" I encouraged them to tell me how my life would improve if I used their products or service. Question three, "What are the questions you'd like to ask me?" Question four, "Give me five reasons why I should use your company" … etc, and I became known for this 'grinder'.

Two great quotes that resonated with me at the time were, firstly, Sir David Simon (of BP), who said, "There were two great cricketers, Gower and Boycott; Gower had a wonderful flair, Boycott a dogged determination, and these were perfect characteristics for business success." Secondly, Richard Branson spoke about, "flaunting conventional wisdom." I knew I would need these attributes and had to 'dare to be different' if I was going to stand out from other business speakers. Working with companies like Stanley Tools, Record Tools and JCB, along with visits to Black+Decker, gave me access to their factory shops and a golden opportunity to kit myself out with tools, including the brilliant Black+Decker Workmate, all absolutely invaluable in my DIY days. I had enjoyed this privilege years ago when visiting Bassetts in Sheffield, and Rowntree's and Terry's in York, and would come home with a terrific selection of chocolates and Liquorice Allsorts.

Opportunity Knocks!

Another new prospect, Spirax Sarco, gave me a booking for an hour presentation at their sales conference on 5th February to be held at a hotel near Grantham, which was to prove to be an important day and another big stepping stone for me. It would be a departure from my usual training sessions and the launch of my hour-long 'Do You Seriously Want to be a Success at Selling?' presentation. For the first time I used my community singing to open, getting everyone to sing what I described as the salesperson's anthem, 'Always Look on the Bright Side of Life', which became my start to all conference presentations. The event was the closest thing to entertainment I had experienced since Butlin's, with a stage and sound engineers. I loved getting mic'd up, I had a room to change into my suit, and the whole thing was even being filmed – I was in my element.

The UK sales and marketing manager, Murdo MacDonald (fabulous name for a salesperson), who booked me, gave me permission to have a copy of my presentation and use it for an audio tape. I made a mnemonic using the letters of SPIRAX to describe the six key attributes of a successful salesperson, and I organised a quiz with a prize for the person with the most attributes correct. The 'S' was for sparkle, something I mentioned earlier; but the 'X' would test everyone, so I called it the X-factor. Can you guess what attribute of a successful person the X-factor might be?

I was invited to stay overnight and treated to the black-tie dinner, where it was terrific to talk to the delegates and hear how this first airing of my presentation had been received. The people who worked in the office or administration didn't agree with my thinking that salespeople were the most important part of the company, but they did enjoy some of what I said, and I duly used this recording for producing my first audio cassette to sell.

In March I attended my fourth ISMM regional seminar in Luton, where I was now presenting for an hour, using the mnemonic COMMUNICATE as the structure for my 'Selling by Telephone' seminar (and another stepping stone). The month also saw the start of a long relationship with Ring Lighting and Automotive in Leeds. I went to Birmingham to work with Aramark and had a marvellous night out on Broad Street with them following the two days' training.

A large stepping stone (in fact, perhaps five stepping stones) took place on 4th, 5th, 10th and 26th of March, with my first 'Customer Awareness' training days for OSTA members, and on 25th I was in Sheffield with my 'How to Set up a Telesales Team' for managers. During March I also went back to work with Britannia Rescue and Croda, and presented my 'Territory Planning and Management' training day for Tyrolit down in Crick.

All this travel gave me an opportunity to introduce another marketing idea; I would buy postcards at the places I visited and send them to clients with a thank-you message, either for a booking or for seeing me to discuss a booking, a very easy way of MMFI.

Spain

Life was about to get a whole lot busier when another huge stepping stone presented itself. The OSTA dealer training days had obviously gone well because Gareth and Brad invited me to be the keynote speaker at their annual conference in Spain – *yes, Spain!* I wish I could remember how I felt all those years ago, but I do know it changed everything for me. This wasn't just a stepping stone, this was a massive life-changing leap. Planning, preparation and rehearsals followed. Gareth came up with the title for my spot: 'GOTBO' – Glimpses of the Bleeding Obvious. Instead of having to take all my props, a slide presentation would be made for me and I could use pictures instead of props. Oh boy, I was stepping up a gear now; this was getting nearer to show business by the day, particularly on top of my successful Spirax performance.

Travel arrangements were made for me and rehearsals held at their Barnsley head office. Obviously nerves and butterflies were present for the next month, and I practised in every spare moment I had (and probably in my sleep). This was a wonderful opportunity to get closer to my goal of standing on that stage at the ICC in Birmingham for the ISMM.

The whole event from 10th to 14th was fantastic. On the first afternoon I walked across the road to the supermarket to buy a pack of beers to enjoy on my balcony overlooking the pool, when I met Ian Callander doing the same; we are still very best friends some 20-odd years later. In fact, I was best man at his wedding to Phyllis in 2006. On a visit last year, Phyllis made the sweetest remark, "It's lovely to see you Barry, you are like a breath of fresh air." They have been very kind to me and are wonderful friends.

By the time it came to my appearance I had made friends with quite a few of the delegates. Some of them I already knew, such as Dale Hollingdrake who, along with Ian at Metrik, had attended the OSTA training days and had also sent some of their people. Dale was very supportive on the morning of the conference, so it made it a little easier when I walked out on stage to close the business part of the conference. I started with my community singing of 'Always Look on the Bright Side of Life', describing it as the business person's anthem. The audience response was fantastic – they joined in with clapping, as well as singing, removing any nerves and butterflies. The weekend that followed was wonderful, swimming in the pool, marvellous food and drink, entertainment, mixing, mingling and networking with the business owners. Ian and I hired a car and visited Ronda and Puerto Banús.

I also made friends with the chairman of OSTA, John Irish CBE, and his wife Isabel. In July they invited me for the weekend along with two other couples to Burford House in Somerset. We played croquet on the lawn, something I hadn't done since I lived at Petits Hall when I was eight. The evening began with a Lanson champagne reception in the drawing room. A formal menu detailed events, which included toasts and speeches by the guests, including me, and wonderful food. As I didn't drink wine, Isabel was even happy for me to put my cans of beer that I had taken on the table.

All this was happening for me and all I had to do was something I loved – speak for an hour. I even got paid, and there was icing on the cake as they allowed me to take away an audio recording of my spot in Spain, thus becoming my second audio cassette, *Do You Seriously Want to Boost Your Business?* Once again, David Hull was responsible for the title, inlay words and artwork. I worked with Sam, a smashing guy at Belmont Recording Studios, Huddersfield, and had these two presentations transferred onto audio cassette (and now available on CD … although cassettes are also now enjoying a resurgence!). So now I had something to sell following my presentations, and I ordered 100 of each cassette to get me going. Ian and Dale joined forces and booked me to present a training course for their people on a September Saturday in Carlisle. I also had a brilliant trip to Dublin with John Heath.

More Associations

When I returned home, I knew exactly what I would do – my telephone cold calling would concentrate on associations and large companies who held conferences with 'motivational business speakers'. The library had books listing such organisations and provided me with lists of suspects; these would now be the target of my 100 cold calls a day. I already had several associations under my belt, so now with OSTA and Spirax, I had quite a collection of testimonial letters to show to new suspects – oh, this was going to be marvellous, I thought.

October 1999 was ISMM conference time again. As a speaker at the regional seminars I now received a complimentary ticket and that year's line-up of speakers included the climber Joe Simpson, author of the book *Touching the Void* (now also a brilliant film); Richard Denny, whose videos and books I have learnt a lot from over the years; Aidan Jones; Ros Gardner and, after being such a hit the previous year, Larry Winget returned. As always, the conference provided me with new ideas and renewed my desire to be on that stage. I kept saying to myself, "I can do that, I want to do that and I will do that."

World Wide Web

In November I bought a new computer and decided that I needed a website. I tried Sage at first, but they just printed a load of words – it was awful. Interprint, with whom I had a fabulous relationship, had set up a web design department and using flair and colour did a marvellous job. The majority of speakers like me went under the heading of 'motivational business speakers', but I changed the emphasis to 'inspirational', which I believed was more in line with the feedback I was receiving and certainly what I was aiming to achieve. I registered my domain name, www.barryyoung.co.uk, and because I am a big-head I am still paying the hosting fee all these years later! I had some new publicity photographs taken and new business cards designed by a brilliant young female designer at a printer's in Cleckheaton. I also found a woman to proofread and edit anything of that nature, which proved to be a very good idea, as she brought to my attention the wrong use of an apostrophe in the phrase, "delegate's comments include" … because there is more than one delegate, the apostrophe should come after the word "delegates'", like so … but I expect you knew that!

Opposite: a few samples of my publicity material at the time

Barry Young
INSPIRATIONAL
MOTIVATIONAL
BUSINESS SPEAKER

Barry's exuberance and verve ensure a memorable and positive contribution to your...

conference   business meeting   sales seminar
convention   training session   ...etc.

Barry's presentations have been described as stimulating, thought provoking, enlightening and, at the same time very, very entertaining.

He adopts a very practical and factual approach in his presentations. Key objectives are to inspire and invigorate, to remind, rekindle and reinstate those essential attributes that will enhance personal happiness and business success.

All presentations are discussed, developed and tailored to suit your business and objectives.

Telephone: (01274) 874302
Email: by@barryyoung.co.uk

Comments from clients include...

"I came away feeling inspired and invigorated"
"Our people left the day feeling more positive about themselves and their work"
"Everyone I spoke to thought the whole experience was exhilarating and they had learnt a lot in the process"
"Your style of presentation is unique to say the least"
"Lifts the spirits" - "Highly recommended"
"Barry delivers his messages in a motivational and individual way, mixing humour and real life examples"
"The brief we set you was not only met, but far exceeded our expectations"
"Our team were thoroughly stimulated, challenged and entertained"
"In terms both of content and delivery, your talk was simply superb"
"Your presentation was likened to an annual service for a vehicle – you don't really notice anything wrong until it has been properly tuned"

Barry boasts an impressive portfolio of testimonials and references for his presentations across a broad range of organisations including...

- The Automotive Industry
- Banks and Building Societies
- County Cricket Clubs
- Chemicals, Carpets and Catering
- Hotels, Holidays and Health
- Motoring and Manufacturing
- Plant Hire, Property and Publishing
- Transport, Tools and Toiletries
- Sport and Leisure
- The Stationery Trade
  ...and many more.

TELEPHONE / FACSIMILE:
01274 874302
—
E-MAIL:
by@barryyoung.co.uk
—
16 Moorfield Avenue,
Hartshead Moor,
Cleckheaton,
Yorkshire BD19 6PG

OR

See and hear Barry on
www.barryyoung.co.uk

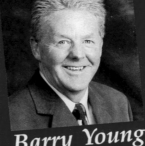

Barry Young
SPEAKER, TRAINER, MOTIVATOR
Seriously Funny, Seriously Successful

Barry Young
Trainer
Speaker
Motivator
Seriously Funny, Seriously Successful

Barry is an international business speaker, trainer and motivator, providing inspirational and stimulating presentations at conferences, conventions, seminars, exhibitions, meetings etc.

He offers a genuinely innovative and refreshing approach and concentrates on subjects that will help you:

FIND, WIN AND KEEP PROFITABLE CUSTOMERS

TO FIND OUT HOW BARRY CAN HELP YOU . . .

Increase sales and profits

Improve internal communication and teamwork

Secure more and better customers

Boost confidence and competence

Make more of your time, telephone and talent

Gain an edge over your competitors

Exceed your customers' expectations

Achieve your objectives and much more

Contact him on any of the ways listed overleaf . . .

Finances

All was going extremely well – my finances were very healthy, money was coming in and not much going out (as I didn't have time to spend any), so I decided to pay off my mortgage. I went to Lloyds in Manchester Road where I told the clerk, "I'd like to pay off my mortgage." She got Helen to speak to me who suggested private banking, who would invest my money in shares, which could exceed what I was paying in mortgage interest. She convinced me and sent John Moody and Mike Cooper to advise me. They amalgamated all my various pots and investments and looked after it all – they sold some shares, kept others, sorted out PEPs and MIPs and pensions etc, and took all that worry away from me. I ended up with a portfolio, with some in shares, some in fixed assets and some in government bonds.

The year ended in this same fantastic, frenetic fashion with bookings with companies all over the country, including: Vendepac, Stanley Tools, OSTA, Mister Minit, Silver Cross Prams, Holset Engineering, Marshalls, WOM, Barlow Handling, Nairobi Coffee and Tea, Hepworth Engineering, Ingersoll Rand, Dormy and Champion Motor Spares. Terry Brooks helped me secure a booking with Oak Tyres and a booking that started over dinner at the OSTA conference was Pilot Pens. In December GAP booked me for four days in Glasgow and I finished the year working with Feb MBT, Saville Group, Federal-Mogul and Mamas & Papas. 1999 also provided a lot of testimonials about what I could do, how I did it and how companies would benefit from using my skills – this became the evidence I could now show prospects.

Background: my headsed paper

Barry Young

SPEAKER, TRAINER, MOTIVATOR

Seriously Funny
Seriously Successful

16 Moorfield Avenue,
Hartshead Moor,
Cleckheaton,
West Yorkshire
BD19 6PG

Telephone/Facsimile:
01274 874302

Website:
www.barryyoung.co.uk

E-mail:
by@barryyoung.co.uk

The wonderful trend for me was that many of these bookings were now for an hour at conferences, and as the year came to a close my sights were set on an even larger conference. It was a time to think big and remember that experience is not what happens to you, it is what you do with what happens to you that matters ... bring on the Millennium.

My lovely neighbours Ian and Helen had invited me over on Christmas morning to join their present opening with their lads Christopher and Nicholas. Ian made bacon butties, I took the ingredients for Buck's Fizz, and it was a wonderful morning. The two boys have now become successful young men and have set up home with their partners, but the three of us still enjoy Christmas morning together.

Great quotes from two iconic American sportsmen mapped out the new year for me: Babe Ruth, the baseball player, said, "Yesterday's home runs don't win tomorrow's games." Wayne Gretzky, the ice hockey player, when asked about his success answered, "I skate to where the puck is going to be." This was how it would be for me in 2000. I could not sit back on my laurels (definition, "to be satisfied with what one has already achieved and stop striving for further success"). I needed to capitalise on the success of 1999 and take advantage of it by skating to where my opportunities would be in 2000.

The Millennium

I am delighted to say 2000 continued as 1999 finished with repeat bookings and new clients. January kicked off with ten bookings, and in February I went to Australia (see 'Adventures' chapter), so I asked Ian and Helen if their sons could look after my cats while I was away – feeding them and emptying their litter trays (although apparently they didn't like the litter trays, so Helen had to do that part!).

I returned home on 9th March to plenty of bookings and I also ordered 250 of my audio cassettes and, because many people now had CD players in their cars, I ordered the same number of CDs from my supplier in Birmingham. My neighbour Ian helped me with the CD inlay design and colours and made a fabulous job of it. They sold well to delegates after my presentations and training days and were also now available on my website.

One of my CDs

Help?

2000 promised to be another fabulously busy year. I had for some time wrestled with the idea of getting some help, either with administration or looking after the home – perhaps a cleaner, secretary or a telesales person. I decided against a telesales person, particularly after comments from clients who said that it was my personality and telephone manner that swayed them to see and book me. No one else would have the same commitment, dedication and belief. A personal assistant was another idea, but I didn't fancy a stranger knowing all my personal and financial matters, so I decided on a cleaner. Suzanne was recommended by my neighbour Ken's daughter, Carol. From the Seychelles, Suzanne worked for several high-profile customers, including the chief of the West Yorkshire Fire and Rescue Service. As well as cleaning, she ironed my clothes and introduced me to tubular shirt sleeves – a much more professional look than the normal crease that you see on shirts (after all, you wouldn't iron a crease like that on a jacket). I introduced and encouraged this idea and look in my training and presentations thereafter.

Busy All the Time

A very significant booking at the end of the month took me to Brands Hatch, just a few miles from where I was born of course. Business Link organised a sales and marketing convention (I am still not sure about the difference between a conference and a convention, but it's another thing to boast about) with "Four world-class speakers" (the literature's line, not mine, although I am not going to argue) "to bring you into the 21st century with the latest in sales and marketing." Little did I know when I lived just down the road 50 years previously, attending my seventh of ten schools, that I would be back at Brands Hatch as a 'World Class Speaker' wearing my jazzy jacket. This is where I crossed paths with Geoff Burch. Using my props I presented my 'Do You Seriously Want to Boost Your Business?'; Geoff was on after me with 'Customers – Who Needs Them?' He began by saying, "Take no notice of Barry with all that positive happy stuff. I am a right miserable so and so, but richer than he is," which received much laughter. We worked alongside each other again in 2001. His book, *Writing on the Wall*, is a very, very funny look at the business world and the people in it.

Leisure

David Hull (sales and marketing director at Allied in Bradford) had been a client, became a friend and moved to Norfolk. I had some lovely holidays with him at his home in King's Lynn, where his wife was MD at Colman's. We went boating on the Broads and had some marvellous times. I have David to thank for the artwork, design, title and words of my first cassette that I sold, *Do You Seriously Want to be a Success at SELLING*.

A fortnightly computer course at Huddersfield University was helping me get greater benefit from my PC. On 6th May I had my first and last experience of paintballing in a local wood. I don't know if I just don't want to remember who organised it, but I can't. I do know my doctor gave me a right telling off when I went to see him covered in bruises. It was great fun at the time, and like most things I threw myself into it, diving over walls and rolling around like I was in a cowboy film.

Top: early cassette artwork
Bottom: later artwork for 'Seriously Boost Your Business'
and 'No Time Like the Present'

A booking in June as a result of the Brands Hatch event was with Line Packaging in Gillingham, Kent, a 'Customer Awareness' afternoon for the whole company. Later in the month it was the British Office Supplies and Services Federation Annual Conference ('BOS') at the Belfry – yes, me on stage at the Belfry. Later that month I was off to Scotland to work with M&S Toiletries for two days, and I did a further two days with them in July at their Wakefield depot. This wonderful variety of venues and businesses continued into the summer.

My dear friend Phil, who had used my training at RL Insurance, had spotted a niche in the market and started his own company, CCS (Call Centre Support), offering just that – telephone support to companies that did not always have enough call handlers at the right times, perhaps following a marketing campaign etc. We have all experienced the frustration of waiting for a telephone to be answered, so these unanswered calls would be re-routed to CCS, thus avoiding unhappy customers or missing a selling opportunity. CCS also offered an outbound call-making service and, following his launch of the business, I worked twice in August with his rapidly expanding team. Phil made a great success of CCS and at one stage employed 80 people. To finish the month, a very interesting venue with Saville was the RAF Museum at Cosford in Shropshire.

Holset Engineering had used me on several occasions and in September I had the chance to add another string to my bow when they asked me to host a communications day for all of their 750 employees. There were rehearsals and run-throughs at the conference venue, which I enjoyed immensely, and then on the day, complete with sound checks and cameras, it was brilliant. I received the following endorsement, "Barry's enthusiasm, his personal style, and his ability to re-enforce our key business messages throughout the day were excellent. He was the 'glue' which held the day together and he maintained a high energy level with our audience." And the bonus for me, I took away a video of the event.

Huddersfield Technical College asked me to make another presentation at their November 'Business Breakfast Briefing' about time management; they wanted to call it 'No Time Like the Present', which gave me two fabulous opportunities. One, to create a new presentation and two, to have the event filmed and so provide me with a third title in my audio tape and CD offering. I booked the video company and set to work on the content; I read and researched everything I could find on the subject, resulting in an hour on time management and much, much more, with the title, 'No Time Like the Present'. It certainly is so important to enjoy and make the most of every moment of our one-off beautiful life.

Vertical Markets

New businesses and repeat bookings kept me busy in September and October; Park House Healthcare gave me the first of many bookings. I was back at Ryzex in Chippenham. Two evenings training at the Bradford Prontaprint shop presented another opening for me, where I learnt that these shops are franchised and have large annual conferences, so I spotted another opportunity and approached their head office in Watford to discuss these events. Dahle Office Products & Equipment had seen me at the OSTA event and booked me for their people in October, and I came away with one of those lovely desktop pencil sharpeners like they used to have at school.

The office stationery buying groups like OSTA were very popular, and it was a vertical market I was set to capitalise on. The next to book me was Officepoint, secured as a result of my success with Kingfield, John Heath and OSTA. It did, however, provide me with a bit of a challenge – the country was in the middle of the fuel shortage, which meant I had to go on the train with my mammoth suitcase. Things didn't get off to a good start, as one of the wheels broke at Brighouse Station, leaving me to drag it rather like a sledge all the way to Kempton Park. I can't remember all the train and platform changes, but I was happy to arrive at my accommodation. The MD, David Langdown, met me and we had a very pleasant afternoon in his garden drinking beer. My conference presentation was followed by a fabulous evening event, and his letter read, "I understand the extra effort you went to in order to get here from Yorkshire. I hope to see you again soon, there's an open invitation extended for another beer in the garden. PS where did you learn to dance like that?!"

Chapter 15: Stealing the Show

There was another seminar for the ISMM in Coventry at the beginning of September 2000. As always, I saw these presentations as stepping stones to my real goal of getting on that stage at the ICC in Birmingham. That took a sudden whole new twist when I received a call from Jennie Harnaman to arrange a meeting with Chief Executive Patrick Joiner. The three of us met at a beautiful hotel near Grantham where they gave me the news that I had been optimistically hoping for and had been working towards for years – they wanted me to present at this year's conference. I tried to be calm and nonchalant, but I doubt I managed to hide my delight! Obviously, I already had plans to attend the conference, so I knew I was available. The only downside, if there possibly could have been a downside to this fantastic news, was that I was only going to be allocated 20 minutes. "But my presentation is an hour," I protested. "Sorry Barry, it's 20 minutes," and, although they didn't exactly say take it or leave it, I realised if I wanted to fulfil my ambition and capitalise on all those stepping stones, I would have to trim the hour down to 20 minutes. I remember a quote from the legendary CEO Jack Welch, "By reaching for the seemingly impossible, you often do the impossible," and it seems I had.

With only weeks to go before the conference, I started preparation straight away. I placed all my props out on the dining room table and made the difficult decisions about which ones to remove. It was important to keep those that had generated the most laughs and had a serious message. I then went walking, rehearsing my shortened presentation and timing it. I got it down to 35 minutes, so I rang Patrick, but he insisted on the 20.

My props were disappearing, I removed some more from the table and went walking again – 30 minutes, and tried Patrick once more. "No Barry,

20," he repeated. This was very difficult — my act was changing so much, two more props and associated business messages went, I walked again, 25 minutes. That was it. I'd say nothing and go with that (perhaps I could talk a bit quicker). Remembering there would be 1,500 people in the audience, I put an urgent order in for my audio tapes and CDs. My producer in Birmingham pulled out all the stops for me to ensure I had them for the conference. Sheila agreed to manage my stand and sell them for me on the day, along with my very good friend Dale from BSS in Lancaster. I had bought a suit two years previously, along with a beautiful pair of Barker 'fine English shoes' in burgundy, both in preparation just for this day. When I had seen it in the shop, I knew it would be perfect as my stage suit, light coloured and very different to the usual dark suits that speakers wore. I had a new pale yellow shirt and colourful tie, and the fabulous shoes finished off the look. With nervous anticipation I continued to rehearse my shortened presentation.

Now the hours spent at the library, the 100 telephone calls day after day, years and years of learning, reading, listening to tapes, paying to watch other speakers, networking, volunteering to speak at events had all finally come to fruition. Some people may have said, "Lucky old you." No, it definitely wasn't luck, which is defined as "whatever good or bad events happen to a person by chance." Well, none of this was by chance, I had made my own luck. Someone once said, "Luck is where opportunity meets preparation." Sometimes at my presentations a company would launch a sales competition with a prize of a holiday. I would encourage delegates to go home, pack their suitcase, get their passport out, put their suitcase by their front door and be prepared ... now go out and win that holiday.

I was prepared — I may have been preparing all my life, and now I met the opportunity! I also read, "You can't become a master craftsman until you are an excellent student; to be a master of your craft you have to be an excellent student first." William Osler said, "To become successful at something, you first have to become interested in it." I think it is important to point out that I didn't achieve all this on my own; I was an excellent student, I enlisted help, I mixed with successful people (I read their books or articles in the *Sunday Times* and magazines). Books like *How to Win Friends and Influence People* by Dale Carnegie and my favourite book of them all, *The Power of Positive Thinking* by Norman Vincent Peale. I bought videos and tapes, spent hours listening to and learning from the likes of Brian Tracy, Earl Nightingale and Zig Ziglar. Yes, I was prepared. "A good salesperson only needs an opportunity; a great salesperson creates an opportunity." I had done just that.

Accommodation for the speakers was at The Hyatt Hotel which is linked to the ICC by a bridge over Broad Street. I asked for a high floor and was given a room on the 17th with fantastic views over the city and Gas Street Basin (where I had finished my Grand Union Canal bike ride a few years before). The windows had one-way glass and, after unpacking and showering, I opened one of the cans of Tetley's bitter I had taken with me, laid back in an armchair in the window with no clothes on and drank my own health! I could not stop smiling and remembering what I had said after last year's conference, "I can do that, I want to do that and I will do that." One quote I read said, "We become what we think about," and that is certainly true for me.

The speakers attended a private dinner with Sheila Watson-Challis, Patrick Joiner and members of the management team. For many of the speakers it was like a reunion, with reminiscences of past meetings and stories of recent bookings, a sort of old boys' club. As the unknown new boy, I sat quietly listening and learning, mainly because no one spoke to me! When I met Robin Fielder, whom I had admired and watched over the years, I almost bowed, but I managed with just a handshake. Dr Denis Waitley, one of the world's top speakers who had counselled Olympic athletes, US presidents and Apollo astronauts, was also there. His audio tape series, *The Psychology of Winning*, has sold millions – I had bought a set myself and gained a tremendous amount of knowledge from them. I didn't even dare to shake hands with him! Meeting all these successful and high-profile people didn't do much for my nerves. As soon as it was acceptable to leave I did ... although it was going to be difficult to sleep. I was so excited, rehearsing my lines over and over again in my head. The night-time view over the city was amazing. I went to bed with a head full of thoughts and expectation.

SUCCESSFUL

Conference round-up

People say the nicest things…

"Full of tips and ideas. What a wonderful day!"
ANGLIA REGIONAL CO-OPERATIVE SOCIETY

"An extremely interesting and informative day"
JOHNSON & JOHNSON MEDICAL

"I came not knowing what to expect. I left full of ideas and inspiration"
TELEWEST COMMUNICATIONS

"An excellent way to reinforce sales skills and re-motivate sales forces"
ASM TECHNOLOGIES LTD

"Very worthwhile and informative yet in a relaxed atmosphere"
IFM ELECTRONIC

"Excellent annual reminder of skills learnt over the years plus a host of new tips for achieving results"
UCB HOME LOANS

"Motivating, inspiring"
FIRST NATIONAL BANK

"Last year's conference changed my life for the good. This year's will change it for the fantastic!"
BRETT WASTE MANAGEMENT LTD

"A day not to be missed. It's like an adrenaline injection"
WEST BROMWICH BUILDING SOCIETY

"Interesting, inspirational, impressive and invaluable. Should be mandatory for anyone serious about a career in sales"
INDIVISUAL COMMUNICATIONS

On 25th October, more than 1500 sales professionals packed the prestigious main hall at the International Conference Centre in Birmingham for *Successful Selling 2000*, the annual conference of the ISMM.

Now in its tenth year, *Successful Selling* is widely recognised as the UK's top sales convention. The conference gives delegates the opportunity to refresh existing skills and to hear some of the latest thinking and newest ideas on selling.

Once again, this year's upbeat, action-packed day was voted a tremendous hit with delegates. Featuring seven inspirational speakers from around the world, it provided a dynamic combination of practical sales training and personal development designed to leave delegates charged up and motivated to achieve greater sales success in the coming year. For those who missed *Successful Selling 2000*, these pages and comments from delegates give a flavour of the day.

▼ **PATRICK JOINER**, ISMM Chief Executive, opens conference proceedings by highlighting the growing number of companies aligning themselves to the aims and objectives of the ISMM

SELLING 2000

Conference round-up

► **ROBIN FIELDER,** one of the all-time greats of sales training, imparts his wealth of knowledge to a highly-appreciative audience

▲ **PETER THOMSON,** Conference Chairman, adds his own brand of down-to-earth business advice

▲ **DR DENIS WAITLEY,** master US motivator, shares insights acquired through his work with many of the world's top achievers

▲ **BARRY YOUNG** steals the show with his hard-hitting yet hilarious presentation

◄ **REBECCA STEPHENS** MBE holds the audience spellbound as she recounts the tale of her triumphant ascent of Everest

▼ **BOB BEVAN,** one of the UK's leading after-dinner speakers, closes the conference in style

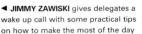

▲ **ANTHONY MORRIS** adds value for money as he shares top sales tips from his native South Africa

◄ **JIMMY ZAWISKI** gives delegates a wake up call with some practical tips on how to make the most of the day

261

On Wednesday 25th October my big day arrived. The first job was to get all my audio tapes and CDs to my stand. Sheila and Dale arrived nice and early to help set everything up. I had an advertising display board made with my name and explaining what I did, plus a number of tabletop stands with details and prices of my CDs and tapes. I left them to it and went back to my room to shower and get ready, although I would not be putting on my stage clothes just yet. A green room was provided for the speakers where I went next to hang up my suit etc. A pre-conference briefing with the morning session speakers was held on stage at 7.30. I also had to set up my props table in the wings, ready to be moved on stage during the morning break. We were given a timetable with headings and times: Barry Young to artiste's lounge 10.50; to wings 11.10; on stage 11.20; off stage 11.40 (that last one was in doubt!).

Peter Thomson, a highly respected personal development strategist, was the conference chairman. He discussed the introduction that he would use, and also gave me some very helpful and supportive advice. He advised that, just before I was due to go on, I should stand in the wings and continually say out loud my opening words. I have always been grateful to Peter.

The fantastic record that was played as the conference opened and throughout the day was 'Proud' by Heather Small. Patrick Joiner was first up, welcoming everyone with a short presentation about the day ahead and the work of the ISMM. Peter was next, opening events, before introducing Jimmy Zawiski, a personal performance specialist. He had been walking round the green room bashing his chest and saying things to generally psych himself up. Whilst he was on stage, I changed into my new outfit. Next up was the immaculately dressed Robin Fielder, and the things Robin spoke about were sound good sense. I was worried about following such a seasoned and well-known speaker, but I knew my presentation was much more animated and with the use of my props more humorous and entertaining. The morning break came next which gave me 30 minutes to check that my table was on stage and the props all in order.

Just before my slot, I did my talking-out-loud bit in the wings, waiting nervously for Peter to introduce me. Then suddenly I was walking out onto the stage in front of 1,500 people. I opened with my community singing, 'Always Look on the Bright Side of Life', which warmed the audience up and helped me calm down. I think it might have been the first time delegates had been asked to sing, and also the first time props had been used. It was an all-action 20 (plus) minutes of nuts and bolts, good old down-to-earth stuff that people could make use of immediately, and they loved it.

I did my new nosy gag … "Do you remember when you were younger you were told don't be nosy?" With my props of a large false nose and policeman's helmet, I put them on and explained, "You've got to be like a policeman, be nosy, find stuff out. I got a bit nosy the other day – when you're in your hotel room there's often a Bible. I looked in mine which had a note in it asking, 'Do you crave the demon drink? If you need help, ring this number.' I rang the number and it was the local off-licence!" The laughter in some places turned to applause at my humorous anecdotes, and the more they laughed, the more I performed – this was my Royal Variety Performance, and I was enjoying every second of it.

At the front of the stage were two lights: green for time on stage, and red for get off, your time is up! I don't remember the lights at all, but I will never, ever forget the tumultuous applause that broke out when I finished with the words, "If you see it and believe it, you can achieve it, thank you." Peter, God bless him, even got me to go back to the centre of the stage to receive more applause and cheers of approval from a delighted audience.

Denis Waitley wound up the morning session and then it was time to join Sheila and Dale on my stand. A crowd were already surrounding the stand and sales of my tapes and CDs were brisk, to say the least. I networked, spoke to and swapped business cards with as many people as possible, before and after an excellent lunch. Many conversations ended with the promise of bookings or follow-up calls. I was very gratified and delighted when one of my heroes, Robin Fielder, came up to shake my hand and compliment my performance.

The speaker after lunch that I particularly wanted to see was Rebecca Stephens MBE, the first British woman to conquer Everest. At the mid-afternoon break and the end of the day we were back on duty at the stand selling tapes and CDs before packing up, loading the car and then heading out for a meal and to analyse the day. Unfortunately none of us could really celebrate as we were driving, but it was wonderful for me to have Sheila there to be part of it and see me achieve my long-time ambition.

There was a terrible anti-climax when I arrived home to a cold, empty house (apart from Harry and Honey that is, who were always pleased to see me). The adrenaline had gone and the come-down was awful. I consoled myself thinking of those brilliant lyrics from the song 'Proud', 'What have you done today to make you feel proud?' Well, I certainly knew the answer to that – all those schools, a less-than-ideal education, struggling to spell properly, but what I had achieved that day undoubtedly made me feel amazingly proud. All those stepping stones I had negotiated, I got there, I did it … "Well done Baz, you deserve to feel proud," I said to myself! Another wonderful mnemonic is PRIDE – Personal Responsibility In Developing Excellence, and I think that is what I have done. That show reel I had produced really did make the boat go faster!

Although there was no fee for speaking at the conference, it was of course a marvellous platform for exposure and publicity. In recognition of my contribution to the success of Successful Selling 2000, I was made an 'Honorary Fellow', giving me lifetime membership. I was also given a summary of the delegates' feedback and a VHS tape of my presentation. The December issue of the Institute's magazine had a conference round-up feature. I was delighted; no, I was more than delighted, to read, "Barry Young steals the show with his hard-hitting yet hilarious presentation." I placed a half-page advert in the magazine for my tapes and CDs, which gave an opportunity to anyone who hadn't bought on the day, and of course created more publicity for me.

I adopted the 'Proud' song into my training days and presentations, expounding the significance and virtues of the lyrics, encouraging the delegates not to just go to work but to go on a mission, to add value to the business, so that at the end of their day they would go home feeling proud because they had made a difference, a contribution.

The aftermath of the conference was tremendous. My career just took off. My bookings diary for November and December was looking very healthy and I was in no doubt that 2001 was going to be a wonderful year. I was now being referred to as 'A Keynote Speaker' and, at these conferences, sometimes had an occasional friendly heckler. I bought a brilliantly helpful book, *One-Liners for Business* by Mitch Murray, full of absolutely classically cutting and humorous stuff. A favourite put-down to hecklers of mine was, "What's your name sir?" "John." "Well, John, let's have an understanding, I work up here alone, a bit like you have sex!"

2nd November was the first outing of my new 'No Time Like the Present' at the Huddersfield Business Breakfast Briefing. Phil was in the audience, along with some other familiar faces from my previous visit. As it was my first presentation using the new content, it was not my best delivery performance, although I believed the material and substance could be as useful as studying for a year at a business school. Even if I do say so myself, the amount of knowledge and information that could be gleaned from it was amazing! With the company hired to have the event filmed I would now have three audio tapes and CDs to sell plus a VHS tape of the event.

There was definitely no time like the present for me – it was onward and upward. As Pope John Paul II said, "The future starts today, not tomorrow."

CHAPTER 16: BOOKS AND FROGS

Barry's Boozy Business Walks (BBBW)

By this time in business I had made friends with a lot of people who were clients, many who lived near me. We'd have lunch together and see each other from time to time. I thought it would be a good idea if I brought half a dozen of them together for a walk and called it a business meeting (which it was, as they had tasks, not just a jolly). For the first one we met up outside Sainsbury's in Brighouse and the group included Terry Brooks (one of my very first customers), Mike Cooper (my financial guy), Phil Hutchinson, Dale Holindrake (who helped on my stand at the conference) and Alan Baxter (from the OSTA conference).

BBBW: Phil, Terry, Alan, Mike and Dale

They mostly turned up ill-equipped, wearing brogues or trainers at the best, and I took them over the muddy moors. We eventually reached Shibden Park, where I took photos of them using a children's playground! I had booked The Duke of York at Shelf for lunch, and we all went in soaking wet from the rain, covered in mud. Approaching the bar to say I was there for the booking, the barman said, "I thought you said they were businessmen!" They took us to the beautiful dining room, let us take our wet clothes off, which they put in airing cupboard, and many of us sat there in our underwear drying out! This was the first of many BBBW.

Bookings as a result of the ISMM conference took me to Cumbria Bearings in Carlisle and Instant Gifts in Tenterden, Kent, as well as the first of 12 bookings with Sovereign Finance in Manchester. December also brought a booking with stationery wholesalers Spicers in Cambridge, once again giving me a chance to do the tourist bit. The month ended with Swan Stabilo Limited in Slough, where the MD wrote, "I can think of a lot of companies who would benefit from your expertise. However, as most of them are competitors, I have no intention of giving you their names. I am more than happy if they lag behind us when it comes to their selling ability! I do look forward to seeing you at future Stabilo events." A marvellous, marvellous year for me and lovely words to finish it with.

2001

I started to think about getting an agent or manager. If I had been a pop star, a manager would promote me and secure bookings, but there did not seem to be such people in my line of business. There were business speaker agencies, but the problem was they simply waited for the phone to ring and sent out a glossy brochure. I might be number 250 on their list, behind politicians, sport stars and the top motivational speakers. So, I decided to carry on as I was – after all, with hard work and determination, I had manoeuvred myself into this great situation, created my own circumstances, and now I would benefit from the consequences in 2001.

More Books

Dr Seuss said, "The more that you read, the more things you will know. The more that you learn, the more places you'll go." January kicked off with a booking at Thirsty Work in

Birmingham before Esselte in Uxbridge, followed by a lovely weekend in Bournemouth working with the publishers Hodder. Marshalls in Halifax gave me chance to catch my breath before a booking with Banner Business Supplies in Norwich at the stunning Sprowston Manor Hotel, Golf and Country Club (which was a Marriott at the time). There were two books in my room, both very useful and one of them very influential. The first, *The Spirit to Serve – Marriott's Way*, was a terrific book for anyone wanting to improve their business. The second was a Gideon's Bible, the perfect introduction and guide to reading, learning and getting help from the good book. I embraced several passages into my presentations, including Matthew 7:1–5. (I have copies of both books of my own now and the Bible has become a comforting and inspirational companion for me.)

My continued visits to antique and second-hand book shops resulted in two more gems. The first was *Wisdom of the Ages* (1936), by Mark Gilbert, with a paragraph on politeness, "The only true source of politeness is consideration; that vigilant moral sense which never loses sight of the rights, the claims, and the sensibilities of others. This is the one quality, over all others, necessary to make a gentleman." The second book, *Manners makyth Man* (1887), by Reverend EJ Hardy, opens with these lines, "Good manners are nothing less than little morals. They are the shadows of virtues, if not virtues themselves. A beautiful behaviour is better than a beautiful form; it gives a higher pleasure than statues and pictures; it is the finest of the fine arts." The wonderful English used in these words helped to make up for my less-than-perfect education and encouraged me to utilise two other books I had bought: *Correct English* and *I Before E (Except after C)* to improve my use of the English language both on stage and in my letter writing. All the driving required for work prompted me to buy a ten-CD multichanger for my car!

Later in the month I drove to London to work with Design Supply at St Ermin's Hotel in Westminster (two nights' accommodation, right in the heart of London – fantastic!). I remember well the last part of the journey from Marble Arch – I hadn't driven in London for many years but I knew my route, down Park Lane to Hyde Park Corner, then down Constitution Hill. However, I had to go round three times before I could get anyone to let me in so that I could turn left and go down past Buckingham Palace, left into Petty France and onto Caxton Street and my hotel. After my long drive I enjoyed a walk around the area. New Scotland Road was just across the road and I remembered that Petty France is where the Passport Office was. I wasn't paying, but I was shocked to know my parking bill was almost £30 for two nights, and that was in the hotel car park!

In February I was *bowled* over by a booking at Kent County Cricket Club in Canterbury, to present my all-encompassing 'Customer Awareness' training day. The day had been initiated by Tim Morton who had seen me at the ISMM conference. Tim ran all the catering at the venue and his team were also involved in the day. The chief executive of the club wrote, "Much of what you cover forces us to look at our own attitudes and behaviour in a critical manner and stimulates us to appreciate our own shortcomings. We look forward to your return in March when you will have the opportunity to speak to our players and stewards." These words helped me secure a booking at Gloucestershire County Cricket Club. I went straight from here to Bournemouth, for my first booking with McCarthy & Stone. I made this into another weekend at the seaside, with walks along the prom and shopping in the town.

As the month came to a close, there were bookings with Spicers and Sovereign, and then Lloyds TSB Commercial in Newcastle. I was back on home turf at the end of the month with a booking at the Hilton Hotel at Dartford. I was on in the afternoon; the delegates had been divided into two teams wearing T-shirts marked with either 'Sparky' or 'Special' – it was a real fun event and I still have my Sparky T-shirt.

Phase Three Training

I had been getting excellent feedback on my Phase Two training day, so I started work on a Phase Three. A phrase from the Marriott book says it all, "Even if you're on the right track, you'll get run over if you just sit there." Another pertinent quote advised, "If you always do what you have always done, you'll always get what you've always got." So it was important for me to be constantly innovating. Sovereign Finance were accommodating me at the Castlefield Hotel in Manchester, which I loved, as my window looked out onto the canal basin and the many bridges for the trams and trains. I even moved my bed so that I could fall asleep watching it all, as it was such a contrast to the very peaceful and rural scene I had from my bed at home. These early training days with Sovereign were, I am delighted to say, prompting fantastically positive and encouraging response letters, and of course all this came from them seeing my 20 minutes at the ISMM conference.

Spain

At the end of April I had booking with a 'federation', a vertical market I had been attacking along with associations. This time it was the National Bed Federation and a booking at the Melia Costa del Sol, Torremolinos, to speak at their annual conference – oh boy, this was just getting better. Geoff Burch was also on the bill, who was always good to chat to, and it was fortuitous that, when we were discussing fees, he suggested I double mine, saying I would get less but better work. It's good to mix with successful people! I returned home on Sunday 29th and on the Monday it was off to Cambridge to work with Spicers again – thank goodness for Suzanne.

Franchises

It was off to the seaside to speak at the Prontaprint national sales conference in Brighton – they even printed the words of 'Always Look on the Bright Side of Life' and 'Proud' inside their conference programme. It was a superb weekend, with the usual invite to the dinner on Saturday night and a chance to explore the 'lanes', and of course a walk along the promenade … and I got paid for all of this!

This booking acted as a catalyst for me. Prontaprint are a franchise, so I thought if they hold a conference for their franchisees, perhaps other franchisors do the same. So when I got back, it was off to the library to interrogate the *UK Franchise Directory*. I also visited the Franchise Exhibition in Manchester, did some investigation and bought my own copy of their directory. Then it was on the telephone to start prospecting. This was to be a rich and very enjoyable seam of business for me, which took me to all sorts of interesting and exciting locations.

I had met Rory Woolridge at the Successful Selling conference who, along with his day job, organised business events down in Worcester. He asked if I would be interested in speaking at these events, so the first event was a business breakfast held at Worcestershire County Cricket Club at the end of June. He arranged accommodation for me at a hotel in Malvern and, with his wife Yvonne, took me out for an enjoyable dinner in the evening. As usual I went down early and had a walk on the marvellous Malvern Hills, which was wonderful new walking territory for me.

Enjoying Myself

After a booking in Warwick I went to stay with my niece Teresa and husband Colin. She had two tickets for Wimbledon, which I'd never been to. We had great seats on Centre Court and also experienced Henman Hill; from there Teresa made a heroic trip to a bar to get us drinks – what a star! Although it started to rain it didn't spoil our day and as a result we went back again next day to watch the famous Goran Ivanisevic–Tim Henman semi-final, which was a wonderful experience that I won't forget.

I recall a marvellous holiday on the Isle of Wight with Dena and Chris. When they first moved to the island in 1976, they bought an old chapel and converted it to a wonderful home. Now they had done the same to another house in Newport. I loved my holidays with them – wonderful walking and cycling, interesting towns and shops, smashing beaches for swimming and of course, superb pubs.

As I have said previously, Sheila and I had five holidays in the Isles of Scilly, and at the end of September I returned. I knew it might be a painful reminder of happy times, but I also yearned for the beauty and peacefulness. I parked at Penzance and took the 2¾-hour trip on the *Scillonian* to St Mary's. I took a tent and camped up at the Garrison campsite. There are daily boat trips to the other four islands, so I visited them all with their peaceful, beautiful walks, wildlife, stunning beaches and great pubs. On St Mary's I had three pubs and made good use of all of them – it was wonderfully relaxing (and writing this has ignited a wish to go back again).

'Coals to Newcastle'

Then at the end of the month I had a real 'coals to Newcastle' booking with Tack. I had been learning from Alfred Tack books for years: *Sell Your Way to Success* and *1000 Ways to Increase Your Sales* are just two from my collection, and he has written many more. Tack were one of the leading training companies who had seen me at the ISMM conference and booked me for a presentation at their UK conference, held at the very impressive and grand Eynsham Hall, just outside Oxford. Bonuses for me were that my presentation was filmed, plus two wonderfully complimentary letters saying what an impact I had. Well, I wouldn't have believed it! Me making an impact at Tack Training … was all this really happening to me? Another song I embraced that had brilliantly meaningful words was 'Search for the Hero' sung by Heather Small, this time with M People; I wonder if this was what I had been doing all my life.

MMFI

September started with three days' training for Shell in Wythenshawe, with accommodation at the Hilton at Manchester Airport. I remember one evening at dinner when I asked the resident pianist if he would play 'Ballade pour Adeline' ('our tune' for Sheila and myself). A few weeks later, as I went into dinner, the same pianist saw me and played the tune again! How brilliant. I used this superb example of 'MMFI' ('Make Me Feel Important') in my presentations thereafter. My friend Graham Thompson introduced me to the branch secretary of his 'federation' and I secured a booking in Bradford for the Federation of Small Businesses. As Graham had a hand in my booking, I was delighted to receive a letter from the branch secretary with this quote, "This was without doubt the best meeting that we have had this year and I think we all went away with a more positive attitude towards our business activities."

Prospecting, Developing and Frog Kissing

With just a few bookings in August it gave me time to catch up with matters at home, to do some walking and some library research. 'Prospecting' was the life blood of my business, because once I had spoken at a conference it was rare to be invited back. More often than not the organisation would have a different speaker at the next event, which is why prospecting had to be regular and relentless.

I will never forget this particular day. I had made 83 cold calls so far but, as it was beautiful and sunny, the cats were asleep under the apple tree and I had two cans of beer waiting in the fridge, I was torn between joining the cats in the garden and making the remaining 17 calls to hit my target of 100. I dialled again – it was a franchisor, Safeclean, part of Valspar Industries. My target contact was franchise director Stan Knights. He took my call and, after the initial introduction and my reference to the other franchisors I had worked with, he said to me, "Well, you have timed that well Barry. I have just come out of a board meeting where we have been discussing the possibility of having a motivational speaker at next year's franchisees conference." When I told Mr Knights he was my 84th call of the day, I will remember forever his words, "Well Barry, sometimes you just have to kiss a lot of frogs." It took another three months of pleasant persistence before Stan gave me the booking for Saturday 17th August 2002 in Coventry. The lack of bookings in August created the circumstances for me to make that call, but little did I know what the consequences of this particular booking would be. I also used some of the time developing Phase Four of 'Sales Efficiency Training' and began an 'A–Z of Success' manual which I thought I could have published one day.

In mid-September I had a fantastic booking with the BANPR (British Association of Nursery and Pram Retailers) at Earl's Court. It was brilliant turning up at the 'tradesmen's entrance', so to speak, with a reserved parking spot. I spoke at two seminars at the Baby & Child Exhibition and they put me up at the Grosvenor Hotel on Buckingham Palace Road. In the evening I was invited to join them on a River Thames paddle boat cruise from Chelsea Harbour Pier to Greenwich and back, with a sumptuous buffet and disco – although I spent the entire trip up on deck watching in awe at the spectacle of the sights and lights of London unfolding as we cruised past.

On 18th December I went to Paul and Barbara's company Christmas dinner up in Skipton and stayed with them overnight – as always it was a fun evening, and it was very kind of them to let me share in their company celebrations. Angie and Dave invited me for dinner on the 18th – I always enjoyed evenings with them: wonderful food, lots of fun and I could walk home, so lots of beer.

The year ended with a booking that took a lot of selling, including a visit to their Telford head office. It was worth all the effort to secure this most marvellous booking with Lyreco Office Supplies & Solutions to present for 600 salespeople at the International Centre in Telford. I was invited to their fantastic Christmas celebrations and cabaret evening and accommodation. Sales Director Mike Hopkinson wrote, "As you know this was our first year with a professional speaker and I do not think anybody could have set a better benchmark for the future." What a superb way to end the year.

There was just some small sadness to all this happiness – I had no one to share it with. Some of the speakers took their wives with them on the trips abroad and I often thought what a wonderful time Sheila and I could have enjoyed. I found consolation in my Bible and remembered the phrase, "Don't worry about what you don't have, be grateful for what you do have." I did just that and looked forward to 2002 and, because life doesn't have a rewind button, I was going to enjoy every moment of my life and relished the circumstances and consequences of 2002. As the Mama Cass Top 10 hit in 1969 said, "It's getting better (better everyday)."

Beauty and peacefulness on The Isles of Scilly

CHAPTER 17: ALL OVER THE PLACE

My first booking of the year began in Longtown, Cumbria, with Jobson's Farm Health, Agricultural & Veterinary Chemists — how did I find and secure this one, I wonder? It was probably my ISMM appearance in 2000. Phil Jobson MD wrote: "Perhaps one of the most striking effects the training has had is making the team think more considerately for other members of the team and this, in itself has a motivating effect." I had now introduced another perfect example of teamwork into my presentations, and that was Formula One pit stops. If you want to see a group of individuals working together under extreme pressure, this is it — just seconds can make the difference between the driver standing on the rostrum or not. I went on from Jobson's to work with my friend Ian Callander's company Metrik in Dumfries and stayed for a lovely weekend with Ian and Phyllis.

In April I was booked on a tremendous adventure. First it was to Birmingham to collect another order of CDs, then on to the Cheltenham Park Hotel for the Superstat conference, where I was booked for two spots — one on the opening day and another to close the conference on the Saturday. On Friday evening there was a dinner for the delegates, although I had to be careful with my alcohol intake, as I was back on stage the next day for my second presentation. On Saturday evening there was a 'Dress to Kill, Licensed to Thrill, Black Tie Gala Dinner' where I had a whale of a time, touting for CD sales, having my ego massaged by appreciative delegates and being bought drinks at every table I visited. On Sunday I went walking and followed the Cotswold Way to Charlton Kings Common and then onto Devil's Chimney, a wonderful walk and a great end to a brilliant weekend.

My calendar for the 11th May reads 'Peter Hawkins', and although he was my ex-brother-in-law he was no less important – I will always be grateful for all he did for me. He and his wife Doreen were throwing a family party for his 70th birthday. I went down to stay with Teresa and Colin in West Wickham and then we went down to Dymchurch for the party, staying overnight at a local pub.

Treats

On 14th I went camping on the Isle of Man. This was my first visit and I loved it. I camped at Peel and visited all the interesting towns and tourist attractions, such as the incredible Laxey Wheel, the Snaefell Mountain Railway and Peel Castle, and of course lots and lots of coastal and mountain walking. An experience here helped me make a decision. One night a terrible storm forced me to evacuate my tent before it blew away. I threw everything into the back of my car and ended up sleeping in the laundry room where the site manager found me next morning. As the site wasn't very busy, he kindly let me finish my holiday sleeping in the television and games room. I would see all the camper van people sitting warm and comfortably, drinking their coffee, and decided then that was what I would get myself. When I returned home after a fabulous holiday, I caught up with Phil Hutchinson for lunch and I am delighted to say we still meet up for lunch many years later.

June began with a two-day GAP Depot Managers' Conference at the Cedar Court Hotel in Harrogate. Then it was an absolute treat for me on Saturday, courtesy of Lloyds Bank. Our host for the day was my private banking manager Mike Cooper, and we were off to Twickenham. Sheila and I were rugby fans and enjoyed the Six Nations competition each year (it is still one of my favourite sports). The match was the Zurich Championship final between Bristol Shoguns and Gloucester. Mike had also invited Terry Brooks. We met at Leeds Station with some of Mike's other clients – there were about six of us. We got on the train and Mike went to get us coffee and bacon sandwiches. On to my second coffee, I was still halfway through it when we arrived at King's Cross. Being as I am, I took the coffee with me to drink on the Tube. It was very busy, with steps up and down, so I became fed up with carrying the drink and, seeing a beggar, I gave it to him. The man said, "Thanks mate," but as we were going along the Underground tunnel he shouted out, "Bloody hell, it's black with no sugar!" Talk about beggars not being choosers!

At Twickenham Mike had booked a restaurant. The previous night Greece had won a European final and so they did not open the restaurant, so poor Mike had to run round to find another venue. When we got to the ground at Twickenham, there was a fantastic outside bar serving Guinness, so we had a few there. We watched the match and then got on the train from Twickenham to central London. In one of those large open carriages, absolutely crammed with people, I stood up on my seat and shouted out, "Excuse me everyone, it's my dear friend's Terry's birthday, would you all help me sing happy birthday" – and the whole carriage sang it to him … and it wasn't even his birthday!

Belgium

In July I had a booking with Integra Office Solutions Ltd to speak at their 'New Horizons' National Conference at the Sheraton Brussels Hotel & Towers, Belgium. I was offered the choice of flying or Eurostar first class. I chose the latter (I am actually smiling away, with tears of happiness, as I type this). It was quite remarkable – I still wonder at all this, I really do. I booked a B&B in Ashford on the Thursday with the arrangement to leave my car there. A taxi took me and my large suitcase full of props, CDs and clothes to the station on Friday morning to check in at 7.45. This would be my first Eurostar experience and, as the train entered the tunnel, the first-class element began with Buck's Fizz and nibbles, continuing with coffee and croissants and, as the train hurtled through the countryside, breakfast was served. I ate admiring the passing landscape – oh, was I loving this.

I arrived at the hotel at 12.30 pm to enjoy the buffet lunch, meet my hosts and other guests. I then settled into my lovely room, showered and dressed for the conference, which began at 3.00 pm. I was the last speaker on at 5.10 pm, so I went down at about 2.00 pm to prepare and set up my props table. I always loved the business of getting mic'd up and having a sound check. I watched the other five speakers from the back of the hall, but I couldn't sit down as it would crease my trousers and that would never do! The early presentations were the important subjects about strategy, finance, manufacturing, market trends and the future.

Just before I was due on stage, I went to use the urinal in the gents. Little did I know my mic was switched on and the audience came with me … I didn't do that again! Then I was on with my 'Find, Win and Keep Profitable Customers'. As always I got things going with my community singing of 'Always Look on the Bright Side of Life' – and of course they were ready to laugh, so I helped them – but as usual with hard-hitting messages as well. I must have done something right because I sold an awful lot of CDs over the weekend.

I particularly enjoyed what happened next – Rick Needle, the chief executive, suggested he and I walk out into Brussels for a couple of beers. It is always pleasant to do something like this after the high I experienced on stage. The evening event was a Belgian beer festival with local cuisine and traditional entertainment. I was pleased I had already done my bit and could now relax. Rick wrote to me with these comments, "Everyone I spoke to was full of enthusiasm regarding your session and I'm sure they all went back to their businesses fired up to knock the hell out of the competition. I am sure that there were lots of Integra members listening to your CDs on their journeys home."

On the Saturday I became a tourist in Brussels, including a visit to the Atomium, which Johnny and I visited back in the sixties, and Sheila and I in the eighties. It is a beautiful city with the Grand Place taking centre stage, surrounded by wonderful cafés and bars (Sheila loved having a brandy or hot chocolate while I enjoyed one of the famous beers). Saturday night was a black-tie gala dinner evening at the Albert Hall complex – I always enjoyed the mixing, mingling and of course the networking and the CD sales of these evenings. Sometimes someone would comment, "Don't you ever stop selling?" and I would quip, "I can't, it's an illness!" Sunday morning provided a last chance to sightsee before the coach left at 1.00 pm for the Eurostar. More first-class pampering on the return to Ashford and then the long drive home to Yorkshire, recounting the fantastic events of the previous 48 hours.

Work and Pleasure

The first engagement of the next week was a second booking with Sidhil in Halifax. On Saturday there was a neighbourhood barbecue with neighbours Sam and Judith, a brilliant evening made even better by just a three-minute walk home. The next weekend I went down to Kent to stay with Teresa and Colin, and as usual had a marvellous time with them. On Saturday night they had organised a brilliant first-time treat for me with a trip on the London Eye, all finished off with a Chinese meal in Soho. Colin builds and flies model aeroplanes and, whenever I go to see them, we go off to his club flying field near Biggin Hill, then in the evening the three of us would go to the brilliant White Bear Inn at Fickleshole.

At the end of the month, Rory Woolridge organised another of his business breakfast events – this time I spoke at the Worcester Rugby Club, he put me up in Malvern again and I had a lovely evening with him and Yvonne. Rory bought me a book, *Walks Around the Malverns* by Roy Woodcock, and I did just that before going home.

1st August it was back to Huddersfield University for an 'Advanced Word' training day and then off to Chippenham to work with Ryzex again. Colin Hughes took me out in the evening to the wonderful village of Laycock – what a delightful place. We visited a couple of the charming and characterful pubs and had a lovely meal before Colin took me back to my accommodation. I did a refresher for my friend and one of my first clients, Terry Brooks, at Rema in Leeds on the 7th.

Not My Best Day

Tuesday 29th October I was at a presentation for the Institute of Directors at the National Coal Mining Museum for England in Wakefield. This wasn't my finest hour – the audience of directors weren't very happy when I told them off for not having a notebook and pen with the remark, "Do you have amazing memories, or didn't you think I was going to say anything worth making a note of?" Well, sometimes you just have to stick by your principles and suffer the consequences … I didn't sell many CDs, but they didn't ask for my fee back. In the future I decided not to make note-taking my problem (and of course it could have been that they wanted to listen to me intently and didn't want to be distracted by making notes). As someone said, every day is a day at school, and so this was a lesson learnt for me. Theodore Roosevelt said, "The only man who never makes a mistake is the man that never does anything."

Then it was that booking I secured back in 2001 with the 'kiss a lot of frogs' man, Stan Knights, and Safeclean in Coventry. In the audience that afternoon was the vice president from the USA. I am told that part way through my presentation he said, "This guy's great, we must get him over to the States, but he will have to moderate his language!"

New Orleans

I mentioned earlier about the wonderful venues that were ahead of me ... well, that was about to go up a gear. I had been booked to speak at a conference in New Orleans – yes, honestly, New Orleans! What a start to November: a flight from Manchester to Philadelphia, and then on to New Orleans. This was the fantastic consequence of that 84th cold call back in August 2001 to Stan Knights, the 'kiss a lot of frogs' man, and the subsequent booking in August 2002 when the VP from America wanted to book me for the States. Well, here I was on my way.

The terminus at Philadelphia is like a mini city. I sat at the counter of a bar drinking beer, wallowing in the fantastic atmosphere, when I experienced the most wonderful piece of customer service (which I have been using in my presentations ever since). The barman came up to me and said, "Are you going to have another one?" I asked for a half, but they didn't serve halves. Nevertheless, two minutes later the barman came back with a smaller glass. I asked, "How much?" but he said it was on the house. Now that's customer care!

Although it was November when I reached Bourbon Street in New Orleans, the atmosphere was just like Mardi Gras. The streets were jam-packed and it was not even the festival time! There were people on the balconies, everyone was dressed up, necklaces were thrown down from above ...! I had lots of free time to explore this fascinating city.

At the event I was very aware of the vice president's remarks about my need to moderate my language. It was a bit like someone saying, "I don't want you to think about pink elephants!" The other phrase that was frowned on was, "God damn it," even though that seemed to be used by

20th August 2002

The reason you are reading this is I guess that you are considering using the services of Barry Young.

After having ran many Franchise Conferences I realize the importance of finishing on a high and needed to fill the graveyard spot from 4pm. Barry, being a man who practices what he preaches, cold called me late one afternoon.

I booked him and what a good decision that was. 137 delegates, who I could see were getting sleepy after a rather substantial lunch, attended my Conference. Barry came on like a blast from the Sahara, hot, gritty and in your proverbial face! I noticed after just a few minutes everybody was now awake and listening.

What followed was a mass of commonsense put over in his very individual style, which as well as being commonsense was very amusing. Barry had done a degree of research into Safeclean so everything was highly relevant and focussed.

I have no problem in recommending Barry Young.

Stan Knights

Franchise Director

Valspar Industries (UK) Limited
152 Milton Park, Abingdon, Oxon OX14 4SD Tel: 01235 444757 Fax: 01235 832975
E-mail: safeclean@valspar.com Website: www.safeclean.co.uk
Registered in Cardiff No. 2360505

cowboys in the movies all the time! It seemed that all the bad language used outside of the workplace was certainly not used in it. Thankfully all went well and my presentation received a standing ovation (my first) and a brilliant letter from Communications Manager Cynthia Allen, "Having been a meeting planner for more than ten years, I can honestly say that Mr Young would be top of my list for all future events. He spoke at Valspar's 2002 Annual Sales Meeting, and I am still hearing compliments from my audience members. His presentation, 'Seriously Boost Your Business', was a big hit." Coming from a highly experienced and already successful sales force, that was quite a compliment. Her letter in full is on my website, and this fabulous response and feedback was to be instrumental in a further sensational booking with Valspar a short time later. (I ought to mention that, in order to communicate with Valspar in America and secure this booking, I had to install email on my computer … one day I might even have needed a mobile phone!)

CDs

I returned to the UK to two bookings with Eurotel, one in Manchester and then one in Birmingham (which was filmed, so I now have a three-hour video of me in action). Then it was yet another franchisee conference, Mr Electric at a super hotel near Kettering. The event was also filmed so I took advantage and secured a copy, using it for a new version of my 'Seriously Boost Your Business' to replace the one from the OSTA conference back in 1999. I was now using the mnemonic SERIOUSLY to define the characteristics and attributes of success, along with added props and new anecdotes. When I went to the studio, we separated the letters into tracks to make it better for the listener and I placed another CD order with my producers in Birmingham. Clive Houlston, UK franchise director, later wrote, "You were billed as our keynote speaker and you certainly did not let us down. Barry I would certainly recommend you to anybody else."

Beautiful Venues

My next special venue was back at the Royal Armouries Museum in Leeds for a presentation to the B&I, then over to Manchester for a new client, Hansar Finance. Terry Cross wrote, "Dear Barry, I had been warned, seriously funny, seriously successful and seriously thought-provoking. Thank you for reminding myself and my team of all the attributes that make a successful sale, a satisfied customer and a profitable business." I also had a booking at the National Motorcycle Museum, then at another of the CSMA events, and stayed at the magnificent Bosworth Hall Hotel in Warwickshire. My superb bedroom suite had a beautiful oak four-poster bed, but I never took any of this for granted and was constantly pinching myself to check I wasn't dreaming! I finished the month speaking at a huge conference for Royal & Sun Alliance.

In December I had a day in the recording studio working on my new CD, and two days working with Super Break in York which at Christmas time was a real treat – the city is wonderful adorned in its festive seasonal regalia. Then it was a very nice trip to Scarborough to make a presentation to the East Coast Export Group. Professor Gerry Bantin wrote, "It is easy to slip into bad ways and become mushy mouthed and accept mediocrity, thank you for reminding us what we must continue to do." It seemed to me that the message coming back from my presentations was the need to avoid complacency and the desire to be reminded of those good old-fashioned principles, manners, etiquette and sensibilities of business and personal success.

I always began my presentations with the Josh Billings quote, "Advice is like castor oil, easy enough to give, but dreadfully uneasy to take." I would tell the audience I was not there to give advice; I would, however, remind, rekindle and reinstate those ideals we could sometimes lose sight of. A delegate from the audience in New Orleans wrote, "Hearing Barry's presentation was just what I needed. I've been in the business for 30 years, and I do find myself in a rut. I've always thought I was as successful as I want to be, so I don't need to change; there's nothing for me to learn … Barry motivated me to try new ideas in my day-to-day sales activity." As someone once said, "The only difference between a rut and a grave is the depth."

Looking Back, Looking Forward

After seven years apart, Sheila had arranged our divorce earlier in the year, and we shared the £120 cost without the involvement of solicitors, so perhaps Christmas would now not be as difficult for me. Sheila married John a few years later and I am delighted to say is very happy. On one of my many visits to second-hand bookshops I came across a signed first edition of John Merrill's fantastic book, *Turn Right at Land's End*. It is the story of his 7,000-mile British coastal walk. I always found books like this truly inspiring, informative and educational – they just made me want to get my boots on and go exploring. My work would certainly be providing plenty of exploration in 2003 and I looked forward to another exciting and exhilarating year. In his book *The IBM Way*, Buck Rodgers quoted an old adage, "Age may wrinkle the face, but lack of enthusiasm wrinkles the soul." He adds, "I believe that; but I think that a lack of enthusiasm wrinkles the face too." So do I Buck.

Andrew Carnegie said, "Do your duty and a little more and the future will take care of itself." Judging by these client comments, that positively seems to be true for me:

As discussed please contact me to discuss training for our lead generation team. In addition we need to schedule stage 2 of your training package for the sales team.

I see these courses as a starting point and not as a single action and thus look forward to developing a continuing programme with you for 1999 and beyond.

I will discuss with Stuart the date for a follow up course for the Pharmacy Sales team.

As you know choosing you to undertake this event was an act of faith on my part, based solely on the air of confidence and positive approach you gave on the phone, we will be in touch with you again to arrange an 'all company event'.

I don't know where you get all this positive energy from but I wish you would let me into the secret. Are you running on Duracell? (they also have a copper-coloured top!) Thank you once again and I look forward to speaking to you in the not too distant future.

CHAPTER 18: JET-SETTING BARRY

A Busy Start

My first trip of the year was to Worcester for a 'Customer Awareness' training day with Discover Travel & Tours, where two nights' accommodation gave me a chance to enjoy this lovely city again. The training went very well, so all in all a great start to the New Year. I spent another couple of days in the studio, a lot of time cold calling and I had been asked if I could do a 'Presentations Skills' training day. A phrase from my existing training was, "Don't tell customers what you can't do, tell them what you can do," so I said I would design one for them and started developing a new training day called 'Present' and, no surprise, I used PRESENT as a mnemonic.

The Franchise Show at GMEX in Manchester at the beginning of February gave me more networking and prospecting opportunities, as well as meeting clients whose conferences I had spoken at. A letter from my next booking at Hodder & Stoughton read, "You were loud, funny and sometimes a bit controversial, but most of all, your presentation was thought-provoking. Thank you for making us all sit up and take notice and to really think about our own approach to this wonderful art of selling!"

In 2002 I had worked with Cash Converters, and so in 2003 I spoke at the Cash Generators Conference. MD Steve Mahon wrote, "I have been inundated with calls from attendees who came away feeling uplifted and inspired." On Saturday 15th I was invited to a match at Bramall Lane by one of the directors of Sheffield United who had seen me speak at an event, which made for an enjoyable day out. The month concluded with bookings with NatWest in Manchester and Girobank in Newbury. I also took my bike and cycled on the towpath of the Kennet and Avon Canal, which put the seed of an idea in my head that blossomed some years later.

Social Life

Living alone means you are your own 'activities director', and with that in mind I invited Helen and Ian to dinner on 1st March, repaying their hospitality at Christmas time. My orienteering club was having training runs for the 'wrinklies' (older runners) on Wednesdays and, if I didn't have a booking, I was able to join them for a run followed by lunch at a local hostelry (which also meant I didn't have to cook that evening).

Brighton was the venue for a Butlin's Redcoat Reunion in April, a great weekend, although unfortunately there was no one from Filey 1975. Nevertheless, I enjoyed walking along the prom and round the town. On Saturday 19th Geoff Burch invited me to his 50th birthday party in Cheltenham, a town I love, where I stayed at a lovely B&B and had a super weekend.

Pembrokeshire is where I spent some of May, and what a revelation this was – the most magnificent coastline that made for fantastic walking, cycling and exploring. I stayed at a B&B in Reynoldston on the Gower. I also had some time walking in Scotland and, along with other mountains, climbed The Cobbler, near Arrochar. Then I went to Wasdale in the Lakes and did the classic 'Threading the Needle' below Great Gable: a frightening experience, especially as there wasn't a soul to be seen. Another first for me came when a group of us from EPOC walked the three peaks of Yorkshire – a very arduous and challenging walk, but wonderfully satisfying.

I was still enjoying plenty of hill walking in the Lakes and the Pennines. I revisited a walk Sheila and I had taken many years previously, Chew Valley at Dovestone Reservoir in Derbyshire. Sheila had taken a fabulous photo of me stood on top of the Trinnacle, featured on the biography page of my website.

I presented an ISMM seminar at the Sheffield Wednesday ground, Hillsborough, Urban Planters employed me again for a Saturday 'Customer Awareness' day with their head office in Bradford and I went back to the Belfry to work with the De Vere Belfry reservations team. This time my room overlooked the 18th green and I was told this is where the top golfers would stay. My bike went with me for more canal towpath cycling, this time on the Trent and Mersey. Professor Gerry Bantin organised another event for me to speak at. I spent three days, one of them a rehearsal day with M&S Toiletries, as they had booked me as master of ceremonies for their suppliers conference. Bill Tempany wrote, "Yet again, you made the day with your tremendous enthusiasm, good humour and professional presentation. It was a great pleasure working with you again and indeed spending some quality time, my colleagues and fellow directors thoroughly enjoyed your company." On one of my visits to Edinburgh the directors took me to watch a local club evening rugby match, which was great.

It was off to Bedford at the start of April for three days with Lenze Ltd, where I did four half-day sessions to accommodate everyone in the company. It was challenging, as I had to ensure that I said all the same things to all four groups to avoid, "He never said that to us ..." etc. Judging by the following comments, I managed it fine – Tom Hardy wrote, "A number of individuals now think of themselves in a different light – I am convinced several members of our team will go on to much greater things in time." This statement became reality – I went back to work with Lenze again a year or so later, when a young man approached me to say thank you. He had gone from being a forklift truck driver to warehouse manager. This was so satisfying and gratifying for me; it was a wonderful feeling to know I had helped someone to progress in life.

Cold Calls

One of my cold calls was to SMG Risk Solutions in Leeds, and by coincidence Mark Minton the MD lived just around the corner, so we arranged to meet at our local pub. This meeting resulted in a booking for an afternoon in June at their Leeds offices. Mark also invited me to join them in the evening for a meal at a Chinese restaurant and said he would bring me home so that I could have a drink – another good result from a cold call. KONE, the elevator and escalator company in Keighley, were also a cold call and interview in April that would bear fruit in the future. A booking with Shell Bitumen in Manchester and an evening at a Tamla Motown-Northern Soul evening with Maggie and Graham at the Ritz Ballroom in Brighouse wound up a fantastic month.

London ... then Prague

On Thursday 3rd it was off to another of those brilliant venues, this time the Tower Hotel in London. I always remember driving down – as I neared Tower Bridge, I saw the congestion warning signs and was not sure what I had to do. Fortunately, and much to my relief, I turned into the hotel car park before the restriction zone started. As always, I asked for a high-floor room so that I could enjoy the views and was rewarded with the most spectacular view right next to Tower Bridge. I was in London for a presentation to the members of Nemo, another of the office dealer groups. My spot was on Friday afternoon, followed by a black-tie dinner with my usual CD selling and networking.

I had to rush home because on Sunday I was to fly to Prague to speak at Blazes' franchisees conference. What a brilliant four days this was, and the beginning of a great friendship with owner Michael Eyre. The event started with a treasure hunt around the city, when one of the clues was to find an actor dressed as Wolfgang Amadeus Mozart and answer questions on his music. Being a big fan I did very well, helping our team win. Michael's daughter was our team leader and carried what she called "walking out money," buying us a beer at almost every bar we passed, which was a tremendous start to the four days of activities.

The conference was on Monday, with my two-hour interactive presentation winding up business proceedings. The remaining days were all fun time, with all sorts of beautiful venues for meals and entertainment. It was a very well-organised experience for the franchisees. I also had time to look round the city by myself and with the delegates, sampling some of the plethora of bars with the local beer at 50p a pint! The main organiser was director Cathy Birchall who wrote, "Your rousing presentation ensured that all those dark corners of our psyche were well and truly illuminated. We have nowhere to hide and no excuse for not getting off our backsides and making life, work, fun, whatever the thing we want it to be."

Kissing More Frogs ...

One of my 'kiss a lot of frogs' cold calls, when it was another case of being in just the right place, was Flexseal. A visit to their head office in Wombwell near Barnsley followed, when I secured a booking at yet another amazing venue … and also on my birthday! On Friday 29th I had a booking to speak at the ABHM (Association of Building Hardware Manufacturers) conference in York. The delegates were from all over Europe, which gave me my first introduction to working with interpreters. It was a fascinating experience, and I had a meeting with the four female translators to discuss the finer points, such as speaking carefully, a little more slowly and waiting for the delegates to understand and appreciate the jokes etc. I was invited to join them in the evening for a wonderful meal on one of the platforms at the National Railway Museum. This booking was the result of pursuing that vertical market of associations and federations, and this presentation would also take me to Europe at a later date.

Varied Venues

Talk about variety of venues – October began with a booking with a society, this time the National Merchant Buying Society Limited, in Athens at the Divani Apollon Palace hotel. I remember sitting with the group in a bar looking up at the floodlit Acropolis – surely I must have been dreaming? The evening black-tie dinner produced CD sales and resulted in bookings with some of the society members. A quote I used in my sales training was, "Just keep putting yourself in danger of getting an order."

McCarthy & Stone were an almost permanent fixture on my calendar, and now I had days in Manchester and York. Regional MD at York, Trevor Walters Thompson, wrote, "Keep up the good work and should anyone have any reservations about using you just give them my number." Bookings at Centre Parcs in Nottingham and Penrith were followed by the first of several bookings with United Utilities. This was four presentations over two days to 500 people (125 people at each time) at their Networks Employee Roadshow, another case of ensuring I said all the same things four times. The first two were at Lancashire Cricket Club at Old Trafford, with the second two at Camelot Theme Park at Charnock Richard … the venues were getting more exciting all the time! MD Chris Marsden wrote, "I will never forget your presentation on Tuesday morning. You created an electric atmosphere that motivated a particularly difficult audience into a reality check, followed by laughter and applause. We were all taken on an extraordinary and entertaining journey, which had us questioning our actions one minute and delving into our emotions the next."

I bought a new stage suit, an Amici from Lakeland (the leather wear shop, not the kitchenware chain!). It was a beautiful light blue/grey, made from very fine cord material, and looked great. At the same time I bought a superb pair of Bally shoes to go with it, which even came in their own individual cotton drawstring bags.

Spain ... again

A birthday I would not forget began on 16th October when I flew to Spain to work with Flexseal at La Manga Club. The training day on 17th began with Buck's Fizz that I had ordered to be brought into the room to toast my birthday, which got the day off to a great start. This fun theme continued throughout the weekend, and the delegates clubbed together to buy me a gorgeous yellow La Manga golfing shirt which I still treasure. The training went so well I was back working with them before the year was out.

I remember a quote which asserted, "Find a job you love, and you'll never have to work a day in your life." After the fantastic events of 2003, that rang so true for me. I cannot imagine how I felt about all this back then, as I am overwhelmed by it all even now ... little did I know that 2004 would be even more elaborately exciting.

2004

Flexseal finished the previous year and started 2004 with Phase Two of 'Sales Efficiency'. This was my only booking in January, giving me the chance to catch up with my personal and domestic matters, and my favourite pastime – winter walking. I did have a very healthy-looking bookings calendar for the year, as well as other prospects to follow up on, so I wouldn't be without excitement.

Netherlands

The excitement began on Sunday 8th with a booking that came as a result of the ABHM conference in York – I was off to the Netherlands. I flew from Leeds Bradford to Amsterdam, where a hire car had been arranged for me so that I could drive to the venue near

Arnhem. This was a bit daunting, I have to say, and I was glad to arrive and check in. The schedule gave me time to take a train journey into Arnhem and enjoy a day out in the town. As soon as I arrived home on the Wednesday, I began packing for my next adventure … and this really would be an adventure.

Las Vegas – Show Time!

When I started writing this biography, this was the period I was looking forward to writing about the most. The culmination of those 50 years, my crowning achievement and, in work terms, my Everest, my No 1 hit, my Oscar. On Sunday 15th February I was flown to Las Vegas to speak at another Valspar conference. Cynthia Allen was true to her word when she had said that I would be top of her list for all future events, and so here I was. The sad thing about all this was that I was the only one who really understood and appreciated just what a personal achievement this was for me. If I had been a footballer playing at Wembley or on Top of the Pops, my friends and family would be boasting about me. However, this business arena which I played in wasn't on their radar, and of course many didn't know my back story either.

I had asked if I could extend my three days into nine at my own expense, and the company very happily agreed. I booked into a motel before and after the conference and they arranged the flights accordingly. Unfortunately I had a nightmare arrival in Las Vegas when my suitcase didn't arrive with me, and a very sleepless night and troubled morning followed. I was very relieved when eventually my case was delivered to my motel. The venue for the conference was the Excalibur Hotel, where I had asked for an upper-floor room and was rewarded with a view right down the strip. Vegas had certainly changed since Ray and I were there in 1972, but it was marvellous to revisit places like Caesars Palace and Circus Circus, and to explore the fantastic new hotels. Two of my favourites were the Bellagio and the Venetian. I spent hours at the top of the Stratosphere Hotel, which I found absolutely amazing, with its incredible views and sights. The 'all you can eat' buffets were extraordinary, but I didn't indulge that often. I still sit here writing almost open-mouthed in amazement at it all.

Las Vegas reactions!

In his book *Wisdom of the 90s*, American entertainer George Burns wrote, "Show business is like sex — you need a good start and a big finish." This would have been the perfect venue for a big finish to my speaking career, although fortunately I still had bookings to do, places to go and people to see.

Back in Blighty

The delightful Belton Woods Hotel, with its two golf courses and health club, was the setting for my booking with Inter-Tel Europe. A story I often recall when I want to highlight negativity is from this event. One of my props was a Bob Dylan LP used to illustrate 'The Need For Change'. I would tell the audience that Bob Dylan had a hit with a record entitled 'The Times They Are A-Changin', and then go on to say, "And they certainly are a-changing." I was in the garden after my presentation when a guy came up to me to let me know that that particular Bob Dylan track was not on that LP! (There is always someone looking for the negatives in life.) Nevertheless, this incident was more than compensated for when MD Chris Harris wrote, "What a performance! You were undoubtedly the high point of our Business Partner Conference at Belton Woods last month — by the middle of the evening many of your phrases and expressions had reached almost cult status amongst the audience!"

Next day I set off to speak at the Institute of Leadership (ILM) conference at the Renaissance London Heathrow Hotel. My bedroom looked directly onto the runway and it was brilliant watching the planes landing — what a treat. A letter from the CE said, "Your presentation, whilst containing a serious underlying theme, was hugely entertaining and gave everyone a boost when they were beginning to wilt under the volume of information we had received during the day. All those present were certainly 'lifted' by your presentation and inspired by your enthusiasm." I went round the M25 to spend a wonderful weekend with Linda and Chris. We had a lovely day out with lunch at The Spotted Dog at Penshurst and then visited Tunbridge Wells, a beautiful town with a brilliant second-hand bookshop which Linda and Chris had to drag me from.

On 6th April I worked with DePuy in Leeds and had a run and lunch with the EPOC wrinklies on Wednesday. Scarborough was the venue for the Butlin's Redcoat Reunion weekend at the Grand Hotel, and at least this time there were some people I knew, including Entertainments Manager Rocky Mason. I took part in the Redcoat Cabaret on Saturday night, performing my Frank Spencer. I haven't mentioned it, but he made regular appearances at conferences and training days, especially in tricky situations!

Inspiring Children

It was another stationery dealer group conference with OFDA (Office Friendly Dealer Association) on Friday 21st, and another franchisees conference, 'Recognition Express', on Saturday 22nd. At the end of May I had one of my most challenging but also most rewarding bookings. I had met Alan at a party at Ann and Martin's. He had explained that he was a teacher and his school were trying ideas to improve performance and results. The previous year they had invited a blind man who had achieved great things to speak to the children to help with motivation. He asked if I would be interested, so I agreed and spoke at the school on two occasions.

I made changes to my presentation to make it relevant, and I had to highlight the importance of knowledge, passing their exams, attitude, enthusiasm and all those other attributes that would contribute to their success and happiness. I felt a bit of a fraud telling them the importance of getting certificates and qualifications, when I didn't have any myself, but people tell me it is very difficult to even get an interview without a degree these days. In addition, telling them to have goals and ambitions – I didn't have any goals or ambitions until I was in my thirties, but I did highlight that people like David Beckham had not become a great footballer without the relevant hard work. I gave them this very easy-to-remember mnemonic: DAD – I told them with every confidence that success is all about Dedication, Application and Determination. I also advised them to ignore teachers and parents when they were told not to be nosy: "Be nosy," I said, "ask questions, seek information, read books." The famous quote is, "Knowledge is power," but that is only half of it, as I believe it is what you do with your knowledge that makes it powerful. It would be wonderful to think that just one or two of the things I said made a difference to those kids.

Barcelona

I was booked to go to Barcelona on 22nd. Harry was so unwell that I arranged for him to stay at the animal hospital, and I bawled my eyes out driving away after taking him there. The booking was a result of my attack on associations; this one was the European Power Transmission Distributors Association (EPTDA) conference. Wow, what a place Barcelona was; I seem to have been on a European city tour. I had plenty of leisure time and walked for miles, visiting the famous La Rambla, La Sagrada, the seafront and generally soaking up the atmosphere, before stopping off for a couple of beers and a paella. What a way to earn a living (although this could not in any way be described as work).

I was to have a brilliant adventure one evening with about six of the delegates, who asked me along to the football with them. It was at Camp Nou, the famous stadium where Barcelona play, so I agreed. They didn't have tickets but there was a window selling returns, so we were stood there when someone came up selling us tickets. "You come with me!" he said, but we were all looking worried, so he added, "You no worry, you no pay until you sit in seat ...", which was reassuring. So we walked round the outside of the stadium and came to a barred metal gate which he rattled and as a bloke turned up they spoke together in Spanish. The gate opened, we went in and headed upstairs through more gates. As we reached the top we came out almost onto the pitch, where we had seats in the front row of the stadium – we could almost touch the players. It was an amazing atmosphere, and we could hear the footballers talking to each other, the boots hitting the leather of the ball – everything! Fantastic!

Marbella

I was booked to speak at the Associated Vending Services (AVS) conference, which turned out to be a fun event, summed up in a letter from CE Brian Tustain: "Barry, I am in your considerable debt for the excellent and very professional presentation you made at the conference. The hard work you put into it, coupled with the very positive life observations, were simply superb! We all laughed and laughed, not an easy feat as our final speaker at the conference when lunch, golf, and warm sunshine awaited our 250 delegates. We particularly enjoyed your company over the whole weekend. You entertained our delegates round the pool and at lunch and dinner, we all felt we had known you for many years – you have become a good friend of our association." This is also when and where I discovered chillout music. Having breakfast I heard this wonderful music being played, so I asked a waiter what it was, and he returned with the name on a piece of paper: Punta Del Este – Chillout Sessions. Later that morning I was enjoying a beer in a bar on the front and heard similar music and a conversation with the bar owner confirmed it was chillout music. I loved it and I now have a huge collection, including six Punta Del Este CDs: perfect music for late-night driving, dinner parties and those laid-back moments – try it.

Cats

Something I have been very remiss about is how important Harry and Honey had been to me since Sheila and I parted back in 1995. Many people, especially those without children, regard their pets as their children, and I was one of them. I was now to experience pain and heartbreak similar to Sheila leaving. Both cats were a good age in cat terms, but they required constant visits to the vet in 2004. My neighbours John and Morag and I had a reciprocal arrangement for cat sitting, but I was growing more concerned about leaving them. Fortunately I did not have many bookings that took me away from home in July and August, except one on 20th July with Elf Business Energy in Redhill, Surrey (a result of being seen at Birmingham).

Honey died in July. I lay with her in front of the fire through her last night, and I dug a grave for her under the apple tree where she had loved to lie. It was heart-breaking, as she had been such a comfort to me and given me so much joy; I consoled myself knowing she had a nice life with us. Knowing how unwell Harry was, I dug a second grave next to Honey. I collected Harry as soon as I returned home from Barcelona, but had to take him in again when I travelled to Marbella, so I had more heartache and tears.

When I collected Harry this time I made a decision I hadn't wanted to make, but realised it was very selfish to let my dear friend suffer any longer, so I had the awful task of taking him to the vet. I buried him alongside Honey, both of them with their favourite blankets and toys. They had been such wonderful companions for something like 15 years and I would miss them terribly. A few days later my birthday didn't have the usual importance or significance.

The Big Event

Rory Woolridge was involved in another event in Worcester. I had spoken at Worcester Cricket Club and Worcester Rugby Club. Now the venue was to be at Worcester Cathedral. Rory was hosting a 'power networking breakfast' at 'The Big Event', a charity day for the Cathedral Music and Light Appeal. The day started at 6.30 am with the networking breakfast. I was guest speaker and later presented with a beautiful, limited-edition painting of the nave, which is where I made my presentation. I wish I had known God then, as I now do, but apart from God I was in very good company that day – Dr David Starkey and Alistair McGowan provided the evening entertainment at the gala black-tie dinner. I did get some work from the event, sold some CDs and enjoyed some walking on the Malvern Hills. Again, business and pleasure, how brilliant and what a marvellous experience – imagine, Barry Young speaking in the nave of Worcester Cathedral!

I hosted the second of my BBBW on my birthday with all the same guys, although better equipped this time, and we went on a pub-crawl walk. We met at my house, started with bacon sandwiches and Buck's Fizz, and I'd put a large sign on the door, "No moaning!" due to the previous experiences on BBBW.

Memorable Marlow

October finished with a second booking at Office Friendly at the Compleat Angler Hotel in Marlow. I went down early and stayed at a lovely B&B at Cookham Dean. The owner was a script writer and had penned many of the *Poldark* episodes, a favourite programme of Sheila's and mine. On a recent stay in Henley-on-Thames I went back to see them, but unfortunately he had passed away. Nevertheless, his wife made me very welcome and we had a lovely chat over coffee and biscuits.

On the day of the conference I was the last speaker of the morning session, before we broke for a buffet lunch. Kriss Akabusi was due to speak after lunch. We were all in this large room with the buffet, where the

Kriss Akabusi

The look-alikes

window looked onto a car park next to the Thames. Someone saw Kriss arriving, and I was stood there with my plate of food when he came in, looked across and said, "Hey Barry, how are you doing?" And I nearly took off with pride. Everyone thought, wow, he knows Kriss Akabusi (and of course, I had met him previously)! The evening black-tie dinner was preceded with drinks at the bar with two professional look-alikes circulating with the guests – Del Boy from *Only Fools and Horses* and Patsy Stone from *Absolutely Fabulous* – and I couldn't resist the temptation, so Frank Spencer joined them for a photograph.

The Hague

It was back on the European tour on 1st November for a booking in The Hague, another result of the European event I had been at in York. The venue was the magnificent Grand Hotel Amrâth Kurhaus at Scheveningen. I flew from Leeds Bradford to Amsterdam and then travelled on a superb double-decker train to Scheveningen. I spoke just before lunch to finish the conference, which gave me plenty of time to enjoy the gorgeous seafront. My hosts accommodated me that night and I had a wonderful meal in the stunning surroundings of the hotel. I had a conversation with the piano player during his breaks, a young man with great musical ambitions. Next morning the plan was for a taxi to take me to the airport, but I had arranged with the organiser a late flight so I could enjoy a day in Amsterdam. The taxi took me to the city and collected me later that day to catch my flight home, so I did my tourist bit with a boat cruise on the canals and a lovely day looking round the city – a marvellous start to the month.

Returning My Fee and Honouring My Guarantee

My hard-hitting and humorous style did not suit my next client. They wrote to me after the event telling me they and some of the delegates were not happy, so I returned their money. Then I received another letter explaining that some of the delegates had in fact enjoyed my presentation (I knew this because I had sold some CDs), and with this in mind they returned half of my fee. This was only the second time (and indeed the last time) I had to refuse payment. The first time had been with a company I had worked with on many occasions, delivering training days and receiving glowing testimonial letters, including the 'Ode to a Sales Workshop' in 2001. On this particular occasion I knew straight away there was an element among the group who had been sent to make up the numbers. They didn't want to be there and didn't think they should be there. Once again CDs were purchased by some and I was disappointed to receive the news of some unhappiness, but returned my fee as agreed, which unfortunately ended a long and happy relationship. It just proves you can't please all the people all of the time.

<u>ODE TO A SALES WORKSHOP</u>

Barry Young is our wacko trainers name
It would appear he wants us to play <u>his</u> game.
We started off with lots of music and noise
But more was to come; sorrow <u>and</u> joys.
There are many books we could read and digest
But Barry is sure that <u>his</u> tapes and CD are the best!
Magic Moments, can we believe there are so many?
Yet wait, apparently power words are two a penny.
What do points make? He asks with a smile
Prizes we reply, if you go that extra mile.
Don't forget, put your hand up, before shouting out
Otherwise your answers are really worth nowt!
Lets look at some words to describe how to prepare
Knowledge, skills, determination, listening: all show we care.
For we really do have our customers interests in mind
It's just that sometimes they're really hard to find.
But that's why Barry is with us this week
To show us how it's done, and <u>not</u> to be meek.
The use of props has proved to be useful
Snooker cues, alarm clocks, batteries, quite a bag full!
Anyway, that's really enough wittering from me
Have you all set your objectives, done your homework, CV?!
Let's hope today really goes with a bang
Return to our work mates, but don't tell them we sang!!

There was one occasion when I actually offered my fee back on stage, at an hour-long conference presentation for a manufacturing company in Sheffield. I was in full flow and I used the 'c' word. I was mortified, stunned – as of course was the audience. I said straight away to the audience of 100-plus, "I am so sorry, I have no idea where that came from. I haven't seen one for years, but I certainly feel one now," which produced a sort of relieved laughter and greatly reduced the tension in the room. Then I said, "If anyone is offended in any way, please tell your managing director at the end and I will not take my fee." No one did and judging by CD sales the rest of my presentation made up for it. In fact, when I said sorry to some young women buying my CDs, they said, "Don't worry Barry, working in a factory environment we are used to that sort of language." I am still embarrassed by that terrible incident, and I hope readers won't think too badly of me. This had been everyday language for all those years that I had worked in the factory – I always found it quite amazing how when we came home, we left the language behind at the factory gates and I am pleased to say I never slipped up in front of Mrs C.

Slap-Up Meals

November finished with another booking for AVS at a presentation ceremony. I had a wonderful Saturday afternoon in Sheffield when I took Susan Browett out to lunch to thank her for all the work we enjoyed at Kingfield, and I did the same with Brad Wilson to thank him for all the work we did at OSTA. I also had lunch with another colleague, Simon Moate of Aramark, when he was up in Yorkshire. Terry Brooks of Rema and I went to the fabulous Bibis restaurant in Leeds. I always remember this was the most expensive meal I had ever bought, but I loved these reminiscing get-togethers. Sheila and I used to go to Bibis when it was a small place in Mill Lane, before it moved to a fabulous place in Greek Street, and now it is under the arches. My bookings ended with Dreams in Halifax: the shop, not the sleeping dreams.

Mind you, with all that had happened in 2004, it had sometimes been like a dream and sometimes like a nightmare … with Harry and Honey passing away, swearing on stage and unhappy clients. However, I know Harry and Honey had wonderful lives, I didn't swear on stage again and I haven't had any more unhappy delegates. I did, however, go to the Netherlands, Marbella, Barcelona, Las Vegas and spoke at a school and a cathedral: all certainly more than I ever dreamed of!

I donned my activities director's hat and hosted plenty of dinner parties over the festive season. I enjoyed bringing three couples together who had never met before, and used getting-to-know-you type games and wearing my prop hats. This year I stayed with Terry and Pauline Brooks for a night, with Helen and Ian on Christmas morning and then up to Kath and Dave's for dinner and overnight.

I had always said I would not buy a camper van whilst my cats were alive, and of course I wished they still were, but in 2005 I started my search. Being a bad decision maker and my enjoyment of research meant I had spent an awful lot of time going to shows, visiting dealers and reading magazines, deciding which camper van to buy. Finally I knew what I wanted, an Auto-Sleepers Trident, and now I just had to find one. With my impending retirement and a camper van, I now looked forward to a whole new chapter in my life.

Fun and food festivities

In memory of Harry and Honey

CHAPTER 19: A RAMBLING RETIREMENT

As previously mentioned, for many years I had it in mind to retire at 50, buy a camper van and set off to see all those places we don't have time to go while still working, but I had been enjoying my work so much – well, you couldn't really call it work, it was so much fun. I was actually 63 when I stopped actively canvassing for work in 2007.

All things come to those who waiteth, providing you worketh like hell while you waiteth!

I have often been asked why I retired from a career that I loved so much, and I have to say it was a difficult decision. I love what I did – all the wonderful places I went to, beautiful hotels, my food cooked, my bed made, receiving all the accolades for doing something I most certainly did love: it had been such a remarkable and rewarding ten years. I remember a quote, "One day you will find a job that suits you," and I believe I had indeed found my perfect vocation.

I was in show business, standing in front of an audience being the centre of attention, the perfect partnership of entertaining and educating. I suddenly realised why I was successful – it was because I loved to see success and happiness, and I had found a way to help people to achieve just that. I had built a reputation for what was my common sense 'Nuts and Bolts' training. There were companies offering sophisticated agendas which included the likes of fire walking and chopping bits of wood with your bare hands, but I stuck to down-to-earth, easy-to-understand ideas that people could put into practice the next day.

However, on my death bed I wouldn't be saying, "I didn't do that or this conference"; instead, it might be, "I never did climb all the Wainwrights." So, I had enough money, I didn't want for a big house, a yacht or any of those kinds of things. (In fact I had never chased money, and it's interesting how many successful people have not chased money either – the likes of Cameron Mackintosh, Anita Roddick and James Dyson never got into it for the money alone. They had a passion for what they were doing and wanted to be successful at it – great theatre shows, animal-free products and a bagless vacuum cleaner were their motivations.)

The other thing that had happened was that my job had become a way of life, a belief and conviction in what I myself said. I loved to see success – there's nothing wrong with that – but I had become too opinionated and I wasn't able to switch off from a 24-hour customer service critique wherever I went. I just wanted people to be better but, sometimes, much to my shame and regret, I was downright rude. Fortunately friends like Phil told me not to be so judgemental, and I will always remember Ian telling me, "Barry, you need to learn to accept and not expect." I did get better over the years after my retirement and, as Frank Spencer would say, "Every day, in every way I'm getting better and better!" Another brilliant quote that has helped me in this is, "Do not give your attention to what others do or fail to do, give it to what you do or fail to do." Wonderfully wise words! (See also Matthew 7.1-5.)

The important thing about a happy and fulfilling retirement, I believe, is to have objectives, things you want to achieve. If you don't, it could be very easy to sit down in an armchair and vegetate. A quote I used often was, "The difference between high and low achievers is how well they use their time." This is as true in retirement as in business, and I resolved to use my time well in the years ahead of me. I knew what I was going to do. Amazingly Alan Evans, from whom I was to buy my van (see below) had done exactly the same – retired early, bought a camper van and visited all those places he hadn't been, setting off on all those explorations and adventures that he didn't have the time to do whilst he was working.

Aristotle wrote, "The end of labour is to gain leisure," and that seemed very appropriate as my life became one of pleasure and leisure. Instead of the *Times* Rich List, I started reading *Mojo Magazine* with lists like 'The 100 Greatest Albums Ever Made' and, instead of self-development books, daily spiritual readings, like Patience Strong's *Thoughts for Every Day*. The thought on 15th January was so pertinent and inspirational:

Life should be a festival of hope and merriment – with everyone in high and happy mood.
Every day that passes should be well and truly spent – and hearts be lifted up in gratitude.

I reflected on how my life had been a festival of hope and much merriment, my heart was certainly lifted up in gratitude and now as I contemplated my future I was, "in a high and happy mood."

Trident Triumph

After a great deal of searching I finally found an advert for an Auto-Sleepers Trident which was red – most caravans and motorhomes are white, so this was a find. I rang the seller, Alan Evans, who lived just outside Warwick. We chatted for an hour during which I learnt how my planned retirement mirrored his story. I arranged to go down to see the van almost immediately and fell in love with it as soon as I saw it on his drive. It looked fabulous and was immaculate, just as the advert had claimed. Alan had obviously looked after it with loving care.

My Auto-Sleepers Trident

If my mind wasn't already made up, a test drive on country roads and the M40 convinced me that I should buy it – no procrastination or deliberation this time. I returned on the train a week later and drove the van home. I have to say it is certainly one of the best things I have ever bought – it has provided me with so much freedom and joy, I love it.

Alan suggested that I join the Camping and Caravanning Club and the Caravan Club, providing me with directories and maps detailing camping sites all over the UK (and as a member giving me preferential rates). I joined both clubs and made my first trip to the caravan club site at Broadway near to the Auto-Sleepers works at Willersey, which gave me the opportunity to visit the factory and get some more information on my new purchase. I also had a week's wonderful walking in the surrounding Cotswolds, including a fabulous day's walk up to Broadway Tower and then on through the delightful countryside to Snowshill, Stanway, Stanton and Buckland. Then I moved on to the most wonderful site, Tewkesbury Abbey, a real delight. I made friends with fellow club members Ray and Linda from Fishguard who encouraged me to take my camper down to the Pembrokeshire coast, which I did later that year.

My next camper van trip was, for me, another unexplored area, the Llŷn Peninsula in North Wales. The owner of the first site I stayed at was a member of the Caernarfon Male Voice Choir and invited me along to rehearsals one evening, which was brilliant. It was a terrific new area to explore, with superb walking and beautiful beaches. I visited Pwllheli to see the Butlin's Holiday Camp, and thanks to two items in a charity shop I began a collection of audio books.

I could see my camper was going to give me a lot of enjoyment and be a great investment. I always refer to my camper as a great big rucksack – you load it up and off you go but, just like my walking rucksack, it demanded careful and considered preparation and packing. Sometimes it could take me a week, others probably do it in a day. The van could be hooked up to electricity; it had a three-way fridge, powered either by the engine, electricity or from propane gas cylinders. A heater ran on the diesel fuel, it had onboard water and most importantly, especially when not on a proper campsite, a portable toilet in a cupboard under the sink (you just have to remember to get it out before making the bed).

One of the reasons for buying this particular van was that it provided sleeping space for two children above the main living area, which would give me lots of space for all my walking gear, rucksack, boots, clothes, maps, books etc. The other great feature was the 'rock and roll' bed – in its closed position it provides seating for eating at a table or two rear passenger seats, but is easily converted to a double bed by pulling out and letting the cushions unfold, rolling out the bedding and in two minutes you can be in bed ... particularly useful when drunk!

The van had a brilliant Sony six-CD auto changer and also a 12-volt, 10-inch TV, although I never made much use of it – the last thing I wanted to do when escaping to the wilds was to watch television!

The first big adventure in my camper van began on 8th June when I set off to Ireland. I took the boat from Holyhead to Dublin, turned left and went right round the coast, through the Wicklow mountains, Wexford and Waterford, and for my guide took a lot of inspiration from *McCarthy's Bar* by Pete McCarthy. I travelled to Castletownbere, featured on the front of that book, carried on round the coast through Killarney, and after a week or so ended up on the Dingle, where I climbed Mount Brandon. I found a spot on the coast and stayed there for nine days, and for first time in my

Brandon, where I learnt to relax

311

life I learnt to relax. I ambled around the coast and sat and watched the tide go out and come in. I went out rowing with the locals in their racing gig and enjoyed the local Guiness! So instead of carrying on round Ireland, I stayed there before returning directly to Dublin – it was a wonderful experience.

I had two further trips to Ireland – on my second trip I went from Cairnryan to Larne and drove anti-clockwise around the coast. I visited the Giant's Causeway, I climbed Croagh Patrick (the Holy Mountain), climbed Errigal in Donegal, went across to Sligo and climbed Benbulbin, visited the famine village on the Inishowen Peninsula, and went down to Galway and climbed the Twelve Pins of Connemara. For the third trip I took the ferry to Belfast and then drove straight across the country to Kerry and climbed Ireland's highest mountain, Carrauntoohill in MacGillycuddy's Reeks. I also visited the cliffs of Moher and the Burren before coming back to the Mourne Mountains where I climbed Northern Ireland's highest mountain, Slieve Donard.

Pembrokeshire

Following the recommendation from Ray and Linda at Tewkesbury, August 2005 found me on the Pembrokeshire coast. The first site was near Strumble Head, a few miles outside Fishguard at Trehilyn Isaf. There were no facilities, so it was the washing up bowl for a wash down and my Porta Potti. I had a couple of great nights out with Ray, using my Brompton (see below) to cycle into the town. However, it was going back that was the problem. It was pitch black, with no street lights and, although the Brompton has a dynamo, it only illuminates the road a few feet in front. I was very drunk and got lost on the myriad of tiny country lanes and had no idea where I was! My diary records that I arrived safe and sound at 12.50, glad to get to bed! I was also glad I had made the bed before going out.

I spent the most marvellous two weeks exploring the beautiful coast, where a brilliant little bus called the Strumble Shuttle runs regularly, allowing me to have a long walk to a destination, stop for a swim and then get back on the bus or vice versa. I stayed at a mixture of proper sites and also had some wonderful nights parked in tiny coves on the water's edge, falling asleep to the sound of the waves. For three nights I was parked on a harbour just across from the boat club, which was perfect for making friends, and in fact I was invited to a 50th birthday party on the Friday evening with food and a band. I tell you what, I was loving my new camper van life, just superb!

Dumfries and Galloway

My tour around Dumfries and Galloway included a visit to the famous 'Book Town' of Wigton. I went to climb Merrick, the highest mountain in the southern uplands in Glentrool. When I got to the top there was a person sat there very quietly – I later discovered that he was meditating. It turned out to be Donald Somerville, and we became very good friends – he was also staying in a camper van, a converted ambulance. My trip continued down to the Mull of Galloway, parking on the edge of the beach at Port Logan where Sheila and I had stayed many years before. This time I saw my first redshank and fell asleep to the sound of the waves.

Donald was like Graham Jackson – fabulous company and we became very good friends, and our love of the mountains and walking took us to some fantastic places together. He taught me the importance of living in the present moment and to this day I concentrate and enjoy each segment of my morning orange, instead of just eating it. Our first day out together was the 'Ring of Steall', a classic mountain route in Glen Nevis combining the traverse of four Munros, scrambling along narrow, rocky arêtes, one of them with the daunting name of the Devil's Ridge. We attempted to climb Ben Nevis but were beaten back by horrendous weather. Donald had to go home but I went back and climbed the mountain via the spectacular Càrn Mòr Dearg Arête.

I continued my Scotland trip up the west coast to Ullapool, where I stayed at a campsite suggested by Donald overlooking Loch Broom. Another of my life's coincidences happened, when I took a bus ride up to Durness on the northern coast and I met John in a pub. I had last seen him on my Mont Blanc trip! I also met Do and Jim Binney from Bury in a pub in Ullapool. They have become valued friends and we have had lots of wonderful times together. I seem to have made a habit of finding lovely people on my adventures who then become long-time friends!

Back Home

I remember a superb New Year's Eve party with all the gang at Sue and Tony's house which, being high up, presented us with a fantastic firework display over Bradford and beyond. I started the year with a new book by Patience Strong, *Daily Strengths for Daily Needs*, which began,

> *Look at life with eyes that see the best things, not the bad.*
> *Cherish in your memory the good times, not the sad.*
> *Choose the bright side of the road where sunshine lights the way.*
> *Walk in the direction of the blue sky, not the grey.*

I purchased a fold-up Brompton bike, following a recommendation in Ireland, which fitted perfectly in the passenger seat footwell of my camper and is brilliantly useful for getting out and about. I also bought a camcorder so that I could film all my trips and transfer them to DVD. I had time for plenty of domestic chores and sorting, social get-togethers and trips away. Thanks to neice Linda, who gave me some *Daily Mail* vouchers for reduced first-class rail travel, I enjoyed a week in Penzance and a week in Edinburgh. Nearer home I had a very interesting boat trip on the Manchester ship canal from Liverpool to Salford.

Romance?

Many romances begin at work or other social circles and, as I didn't really have either, in an effort to find a girlfriend I responded to an advert for the Oddfellows that read, "making friends, helping people." My local Huddersfield branch produced an events diary with everything from ten pin bowling to pie and peas quiz nights, as well as weekends away. My first events were a wine tasting evening and then a trip to greyhound racing. I didn't find a girlfriend, but I had a great time and, of course, 'Frank' got an airing to a new audience. Canal barge cruises were a favourite for me and a few years later I attended members' weekend in Lytham. I also responded to an advert in the *Yorkshire Post* to meet a woman, which was a waste of money and time – I got left with the bill!

314

UK Trips

As you can imagine, travelling and walking would be my major pastimes. The retirement years were to allow me many trips around the UK and elsewhere, too many to mention them all specifically. Some of the highlights included Hebden Bridge, one of my favourite local destinations. I remember one particular day coming to a wide stream which I had to throw my rucksack across and then leap across myself. I thought to myself, life is like that, making commitments and then following them through – Memorable Maxim. Also worth mentioning was a walk along the Calderdale Way – along with five other guys I walked the 50-mile route: 18 miles on the Saturday and 32 on Sunday. It was quite a challenge, but a fabulous experience, even though my legs ached for a while afterwards!

Back to Wales

I stayed in Caernarvon for a week, where the local Sherpa bus took me to climb Tryfan, Snowdon and many of the other Welsh peaks. I also bought H Mulholland's Guide to Wales' *3000-Foot Mountains: The Welsh Munros*, then set myself the challenge of climbing all 15 of them and (as with the Wainwrights – see below) this guide took me to places I might not have otherwise visited. It was here that I was introduced to world music. I had gone into the Galeri on the waterfront for a drink one evening, where a folk group were due to play later in the evening. During the interim a DJ was playing a style of music that I was not familiar with which I discovered was 'world music' and he suggested CDs compiled by Charlie Gillett, a well-known Radio 3 DJ. This wonderful diverse music has become a firm favourite and I now have quite a collection of CDs.

Isle of Wight

A week in my van at Adgestone campsite and the rest with Chris and Dena. Staying with them I mentioned to Chris that I'd always wanted a Rolls-Royce, and he told me that there was one in a garage on the island, so I went to have a test drive. I was so impressed, and it was a competitive price, but after discussing it with Chris who mentioned that I already had a camper van and a car, I decided not to buy it ... and regretted it for ages. Later on when I stayed with Ian and Phyllis in Dumfries, I said to Ian that I'd always wanted a Rolls-Royce. He told me there was one in the town, I went for a test drive, loved it, we discussed it ... and once again I decided not to get it!

On the way home from the Isle of Wight, I called in to see Ros at Pulborough and we had days out in Brighton, Chichester, Arundel and the Sussex Downs. (In 2002 I had been invited to the wedding of her daughter Hilary to Jason at the magnificent Eastnor Castle in Herefordshire; a fantastic venue and a brilliant day.)

Best Man

On 11th August I was best man at Ian and Phyllis's wedding in Gretna Green; a wonderful day which I recorded for them (they still enjoy watching this, usually with a bottle of bubbly on their anniversary). Like a lot of my family and friends, they were concerned about my welfare when walking alone in the mountains and so they very kindly gave me my first mobile phone. When I look back, it seems amazing – almost inconceivable – that I had succeeded thus far in business without one. Ian had spent some time as a volunteer with the Samaritans and he and Phyllis were to help me with my problems a few years later.

During July and August, I was training hard for a trip with Exodus for a week of Via Ferrata in Northern Italy. I was never a fan of such guided trips, but my desire to experience moving from hut to hut through the mountains using Via Ferrata helped my decision. As I could have possibly been the eldest member of the group of six and didn't want to be the one holding everyone back, I put a lot of effort into being prepared physically. As we had to carry everything for the week's trip, I spent some time on my rucksack organisation. However, I needn't have worried as, despite the literature stating that the trip was for people who were fit and with some climbing experience, there were still people who shouldn't have been with us. I am still friends with Richard Graham, a physiotherapist who administered some much-appreciated chronic cramp relief to me on the trip. We have been walking in the Lakes and I have been down to stay with him in Suffolk and enjoyed some great days out in that wonderful part of the country, including a trip to the coast where I saw my first avocet.

Health, Wealth and Technology

Thankfully my health has been good, but I would like to say a big thank you to my doctor and indeed all of the NHS staff who have looked after my health ... especially following my Mercedes accident when I was nearly killed, various minor complaints such as having varicose veins removed and injuring my shoulder when I fell on ice.

I ought to say that, whilst the NHS has looked after my health, I also want to thank the people who have looked after my money, most notably Mike Cooper who had moved from Lloyds to Investec Wealth & Investment and, because of the marvellous relationship we had formed, I was delighted to move with him and become his first client. He would now be my investment director and we have certainly been through some turbulent times together, but he has been a great support to me both financially and personally.

Someone else who has been very important in my life is my brilliant barber Brent. Thank you to him, and also, to Brighouse Computer Centre, a lovely family company who have for many years looked after my technology wellbeing, supplying computer hardware, software, hosting my website, along with superb and friendly support.

Overseas

On 7th November 2006 I flew to New Zealand for six weeks, where I joined the New Zealand Youth Hostel Association – a brilliant organisation with fabulous places to stay, but the nightmare was sharing rooms with people snoring their heads off! A map of their locations brilliantly corresponded with all the major towns and important places to visit. The great thing about New Zealand is that there are no deadly bites or stings to worry about.

Before I went my niece Teresa said, "Whatever you do Uncle Barry, don't come back wishing you had done something – spend your money and do everything that you want to do" ... and I did. I took a helicopter flight at Milford Sound, an overnight cruise from Te Anau, went on a ski plane landing on the glacier on the slopes of Mount Cook, saw hot springs and geysers, went to a Maori event and I walked the Keplar Track, staying in huts overnight. I visited both islands and all the major centres, including Auckland, Wellington, Dunedin and Christchurch.

I returned via Tasmania (my second visit) to stay with Pauline and Ray for Christmas and New Year; that was followed by a week in Sydney with Mike and Kirstin, where I discovered the fantastic music of Buddha-Bar playing in a harbour side gallery; and finally a week in Perth, which has to be the tidiest, cleanest city I have ever been to.

The Lake District and the Wainwrights

Returning from down under, there were no professional bookings to worry about, so now it was all recreation and relaxation. I mentioned earlier about the need for objectives to fill this tremendous void. I had an idea in my head that I had contemplated for many years and that was to climb all the 214 Wainwrights. Sheila had bought me the complete set of the seven *Pictorial Guides to the Lakeland Fells* that Alfred Wainwright had spent 13 years hand-drawing and writing (they are wonderful works of art in their own right). Over the years I had used them on many walking outings as guides for climbing individual fells.

With the words of Charles Schwab in my mind ("A man can succeed at almost anything for which he has unlimited enthusiasm"), I began my adventures on Wainwright's Lakeland Fells, beginning with book two, *The Far Eastern Fells*. Now his influence really began, because his guides took me to fabulous areas of the Lake District where I hadn't walked, wonderfully remote and peaceful places where some days I never saw another soul.

My camper provided perfect flexibility to access these out-of-the-way locations, and it also meant I could park up and climb a number of the fells over several days and then move on to another area in the guidebook. Staying overnight in these lonely, beautiful places encouraged me to listen to more calming classical and ambient music and read poetry books. I took my *Palgrave's Golden Treasury*, and of course William Wordsworth.

It was on 30th June 2008 that I achieved my objective of climbing all 214 Wainwrights. I had started with book two, *The Far Eastern Fells*, and book seven, *The Western Fells*, was where I would finish. 'The Final Three', as I called them, were Middle Fell, Buckbarrow and Seatallan (I always did like that name). All of them were covered in thick cloud and I was glad to have my GPS to aid navigation. I have to say it was a wonderful feeling of achievement when I reached my 214th fell. I celebrated with a cup of coffee and a chocolate biscuit. When I started back in September 2007, over the previous 20-some years I had already visited 97 of the 214. These remaining 117 had taken me just 46 walking days.

However, there were 60 where I didn't have a camcorder, so I was able to create a new objective of going back to film them. I also did 'The Final Three' again in bright sunshine. Joss Naylor, the legendary Lakeland fellrunner, had set a record by running all the Wainwrights in just seven days, so now for mental exercise I also learnt to recall his route list of all 214. This became my new party piece, which made a change from the beret!

This reminds me of the 50 items story. Because my dear sister Barbara, brother-in-law George, sister-in-law Rita and niece Dena have all suffered from dementia, I had been worried about my own memory. One of the speakers I listened to at a conference, David Thomas, was a memory man, so I rang him and told him about my sister. He told me how to remember 50 items, and so one time I asked Graham Jackson to bring a list of 50 items onto the moors with us. He started reading it to me, giving me all 50 items and, when we sat down for a coffee, I read them back to him – I got 49 right and he was absolutely astounded! So the 50 items and the 214 fells were in response to concerns about dementia.

WWJ ('Walking with Jacko')

This was just one of the many moments that formed part of one of the most exhilarating and exciting periods of my life – years of wonderful walking with my friend Graham Jackson. I could fill a book with these tremendous days out. Graham is a marvellous friend and influencer who is also a comforting confidant and invaluable at putting me right.

Our walks took us from the remote and beautiful reservoirs high up in the Pennines with great names like Widdop and Gorple, to the wild plateau of Kinder in Derbyshire. There were so many memorable events, lost maps, getting lost, missed last buses, forgotten boots, flasks left behind … but above all lots and lots of enjoyment. There are not many people I would walk with, but Graham was one. We could walk for long periods in silence, and he was also so knowledgeable, covering everything from flora and fauna, to military and social history. He also had a brilliant ability to spot wildlife, in particular birds, and two of the many highlights for me were watching a pair of hen harriers high on the Pennine Moors and seeing mountain hares. It was an education and an absolute joy to walk with him (although he almost bored me to death by rabbiting on for three or four hours about the Dambusters and Barnes Wallis!). The great thing for me was that Graham liked to plan the routes, which was a real treat as I could relax and follow him – and he certainly took me to some wonderful places. We are indebted to the work of the Ordnance Survey for their brilliant maps, we can spend hours studying a map like some people read a book, and both of us love to feel the soul of the countryside through the soles of our feet.

In the mid-nineties my quest for second-hand Yorkshire topography books had led me to Tom Burns, an enthusiastic walker, author and lover of the Dales and a huge fan of Yorkshire author AJ Brown, many of whose books I own. Tom helped me with my book search but he would also became instrumental in introducing me to an even greater appreciation of literature and the countryside. I had some marvellous walks with Tom, such a wonderfully interesting character who introduced me to a completely new way of exploring the hills. We would ignore the footpaths and, as in the title of an AJ Brown book, go 'Moorland Tramping'. Now Graham and I would enjoy our adventures this way and discuss the wonderful writings of AJ Brown (Brown walked everywhere in his brogues and a tweed jacket). Another beautiful book about the Yorkshire Dales is *Yorkshire Heritage* by Ella Pontefract and Marie Hartley which describes a bygone world full of charm and traditions.

Graham kept some notes about our walks together …

Between 2007 and 2014 we completed 79 walks together, totalling 898 miles.

Highlights include:

1. Our first (and one of my favourites) was a walk around the Dove Stones with a visit to the Trinnacle and the Chew escarpment, with the most wonderful revelation of some amazing walking country in an area I would have previously dismissed as dreary and featureless.

2. Taking me for a walk in April 2007 over Kinder Scout for the first time in 50 years, after swearing at age eleven that I would never set foot on that 'bog-infested hell hole' ever again. Being thus re-introduced to a walker's wonderland after much persuasion, followed by many fabulous return visits. [Barry adds: On one of these return visits to Kinder Scout, we attempted to cross the Kinder plateau in thick fog by using my compass but, after an hour or so of wading up and down wet, black peat groughs, Graham asked me if we were lost. "No," I said, "I am just temporarily uncertain of where we are!" It was some time later we found ourselves back where we started and, as usual, we were able to laugh about our situation as we tried again, successfully this time. It was soon after this adventure with Graham I invested in a GPS!]

3. Walking along the Pendle Way below Lad Law where you tearfully and very movingly told me of your troubled childhood, something you'd never talked about to me before.

4. Climbing Ingleborough from Horton in the snow on a bitterly cold but glorious March day, and sitting on Simon Fell watching a walker approach dressed in shorts and t-shirt.

5. Talking you out of selling up all your investments after the 2008 stock market crash. [I had been distraught after working all those years to see it all disappear.]

Graham's interest in military history also involved us in the location of aircraft crash sites, wandering around in tussocks and bogs trying to find some bits of aluminium. Graham writes:

To me, walking to find aircraft crash sites had two purposes:
1. To see how good our navigation was, and

2. To honour the poor souls who died, often on our behalf.

Government sources state that more than 10,000 aircraft crashed in the UK between 1939 and 1945. On average ten aircraft per day were falling prey to mechanical problems, navigational errors, enemy action, or inexperience. A large proportion of the downed aircraft fell in high ground in the Pennines, Yorkshire Dales, Lake District and Welsh or Scottish mountains. Many inexperienced pilots crashed learning to master the complexities of flying an aircraft, learning to navigate or how to use it to fight the enemy.

The most memorable day wreck hunting was obviously when I broke my leg on Close Moss (not for the two wreck sites we visited). One of the crash site walks I enjoyed the most was when we traversed the full width of Ilkley Moor from Steeton to Burley in Wharfedale, visiting two site memorials en route. Another was when we explored Kinder Scout, this time climbing up via Jaggers Clough and descending via Broadlee-Bank Tor, locating four of Kinder's many crash sites that day. These included Wellington Bomber X3348, Halifax Bomber HR727, Wellington Bomber W5719 and Heyford K6875.

Unfortunately, Graham's wife Judi wasn't very well, and this wonderful walking partnership had to come to an end. However, we talk about our fabulous times together with great affection and Graham has his photographs and his walks diary and I have my videos to remind me of this unforgettable period of my life. He is also a fantastic knackler.

Graham sums up our walking together like this – always finding and sharing simple companionship together by being out for hours in some of the finest scenery in Britain, going 'off piste' to explore new areas, being a 'good fit' together, sharing problems, troubles and triumphs. I couldn't have put it better; thank you Graham for your fantastic friendship, you have added so much to my life.

More BBBW

There was another BBBW in March 2008, which as always was a fun-filled day. Terry's son Stephen was with us, and there were eight of us having a boozy, boisterous lunch in The Bottomley Arms. When a young couple got up to leave, the very attractive girl came over and passed a note to Stephen that read, "I really like you, here is my number please call me." We couldn't believe it! I said that the note was really meant for me! None of us had known anything like this before. Stephen did call the girl, they became engaged and moved in together, although unfortunately they separated a few years later – nevertheless, a great story.

Walking with Family

I arranged a trip to Keswick where, much to my delight, my nephew Guy and nephew-in-law Peter came up from Kent for a weekend. We did Scafell Pike with cloud and snow on the top, but things improved as we descended. I took them to the climbers' bar at the Bridge Hotel in Buttermere where Guy loved the place and the ale so much that, very kindly, Peter offered to drive Guy's car back to Keswick. On the Saturday we did the Newlands Round when it was windy but clear and fine. We had two brilliant days on the fells, followed by fabulous fun evenings out in the town, and it was great for me to have two drinking pals and to be able share my love and passion for the Lake District with them. They joined me again in 2009 to climb Mount Snowdon. I also took Guy and neice Sally on part of the Pennine Way when they came up to stay with me.

Whilst in the Lakes I visited an exhibition at the Rheged Discovery Centre entitled *The Wainwrights in Colour*. The artist Andy Beck had started to paint all of the 1,500 sketches in the seven Alfred Wainwright pictorial guides. I reserved a copy and in 2017 went to Kendal to the book launch and collected my copy, No 430 of 5,000. It is fabulous and a truly epic piece of work.

I must mention the hospitality and generosity at the campsites I've visited. Over the years I have met some wonderful people – I shall never forget the brilliant morning I had in Wetherspoons in Barnstaple with two doctors and a nurse who had just finished an A&E nightshift.

The Close

Avery significant event happened for me in 2008. There are not many changes of residents in the close, but this year we got two wonderful new neighbours when Matt and Marina moved into No 6. It was obvious to me early on what fun-loving, gregarious, wonderful human beings they were. They started with a BBQ to get to know the neighbours, which went on into the early hours and almost became a yearly event. Matt's firepit was legendary – I am sure on one occasion when he ran out of wood he nearly started on his shed! Matt and Marina have been so generous and kind to me and, due to some of the outlandish (bordering on rude) remarks I make from time to time, Marina has even invented a word for them: 'Barryisms'.

I enjoy a fabulous friendship with them, sharing dinner parties, but I also knew that if I just wanted a chat, I could go over to see them and would be made welcome. Marina reminded me this happened regularly when I came back drunk on a Friday afternoon, turning up with a couple of cans of beer in my pockets, although I never overstayed my welcome. They have two lovely children, Archie and Evie, and over the years I have been invited to join them on Christmas Day and have had the most wonderful of times along with their parents. I am truly blessed to have them as my friends.

Ten years on and in the close some houses have changed hands, but today there are still about eight of the old guard, and it still retains its wonderful neighbourly friendliness. Jordan and Rachel separated – he stayed on and became arts director of *Emmerdale* and is a good friend.

Love Again?

Then in August 2008 I began what was probably the most traumatic experience of my life … well, it felt like it at the time. After 13 years on my own I fell madly in love (or was it lust?). Unfortunately, I didn't comprehend that she just wanted a casual relationship and that I would be on call as and when she wanted. I, on the other hand, wanted to be with her every moment of every day. I just loved everything about her. I also think I was worried that this might be my last chance to meet someone.

I was besotted. She liked going on cruises, which had never been on my agenda but, as there was no way she would go away in my camper, I even had it in mind to sell the van, give up my walking and go cruising. What was I thinking? I am not keen on children, but she had five young grandchildren and even that did not put me off! I felt so good going out for meals or shopping, holding hands with her. I showered her with presents and love notes, we had day trips out (stupidly to places where Sheila and I used to go), and I introduced her to all my friends. I was so happy and was somewhat reluctant to set off on my biggest and most challenging adventure yet.

Dolomites

With my continuing yearning for Via Ferrata in the Italian Dolomites, I planned what would be my most adventurous and certainly demanding camper van trip. In September I drove 900 miles to Lake Garda. The planning and preparation was, as usual, meticulous, including ferries, campsites, routes, rules, regulations, plus all the equipment – crampons, ice axe, helmet etc. I had pages and pages of notes about my route on the passenger seat!

I spent the first two weeks in Madonna di Campiglio enjoying the spectacular mountains and Via Ferrata, sometimes going for two- or three-day excursions and staying overnight in the mountain rifugios. On a rest day I caught the bus to the lovely town of Trento, where a market was in full swing and I bought four fabulous Etnica world music CDs. I then moved down to Arco for a few days and finally to a site on the shores of Lake Garda, continuing on the Via Ferrata in the surrounding mountains. I spent a lot of the time thinking of my new love life, telephoning her, buying presents for her and sending postcards. Nevertheless, I had a fabulous time, which is just as well because driving 900 miles each way through several foreign countries on my own was incredibly challenging. Nevertheless, the rewards of the magnificent mountains made up for all the effort – "No pain no gain" they say. On the way back I had a few days in the lovely city of Luxembourg.

Heartache ... and Revelation

When I returned home the turbulent and tempestuous affair resumed and continued all through what was to be my unhappiest Christmas, into 2009. We even planned a holiday to the Isles of Scilly (somewhere Sheila and I had been to on five occasions). Fortunately the whole unhappy affair came to an end in March 2009, before we went to Scilly, and so my wonderful memories of Sheila and I together were not sullied.

Although part of me was glad it was over, I cried every day for a month – I was lost, miserable and despondent. Then one day as I cried, my legs gave way from under me and I crumpled to the floor. As I lay there in despair, I felt a hand on my shoulder that lifted me up. It was God.

The Holy Spirit came into me and God has been with me and been my constant friend ever since. If I am asked what I am doing on Christmas Day, I reply that I am spending it with the 'Birthday Boy' (although it's amazing how many people don't grasp who I mean).

The outlook was a gloomy one, and I had lost my way.
I saw no hope no sign, no sun,
But that was yesterday.

Patience Strong

I had been brought up as a Christian at the schools I attended. I have always believed in Jesus and Heaven. I prayed before I went to sleep each night and I knew the Lord's Prayer and Psalm 23, but I am not sure all my behaviour had always been that of a true Christian, even though I had endeavoured to adhere to the Ten Commandments and other Christian values. I had heard of God, but now I came to know him.

I have had many engaging conversations with nonbelievers, discussing the dictionary definitions of atheists and agnostics and humanitarians. I like to believe humanitarians live in a very Christian-like way, with a 'do unto others' attitude.

I am often asked whether I attend church, which I don't. However, I do pray, and can be found on my knees several times a week, in mud on top of mountains, at home and at special places such as in woods where I walk.

326

Very, very rarely do I ask for anything – my praying is almost always to say thank you to God for everything – my health, happiness, the strength to climb to the top of mountains and to see the bountiful beauty God has given us. I also say thank you for all of those people who have comforted me through challenging periods of my life. Speaking about church, several years ago during the period of Lent, instead of giving up something, I followed some advice to do something different, so I went to a different church each week during the fasting period.

Another time I remember kneeling, praying in my kitchen and had a very serendipitous moment when one of my 30,000 random tunes came on my system: Marvin Gaye's 'How Sweet It Is (To Be Loved by You)'. I couldn't have put it better – it is wonderful to be loved by God. The wonderful thing I love about God is that He is consistent. I was working hard at becoming the kind of person that He would be pleased with, learning to be more patient, courteous, considerate, thoughtful, gracious, compassionate and, most of all, tolerant. It would be a constant goal that I am still working on today, but I am trying very hard and God knows that.

Every cloud ... as they say, and a further gift of this unhappy affair was to meet another of my life influencers, Damian, at one of her amdram nights out. He has become a wonderful friend, comforter and confidant. His entertainment background as a professional magician and member of the Magic Circle certainly helped produce an entertaining video presentation for my 70th birthday party! His talents also include painting, and he produced a wonderful portrait of me as a birthday present. He has introduced me to the works of Kahlil Gibran and his book *The Prophet*, as well as to Eckhart Tolle and his international best-selling book *The Power of Now*.

As I slowly got over the heartache and dried my tears, I resumed my travels with another trip to the Isle of Wight and two weeks in Wales. Here I climbed Cader Idris and rescued a sheep entangled in a wire fence that otherwise may have died. I also revisited some of my Snowdon-to-Gower walk and was bitten by a dog at a farm campsite, forcing me to visit a doctor for a tetanus injection. Remember the previous dog-bite story from the 1980s? Dogs just don't seem to like me, as I always seem to be having altercations with dogs when I am out walking. Their owners often say, "Oh don't worry, they won't hurt you." "That's what the owner said about the dog that bit me in the b*!!@&$s," I reply!

Scotland

Later that year it was back to Scotland where I met up with Donald in Cannich, and at the age of 65 I saw my first adder. It was also with Donald on the Rum Cuillin where I saw my first white sea eagle. I had seen golden eagles on my visit to Mull and Iona as I was climbing Ben More, and it was on another Scottish island, Jura, that I had seen my first otter.

Donald had to return home, so I continued on to the Isle of Skye where I climbed in the hills surrounding the Old Man of Storr and the magnificent Black Cuillin. Sometimes I had to sit in my van for days, waiting for the rain to stop, so for variety I used the idea of reading three books at a time. One of them was *The Pilgrim's Progress*, which I had last read at school, but understood and enjoyed more on this second reading.

2010

The sun above the mountain's head,
A freshening lustre mellow
Through all the long green fields has spread,
His first sweet evening yellow.

These wonderful words of William Wordsworth inspired me to set off and continue my camper van adventures. Northumberland was my first trip, a beautiful area of Britain, where I went out to the Farne Islands to see the puffins and visited the Holy Island of Lindisfarne.

And in December it was a change of pace – my first Shearings coach trip, which turned out to be marvellous during the non-camper winter months. I had many trips, including Durham, Eastbourne, Morecambe, Torquay, Weymouth and Bath. I was obviously still showing off and enjoying doing my Frank Spencer impersonation because a few weeks later I received a letter with these words, "What a character you are, I think you brought a smile to everyone you met. What a wonderful gift you have. I do hope we meet up on another holiday. Look after yourself Barry, keep making them laugh. Jenny & Ken."

House Renovations, 2011

It all started with the idea of putting a conservatory on the back of the house. My neighbour Robert, along with his partner Richard, was involved in this kind of building work, so I asked him for a quote. Although he maintains that he is not a salesperson, his ideas and enthusiasm inspired trust and confidence and meant that what started with thoughts of a £5,000 conservatory ended up as a £100,000-plus complete house extension and renovation! The phrase is, "salespeople shouldn't sell, they should aid a purchase," and that is exactly what he did.

However, since 1970 I had not spent a penny on the house, except for occasional DIY work. Virtually everything was as it had been in 1963 when it was built – I even still had the original cooker. I expect other people may have had two new kitchens and a bathroom in that time. So, as "you can't take it with you," I invested my pension fund to give myself a beautiful home from which to enjoy that lovely view. The other good news was that Robert had spent a number of years obtaining planning permission for his own extension, making my plans (drawn by his dad, George) more likely to be approved. I spent an inordinate amount of time researching and planning, which has had the benefit of there now being nothing I would change or wish I had done differently. My friend Angie helped me with designing the kitchen and husband Dave provided the internal doors. I also learnt a lot by visiting kitchen and bathroom retailers, along with window and sliding patio door manufacturers, and the TV programme *Grand Designs* was essential viewing.

All those years of memories meant I struggled when it came to donating all the unwanted or inappropriate furniture to charity, but it had to be done – everything would be new, re-wired, re-plastered, re-plumbed, re-carpeted and re-roofed. With new patios front and back, I even had false grass to make my life easier, and underfloor heating to make it more comfortable. After all those years of frugality it was spend, spend, spend! I was also going to hard-wire speakers throughout, but I then

329

discovered the Sonos wireless sound system, which saved all that. Nevertheless, I did use the opportunity to put in HDMI cables etc.

The whole renovation took just short of two years. I stayed in the house and moved round it as the work progressed. I helped by moving my furniture, white goods and my possessions, including my 1,000 books, from room to room, or donating them, almost on a daily basis. I enjoyed being involved with it all, even wheel-barrowing cement on occasions. I did or thought about very little else during this period, which helped me forget about the romance. It proved to be a renovation for me as well. Mike and Val across the road very kindly let me park my camper van on their drive, Marina helped me choose a new three-piece suite, and Jacko helped with the choice of patio door supplier. Robert and Richard's expertise, attention to detail and excellent craftsmanship has resulted in a wonderful, wonderful home – they did an absolutely marvellous job.

Whilst I was in the spending mood, I treated myself to another piece of music-playing equipment that I had always wanted: a juke box from Sound Leisure in Leeds. It was a Wurlitzer look-alike on which I could play all those 45s I still own from my DJ days. With regard to my long-held

The Rolls Royce

yearning for a Rolls-Royce, I bought one of those as well from someone in Leeds, a red pearl 1995 Silver Spirit III. With just 47,000 miles on the clock, it was immaculate, and I don't think anyone had ever sat in the back. I went the whole hog and got some personal number plates, although the closest thing I could afford was 'E19RRY'. I didn't keep the car very long because it disturbed my peace – it was a struggle to get in the garage, I could never relax parking it anywhere and it was completely impractical, so I sold it. Yes, I lost money, but not as much as I will on my Honda Civic if I sell that … but at least I had achieved a goal and drove round in a Rolls-Royce for a while!

My explorations continued with a trip out to the Western Isles, taking the ferry from Oban to Barra, and I then spent three weeks island hopping, working my way up through South Uist, Benbecula, North Uist, Berneray, Harris and finally to the Isle of Lewis where I caught the ferry from Stornoway to Ullapool. Wild, windy and wonderful is how I would sum up the trip, and once again I met many marvellous people. This camper van certainly is a terrific purchase.

After the trials, tribulations and turmoil of the last few years, the house renovation and the romance, I seemed to now settle into a wonderful period of my life. I had a beautiful home, my health, my music, and I was blissfully happy. I also started to go to the cinema, enjoying a whole variety of films. One which I really enjoyed, thanks to its 'against-the-odds' story and fabulous music, is *Eddie the Eagle*. I still enjoyed watching *The Apprentice*, *The Money Programme*, *University Challenge*, *Mastermind* and documentaries about successful people. I always liked to feel that I had gained, learnt or added something of use to my life by watching TV and in fact still do.

On a visit to a second-hand bookshop I found the beautiful book *The Call of the Open*, which included 16 gorgeous watercolour illustrations. This wonderful period of my life is summed up in this poem by Robert W Service:

There's sunshine in the heart of me,
My blood sings in the breeze;
The mountains are a part of me,

I'm fellow to the trees.
My golden youth I'm squandering,
Sun-libertine am I;
A-wandering, a-wandering,
Until the day I die.

In January 2014 I returned to Tasmania to visit my friends. Mike Cooper suggested I should treat myself and fly business class, and what a treat it was, even including a bed! This time I combined it with three nights in Bangkok (what a place that is) and three nights in Melbourne (my third visit there). It was summer time so the weather was great, and I hired a car, toured the island and climbed Cradle Mountain, their highest peak.

Back home, from John o' Groats to Land's End, my camper van adventures continued. Stockton-on-Tees was another destination, where I stayed at White Water Park on the Tees Barrage, and the town has one of the best second-hand vinyl and CD shops in the country, Sound it Out Records.

70th Birthday Celebrations

Meanwhile I was also busily making plans for my 70th birthday party. As I mentioned Damian helped me, not only with the production of a video about my life (a 25-minute pictorial and musical biography about my 70 years), but also with general organisation and by acting as compère. Marina was tremendous; she sent out email invites for me and dealt with the responses. I had planned to have 70 guests, including my family. Graham kindly agreed to film the event for me; Harvey (whose father Robert, along with Richard, had been responsible for my home renovation), who was a DJ, would provide the music. I made several playlists for the evening for him to use, all of my favourites, with everything from easy listening to disco. My friend Do made a beautiful cake and composed a wonderful poem which she read out on the night. I made two very drunken speeches, fell over outside onto my face and finished the night in hospital until 4.00 am. A big thank you to Ann Marie and Robert who took me and brought me home!

Up and Down the UK

Over the coming years my trips took me to the Brecon Beacons, Cleveland Hills, North Devon and Exmoor, and more cities, including several visits to London where I could catch up with my family. I stayed at campsites with good public transport links and had a wonderful time discovering the likes of Shrewsbury, Chester, Carlisle and Birmingham, with its fantastic canal network. In the Birmingham Art Gallery I saw a painting entitled Work by Ford Madox Brown, which led to my becoming a big fan of the Pre-Raphaelites. In Liverpool I always had a pint in The Cavern Club listening to the music of The Beatles.

In Oxford I bought a most beautiful book: not only visually, but because its content has helped me enormously to strive to become a better person. First published in the 15th century, this edition was printed in 1886, and after the Bible this is the most widely read Christian devotional work: *The Imitation of Christ* by Thomas à Kempis. Echoing sentiments in this wonderful book, an entry in my "In Green Pastures" daily readings has these words:

> *Be patient even with people's faults. Let us train ourselves to find the best we can in every act of others, to believe the best always of people and their actions, and to find some beauty in everything.*

Edinburgh and Glasgow were favourite destinations of mine, including cycling on the Forth and Clyde canal from Bowling to Falkirk, with its famous wheel, and then the Union canal to Edinburgh, and walking on the delightful Pentland Hills. Other highlights included walking from a campsite at Cirencester and finding the source of the Thames, and cycling the Kennet and Avon Canal from Henley-on-Thames to Bath.

During the school holiday period I didn't go away, giving me time to catch up with all that other day-to-day stuff. I did come out of retirement once more to make a presentation at my accountant's end-of-year company bash, which I have to say I enjoyed immensely. I videoed my presentation and called it 'Barry Comes Out of Retirement'.

When I was at home, I met up with Phil for our usual fun-filled lunch get-together. He has had such a challenging time. His son Chris, who was born with a brain tumour, has epilepsy and learning difficulties. Phil has had to close his business, concentrate his efforts on Chris and become a full-time carer. I have never seen a man who loved his son as much and I know I am not alone in admiring his strength of character. One of the many wonderful things I love about Phil is that he encourages my Frank Spencer impressions and, like Sheila, says it gives a lot of people a lot of enjoyment. Just one of the many incidents with him that I remember is thumbing a lift on the way to meet him once, when a police van picked me up and let me out of the cage at the back, right outside Wetherspoons. We still laugh about that, Phil has given me a lot of joy and he has certainly enriched my life.

Donald had married Helen and has a fantastic house and croft in the most wonderful remote location up in the Scottish Highlands near Glenelg (a place that Sheila and I had visited). Donald taught Taiji and Qi Gong, whilst Helen taught yoga. In 2016 I went up to stay with them for a few days and then carried on to my second visit to Skye, this time camping at Glen Brittle.

One day I climbed up the infamous Great Stone Chute to the highest mountain, Sgurr Alasdair, at the southern end of the Cuillin Ridge. I had lunch sat on the top point, which is just about wide enough for two people, when another climber joined me. We chatted and I was delighted to find out my companion was Robert Kelso Smith, a guide who specialises in Antarctica and Himalayan adventures and who had been to the top of Everest twice – what a lunchtime I had! Robert lives in Fort William and we hope to meet up when I am up that way.

For years Graham had been urging me to have a walking holiday in Grindelwald in Switzerland, telling me about the superb transport system and recommending the wonderful Derby Hotel. What a fantastic two weeks I had, watching the north face of the Eiger from the hotel windows, taking the mountain railway to the summit of Jungfrau at 13,642 feet and having the most superb days out in Bern, Interlaken and Lucerne on the excellent rail system. A real treat for me was when Guy, Karyn, Sally and Pete came up to Yorkshire for a holiday and we spent some time together with some fabulous days out.

Charity gets on-the-ball expertise

A MOTIVATIONAL speaker who has inspired business people all over the world is coming to Bolton later in the year.

Barry Young will be helping the local branch of the Variety Club of Great Britain's efforts to help disadvantaged children when he speaks at an event at the Last Drop Hotel at Bromley Cross on September 22.

Based in Yorkshire, Mr Young has helped companies improve sales and service with his blend of humour and business knowledge.

He said: "I left school at 15, without a single qualification. I went into engineering but wanted to go into entertainment so became a Butlins' Redcoat."

He progressed to become deputy entertainment manager, planning entertainment for up to 10,500 guests.

When he left to become a salesman, he quickly rose through the ranks to become a manager before forming his own company selling computer supplies and stationery.

After 15 years, he formed a separate company and moved into training and motivation full time.

● Tickets for the seminar "Seriously Boost Your Business" cost £39.99 each including a buffet lunch. To book, contact Lynn Griffiths on 08000 832 196.

MR MOTIVATOR: Barry Young

Article in the Bolton Evening News about the Variety Club event

Remaining Bookings – The Final Curtain

These included a very nostalgic trip booking at Butlin's in Skegness with the Johnson Service Group conference. Staying in a chalet, I was flooded with memories of my 20 weeks with Sheila at Filey. The second was a charity event for the Variety Club of Great Britain at the Last Drop Hotel in Bolton.

Back in 2004 I'd had a booking for Chem-Dry in Cardiff, which led to a challenging and life-changing booking a few years later. Phil Smith, who ran Chem-Dry, rang me one day asking me to host his wife's 50th birthday party. I told him I wasn't a comedian, but he didn't want a comedian, he wanted me. Phil was a Mormon, and he wanted my presentation for his congregation, all of whom were aged between 4 and 90 years old! "I want them to be more positive like you," Phil explained. We met and he clarified

335

the rules – no swearing, no toilet humour, no talk of sex – well that was half my act gone! However, I decided to do it. I managed not to swear on that day and have tried not to swear since.

Following my Prague presentation, Blazes had asked me to make another at the Chevin Lodge near Otley, where I participated in a management team-building exercise, constructing rafts out of steel drums, wood and ropes before racing them around the lake – great fun, with lots of falling in. A brilliant evening with an ABBA tribute band and an overnight stay in one of the lodges making this a memorable day. Director Cathy Birchall sent me what was to be one of my very last testimonial letters:

> *What a delight! What a wonderful Wednesday we're now experiencing after benefiting from your words of wisdom, wit and wackiness! Thank you for interrupting your well-earned retirement to help us out at our annual conference with your inspirational and thought-provoking presentation, it was pitched beautifully.*

As was Cathy's letter – it was just tremendous for me to finish my speaking career just as I started by enlightening, entertaining and, most importantly, making a positive contribution to people's lives.

Guernsey?

In October 2019 I put the cover on my van and on a put it on a SORN, and I booked a ferry and a campsite to travel to Guernsey in my van in May 2020, with also a B&B on Sark, and looked forward to 2020, blissfully unaware of what lay ahead for all of us.

Andnd so it was in 2020 that another of my life's adventures began and this book is the result. Andrew Gide said,

> *It is only in adventures that some people succeed in knowing themselves - finding themselves.*

The Trinnacle

Our deeds determine us as much as we determine our deeds.
George Eliot

Via Ferrata, Lake Garda

Exploring the Brecon Beacons

338

CHAPTER 20: ADVENTURES

The definition of 'adventure' is an exciting or remarkable experience and uncertainty of outcome. My whole life has been a lot like that, and there have been many fascinating events, exploits and experiences that fit that definition. They come in all shapes, sizes and intensity, everything from my first ride on a trolley bus, seeing florescence on the sea at night, to flying over Niagara Falls in a light aircraft.

Pennine Way (270 miles)

Following the challenge and satisfaction of walking the Dales Way, I set my sights on what for many walkers is their equivalent of a runner's London Marathon, the 'Pennine Way'. Sheila would certainly not be accompanying me on this one, but she was incredibly helpful and supportive. I would take with me this time Wainwright's *Pennine Way Companion*, in which he describes and details almost every step of this 270-mile walk. He writes:

The Pennine Way offers you the experience of a lifetime, which is not to say that it offers you continuous enjoyment. It is a tough bruising walk and compensations are few. You do it because you want to prove to yourself that you are man enough to do it. You do it to get it off your conscience. You do it because you count it a personal achievement, which it is, precisely.

The trip required meticulous packing and planning to be able to carry everything for 20-odd miles a day. I laid everything out on the bed, had many lists and maps and took self-addressed envelopes so that when I finished with a map I could put it in an envelope and send it home (so that there was less weight to carry). I needed a torch and a first-aid kit – my

All my kit ready for the Pennine Way

two life-saving pieces of first aid were Deep Heat and Zam-Buk (for feet), although they both stink like hell! I had prebooked all my B&Bs, which meant I was committed to the route, whatever the weather. I had to have confidence in my fitness, map reading and planning skills. This would be a serious undertaking and deserved a lot of respect. I'd read all sorts of horror stories about people who had set off ill-equipped and ill-prepared, and consequently failed to get very far. It is a high-level route following the main watershed up the backbone of England, and also quite a wilderness walk. My biggest challenge would be the fact that on New Year's Eve, the beginning of this year, I had given up drinking for a year, so I would have to walk all this way, sometimes staying in pubs, and not have a drink. I decided that I would be sponsored to raise some much-needed funds for the RSPCA – this might be more of a challenge than the walk!

The route starts at the Old Nags Head in Edale and finishes at the Border Hotel at Kirk Yetholm in Scotland. Sheila drove me to the start, met me at the end and she also came to see me at two places along the way (as they were quite near where we lived). A walking friend of mine, Mel, joined me for the first five miles, but after that there were days when I hardly saw a soul. I took a Dictaphone with me and recorded the whole journey onto tape, which is marvellous to listen back to as my mood swung during the walk.

At 9.30 am on Monday 4th May 1987, I kissed Sheila goodbye. It was an excellent sunny day and at that time I was using a 35 mm camera. AW and others talked of the deep peat groughs filled with black slime ahead of me, but I had been blessed with a very dry April, so they were dusty rather than wet, which was an absolute blessing. I have to admit I was very nervous and daunted by what was ahead of me and, when Mel turned back, I felt very lonely. I understand that you are never more than five miles away from a road, but it doesn't feel like that. It was a reasonably easy baptism for the first 15 miles, although up on Kinder plateau I did have to utitlise my compass and map skills. The first leg took me to Crowden Youth Hostel, the first ever hostel I'd stayed at, where I learnt that all guests had to share tasks. I had a meal and an early night to prepare for 22 miles the next day, which included the infamous Black Hill, but I was woken up by some late arrivals — ill-prepared and ill-equipped. I think instead of maps they had one of those tea towels of the Pennine Way!

Day two — I was grateful that it was a dry day. Black Hill is well named, as the broad top really is black. "This is peat naked and unashamed"; "After a respite of a few miles of firmer ground … featherbed moss repeats the worse torments of Black Hill" (Wainwright).

I arrived at my next YH at Mankinholes, above Hebden Bridge, where Sheila came to see

Peat naked and unashamed

me for the evening and we went out for a meal. Days two and three were very familiar ground – day three was 25 miles to Lothersdale, over Stoodley Pike (commemorating the Battle of Waterloo), past Top Withens (famous for the Brontës), and I arrived at Mrs Hardy's in Lothersdale where she gave me several pots of tea and biscuits. I went out for a pub meal (no beer), and then, as was my custom, I went to look at the start of the next morning's walk (there's nothing worse than getting lost in the first half a mile when you start a day's walking!).

Day four went from Lothersdale to Malham: 18 miles, joining the Leeds and Liverpool Canal for a few miles. In Gargrave I stopped to sort something in my rucksack, put my book down, but then later realised I'd lost it. I really panicked, but thankfully where I'd stopped I had put it on a window sill of a building and was glad to find it again when I returned. I stopped for a swim at Newfield Bridge, near Airton, which was a wonderful spot for swimming. I reached Mrs Sharp in Mallam, who washed and dried all my clothes for me, gave me a meal and a packed lunch for the next day – all for £15! The only problem washing everything was that my clothes were a bit tight the next morning, but it was very welcome. It should be pointed out that, at this stage of my walking life, I was wearing breeches, cotton shirts and two pairs of socks, one long inner and a thick-knit outer pair.

Day five took me to Horton in Ribblesdale via the stunning Mallam Cove and onto the limestone pavement at the top, and I was still on very familiar territory. It was a very special day, as Sheila and her stepmother Joyce joined me for the walk over Pen-y-ghent. It was such a glorious day they were in shorts and t-shirts and, when we got to Horton, Sheila had surprised me by booking into the same B&B, so we had a lovely evening together and after a meal in The Crown she stayed the night. In the morning the next day she came a short way with me, up the lane out of the village, and then turned back. I cried for about a mile and questioned myself about this solo walking … it was 26 miles to Thwaite in Swaledale on less familiar ground, although I was glad to enjoy exploring these new areas.

The Pennine Way crosses the Dales Way at Cam End, through the little town of Hawes (where they make the famous Wensleydale cheese) and I relished crossing Great Shunner Fell, the highest point thus far. I stayed at

On day seven I met and chatted to Hannah Hauxwell

a B&B in Thwaite with an evening meal at Kearton House (where I had stayed when I'd worked for English Wanderer).

Day seven, a Sunday – 24 miles to Middleton-in-Teesdale, via Tan Hill Inn, the highest pub in Britain, where I spoiled myself and had an hour watching the London Marathon before setting off again – I must have felt a bit confident! Wainwright writes, "At the best of times even in sunshine this crossing of Sleightholme Moor is like walking in porridge, and after heavy rain is like walking in oxtail soup." The route crosses the A66 here and at Baldersdale. I had two treats – firstly the halfway mark at 135 miles, and secondly at High Birk Hatt Farm I met and chatted to Hannah Hauxwell, subject of a 1972 documentary *Too Long a Winter*, about living on her own on the farm without electricity and water (the film is well worth a watch, or read the book, *Hannah in Yorkshire*). Geoff Bedford, my neighbour's son, who lived in Sunderland, came up to meet me here and walked with me for a few miles.

The hardest 20 miles of the whole walk took place on day eight, but it included two magnificent landmarks, High Force Waterfall and High Cup

Nick, near Dufton. This is the only day when I didn't walk north but, in fact west, right against all the elements – I had high winds, lashing rain, with nowhere to shelter in the midst of a flat barren moorland. I was glad to get to Dufton. I had worn my waterproofs all day, and was glad to reach Mrs Hallicot at Gill View B&B and enjoy a good meal at The Stag Inn. This was one of my most demanding days, that's for sure.

Day nine – 20 miles to Alston, via the highest point of the Pennine Way, Cross Fell. I encountered thick cloud and snow showers, but I was delighted with my compass navigation. I found my way down to the famous bothy, 'Greg's Hut', and the day continued with waterproofs on and off. I was very pleased to arrive at Alston – still no beer – and stayed with Peggy Bell at her B&B.

On day ten I met Ron Gell at the start of Hadrian's Wall. He walked with me for a few miles to Once Brewed. Arriving at Hadrian's Wall marks 200 miles (24 miles walked that day). Ron told me that he always walks alone and this was his fourth time on the route. He worked at the Player's Factory in Nottingham, where a friend had nagged him to go along with him. In the end Ron gave in and took the guy with him, but his nagging friend bothered him for the whole 270 miles – it was too dry, too hot, too wet, too windy … so Ron said never again! Sheila and I became very good friends with Ron and his wife, Rita.

Day 11 saw 17 miles to Bellingham, where Mrs Gaskin gave me tea and biscuits, and I had a lovely hot bath. Unfortunately, Zam-Buk and Deep Heat leaves an embarrassing odour when you leave the next day.

16 miles to Byrness for day 12. I stayed at a B&B where I asked the landlady for an early breakfast, as I wanted to be off at 6.00 am. This is the day everyone thinks about during all the previous days of walking, the most daunting day since I'd started: 29 miles to Kirk Yetholm, and the end. I remember I was in and out of Scotland and England as the way crosses the border fence, and I recorded on my tape recorder, "Black stinking ooze go away!" I was up to my ankles in it, clinging to the barbed-wire fence to try to keep out of it!

Sheila and our friends Chris and Moyra came to meet me at the finish. Wainwright had put money behind the bar for when you get there for a congratulatory pint of beer or lemonade (not whisky, and only the one

At the end, at The Border Hotel

mind you). You're supposed to say, "Charge it to Wainwright, cheers." But the following postscripts had been added: "PS – Better have some money of your own. PPS – for pint read half-pint: inflation you know."

On completion Wainwright says:

You have completed a mission and achieved an ambition. You have walked the Pennine way, as you dreamed of doing. This will be a very satisfying moment in your life. You will be tired and hungry and travel-stained. But you will feel just great, just great.

He was absolutely spot on.

More Adventures

Completing the 214 Wainwrights had given me an exciting experience and I had many more superb, scary, adrenaline-fuelled adventures on my beloved Lake District fells: climbing Jack's Rake on the way up to Pavey Ark; along the treacherous Sharp Edge to Blencathra and Striding Edge to Helvellyn; and venturing into Lord's Rake and the West Wall traverse to the summit of Scafell. One of my most memorable moments was being lost in a blizzard on the flanks of Allen Crags. I had read about white-out conditions and this was it – the wind and snow made using a map impossible, and when I fell through a snow bridge into a mountain stream and up to my knees in ice-cold water, I felt very alone and very frightened. Thoughts of mountain rescue came into my mind. However, I spoke strongly to myself, gathered my thoughts and once again God's hand was on my shoulder when I met another climber who knew where he was – and, more importantly, where he was going.

Other memorable exciting memories include my first winter ice and snow climb on Tryfan and Snowdon with Mel, which certainly tested my nerves. Leaving my rucksack to climb to a summit of a mountain and not being able to find it on my return was awful. I was running round like a headless chicken before, much to my relief, I found it.

One of my most painful experiences was on the top of a fell in Bowland, I developed chronic cramp in both of my thighs and both calves. I struggled to walk and lay in agony crying out for help. It took me many hours to get off the fell, as I went up to my knees in an unseen bog, waded across a river and eventually reached a remote farmhouse. The wonderful farmer's wife kindly drove me 30 miles (only ten miles as the crow flies) back to my car. I gave her all the money I had to thank her. Luckily my automatic made the 50 miles home just about bearable. It took all next day to wash and remove the black peat from my boots and clothes.

My wettest adventure came when Damian introduced me to his Canadian canoe and we had a trip on the Calder and Hebble Navigation. To begin with, it felt large and heavy. I struggled just to get it into the canal, but then we had to lift it out, carry it around the locks and lower it back in. However, it was lovely paddling peacefully and gently along the canal. We moored up for our picnic lunch and even had a pint at the pub before setting off for the return journey but, as I attempted to get back in, I capsized the canoe, tipping myself into the canal. Damian helped me out and, now soaked, I got back into the canoe and we set off. Suddenly I noticed one of our foam seat pads in the canal, reached to rescue it, and promptly turned the canoe over again, this time tipping us both into the water! An angler on the bank was not best pleased at us disturbing his fishing and he certainly did not offer any assistance. Despite all the heavy lifting and risk of drowning, we did have another marvellous day out on the Rochdale Canal.

1973 and the 'Three-Day Week' provided another adventure. When the factory was closed, I got a job for the other two days at the coal yard with Sheila's dad Don, driving a crane and loading the wagons with coal. I thought this was a marvellous change from being stuck in the factory – talk about big boys' toys!

Sheila prompted two journeys into the unknown for me when she bought me the *Easy to Cook Book*. The recipes were all for two people, so I began to learn a new skill and would cook dinner on Sunday evenings. Sheila would be upstairs in her sewing room and sometimes would become impatient and start shouting, "When will it be ready?" The other journey into the unknown was when we went to learn to ballroom dance. After weeks and weeks I can still only just about do an excuse for the cha-cha-cha … and of course jiving. I also completed a Jiu-Jitsu course, but I still can't speak a word of it!

I am reminded of some of the exploits we had as teenagers in the large department stores, such as hiding in the huge hanging racks of carpets and frightening the shoppers, then getting onto those kids' rides that they had. Sheila and the store assistant were not impressed when I did this many years later in Sheffield. Other events included being snowed in at a campsite in Llangollen for several days in March and having to dig myself out also sticks out strongly in my memory bank of tricky situations, as does test-driving a new motor scooter when I was 70 years old – boy, was that scary!

Side-stepping the advances of a beautiful woman at a conference was certainly a remarkable experience which scarred me! I used all the excuses I could muster to extricate myself from the situation. She did suggest we went back to our rooms and she would talk me through it on the telephone. Oh wow, now I was on unfamiliar territory, and on top of all that she was married – imagine what the consequences of that might have been. An experience that could have become an adventure that had 'uncertainty of outcome'.

347

Coast-to-Coast Walk

1988. When I was walking the Pennine Way as mentioned, I had met Ron Gell on the Hadrian's Wall section and walked a few miles with him: my only companion of the whole walk. He was staying at the youth hostel at Twice Brewed while I was at a B&B, so we had met at the inn for dinner in the evening. In the pub that night he talked enthusiastically about the coast to coast and convinced me that this should be my next big walk. So in May 1988, Sheila drove me to St Bees Head in Cumbria (readers will remember Sheila's and my previous debacle here on the cycle trip). Just like the Pennine Way, I took Wainwright's coast-to-coast book, six maps and five prepaid envelopes with a list of where to change the maps and post them back. Again, I committed myself and prebooked all the B&Bs and, after the Pennine Way preparation, rucksack packing had become a fine art.

The good news was that, just as the Hi-Fi industry kept re-inventing itself, walking clothing was continuously improving, with the advent of breathable, wicking, quick-drying fabrics and the introduction of Gortex and better-fitting quality boots and socks. All this made the exertions and endeavours less arduous and added to the enjoyment of these escapades.

Sheila was a hero, driving me all the way to Cumbria so that I could start walking at 9.30. I waved a tearful goodbye and picked up my pebble (it is customary to take one with you and throw it in at Robin Hood's Bay, on the other side of England – in fact, I took two in case I got attached to it). The first day for most walkers is 15 miles to Ennerdale Bridge, but I decided to add eight miles to get to Black Sail Hut. I had a swim in Ennerdale Lake before I got to the youth hostel. What a place Black Sail Hut is, in the middle of nowhere. I stayed the night there with the warden, a young guy called Jim, and I could have a beer this time because I was not on my year off alcohol!

Day two was 23 miles to Patterdale. I got to Rosthwaite in Borrowdale where it was time to change my map and post one back, which I did at the post office. However, when I posted it I realised I'd posted the one I was about to use back. I had to wait an hour and a half before the postman came to open the box to get my map back! I went on to Patterdale and when I arrived I had actually done the first three days in just two – mind you, I was only 44 and did a lot of walking back then!

Black Sail Hut

Wild water swimming

Nine Standards Rigg

I know where I'm going!

16 miles on day three took me to Shap, with some steep climbing over and through my beloved Lake District. Day four: 20 miles to Kirkby Stephen, another place Sheila and I had cycled through, and I had another swim this day as well. I stayed in a lovely B&B in Kirkby Stephen, complete with home-made food for dinner.

Day five was the section I was not looking forward to, over Nine Standards Rigg – 24 miles of remote, tough and very wet underfoot walking. I was glad to get to Reeth. Thankfully the next day was only ten miles to Richmond, a rest day, giving me an opportunity to go to the laundrette etc.

Day seven took me through a very flat area, much of it on lanes. Wainwright again, "The best way to cover these 20 miles of rural tranquillity is to get them over quickly by the use of country lanes and roads which are quiet and traffic free." I felt reinvigorated, with clean clothes from the launderette, and walked for 6½ hours non-stop, completing 23 miles to Ingleby Arncliffe. The B&B there was only £8 for the night. (The whole trip, including B&B and packed lunches, cost me the total of £87.) I went out for a meal that night to The Blue Bell Inn.

The eighth day covered the Cleveland Hills, with 21 miles to The Lion Inn at Blakey, before the ninth and final day on 21st May, the longest walking day, 29 miles, to Robin Hood's Bay. I set off with great excitement at finishing and seeing Sheila, who was meeting me at the end. As I walked down the hill to the sea to throw my pebble in, I wanted to shout out to all the holiday makers that I'd just walked 190 miles from St Bees Head. I reached the beach and met Sheila, which was lovely, and threw in one of my pebbles (and kept the other one). Another great walk and achievement, a total of 64 hours of walking, but it was good to get home and into my own bed!

Snowdonia to the Gower

1990. I saw a coffee-table book called *Snowdonia to the Gower* by John Gillham. The book intrigued me – having witnessed the ghastly scars of erosion on the well-publicised waymarked ways, he explained that he had devised a route from Llanfairfechan (west of Conway on the north coast of Wales) to Three Cliffs Bay on the Gower Peninsula. In 1990 I decided to do this walk down through the Welsh heartland. He offers two routes – one high level over the mountains, or a low-level option. Even the lower route involves more ascent than the Pennine Way. It was an unknown area for me, it wasn't waymarked (like you get on the Pennine Way) and at times there were no footpaths at all. Gillham had written fancifully about camping and waking up to the sunrise, so I thought I'd camp, offering me greater flexibility and freedom. I had to borrow a much bigger rucksack to put everything into it … but I couldn't lift the blooming thing off the floor, so I had to take everything out and start my packing again – to the extent of cutting my toothbrush in half (I used to joke that I took the wrong half!).

Sheila drove me 3 hours along the A5 to the start, where she helped lift the rucksack onto my back. I had my route notes in one hand, my map in the other, and because it was pouring with rain I was wearing my full waterproofs. I walked up the lane, came to a large metal gate which was all wired up, so I had to remove the wire, walk through and rewire the gate … but I'd left my map on the other side! Not a great start! It was 15 miles that day to a campsite in the Ogwen Valley. I didn't stop until about 3.30 pm as if I got my pack off I thought I'd never get it back on again.

I remember I reached the end of one path, looked up at a hill in front of me and thought I couldn't make it – I'd have to go back. I gave myself a talking to – if it takes two hours, the campsite is only over the other side – so I set off and 20 minutes later I was at the top. I collapsed, put my rucksack on the slope and took some chocolate raisins from the side pocket. However, as I opened the packet they flew everywhere, so I was lying there picking up raisins and eating them, when I suddenly realised I was about to put sheep droppings in my mouth!

The route was horrendous, with no paths and water flooding down the hills. I got down to the road and my campsite was just across on the other side, but I thought I couldn't do all this – having to put my tent up, soaking wet morning and night, not able to get dry etc. Right at that moment a lorry was coming along, so I thumbed a lift. He stopped and picked me up, and I asked him to take me to Llanrwst Railway Station, a request stop, where I stood until the train came. The lorry driver told me I'd be back! Anyway, I caught the train to Llandudno Junction, to Crewe, Manchester and then Huddersfield. When I reached home Sheila wasn't there because she had gone out for the evening. When she came home later that night she found me in bed and went ballistic, "I drove all that way for you and you've come home!"

Two years later in 1992 I had another go at the route … but without the camping! I was going to use B&Bs this time, so I booked the first one and Sheila booked the rest as I went along. She took me to Huddersfield Station where I caught the train at 6.25 am. The first day had thick fog and it was difficult finding the route. Swearing at the author, I was thrashing about in bogs looking for a stile into a wood, but this time I knew I had a warm B&B at the end.

It was an epic journey, right down the backbone of Wales, through Snowdonia, the Moelwyns, the Rhinogs. I stopped at Trawsfynydd for the first night in a pub (which didn't do any bar snacks, so I had to make do with a bag of crisps), then went to Barmouth to stay at a B&B run by Christians. I then carried on down through Wales, passing near Cader Idris and staying in Machynlleth where the farmer asked me, "Where are you going next?" "Pumlumon," I replied, and he said, "You're going into the Welsh desert there boyo." (Plynlimon is the source of both the River Severn and the River Wye, and a few years later I went back and found them both.) I came down from there into the Elan Valley, where I saw red kites flying overhead. A highlight a few days later was going over Carmarthen Fan, the source of the River Usk. I came to a place called Dan-yr-Ogof and my stop that night had a swimming pool, and I dined at a pub where I had a lovely night with Canon Brian Howell-Jones and his wife Monica! Then I crossed the M4 just north of Swansea, heading down to the Gower to finish at Three Cliffs Bay. From there I got a lift back into Swansea where I took the train home to Huddersfield where Sheila picked me up. A fantastic expedition, very tough, but an incredible walk.

Grand Union Canal

I developed a liking and love of canals up in the North, as there are many of them around my local area. They include the Leeds to Liverpool, the Huddersfield Broad and Narrow, Aire and Calder and the Calder. I had done a lot of walking and cycling on these and found them fascinating. They bear witness to a wonderful industrial heritage, as well as being beautifully rural. The Grand Union Canal became my Pennine Way of canals. My nephew Kevin sold me a Pro-Flex 550 off-road bicycle with suspension, which had a small rear carrier, but for this trip I had to use bungees to attach a small rucksack. All I needed was a change of socks, underwear and toiletries. I purchased the 'passport' and British Waterways key, which opens ten boxes along the route. You can then use a stamp inside to mark your passport and to prove your visit.

The distance to Birmingham is 137 miles, with 4,528 feet of ascent. I set off from Little Venice near Paddington (close to where Richard Branson lived in a houseboat). The journey was a wonderful adventure, full of surprises. It included the Blisworth Tunnel, which is 1½ miles long with no tow-path, so that when you reach the tunnel you have to go over the top (as they used to do with the horses, while the boats were propelled through the tunnels by leggers). Cycling along, I headed west out of London, often cycling next to and under the A40, then turned right at the end and suddenly found myself heading through Hemel Hempstead, Leighton Buzzard, Milton Keynes and Leamington Spa. Hatton Locks in

Pedal power on the Grand Union Canal

354

Warwickshire has 21 locks spread over 2 miles – amazing. I always knew I was coming to a town as I would start seeing shopping trolleys and other rubbish in the water! The countryside was beautiful, with tranquil sections full of wildlife, Victorian architecture and engineering. I passed over 80 locks on this journey and, although some of the areas were less salubrious, in others I saw kingfishers and herons.

The first day covered 60 miles from Little Venice to Ivinghoe (not far from Aylesbury), where I stayed at an old brewery turned into a youth hostel. Day two I cycled to Nether Heyford, 50 miles in total, but I had punctures at the end and had to keep pumping the tyres up every mile or so to get me there. I stayed in a lovely B&B, and in the morning the owner took me to a bike shop in Northampton to get the tyres repaired. Unfortunately one of the inner tubes had nine puncture holes, so I put new tubes in with protective tape to stop bramble thorns making all the holes. I also used a green slime inside the tube which self-seals in the event of a puncture.

I passed many beautiful pubs along the way, but unfortunately I couldn't hang around – I had a long way to go! I did 30 miles on day three to Warwick, although I couldn't find anywhere to stay near the canal, so I decided to walk through the night, pushing my bike. I came to a canal-side pub just outside Warwick and asked for accommodation, but although they didn't have any they rang round and found me the Warwick Arms Hotel, probably the poshest one in Warwick. Anyway, I had to cycle all the way back into Warwick, walk into this posh hotel all covered in mud, and they put my bike in the garage. The price was £30 because the shower didn't work ... "Surely you could do £25?" I asked, and the receptionist said, "Go on then!" I went up to this beautiful room where I even managed to make the shower work!

When I reached Birmingham, I stamped my card at Gas Street Basin and then carried my bike through the ICC (I wasn't allowed to wheel it) and caught the train home from New Street.

One of the hazards of cycling along canals is the anglers with their great long poles for reaching the other side of the water. I used to joke, why didn't they just go to the other side? Cycling along they don't always hear you coming when they're pulling the pole across the path. I used clip-in cycling shoes and once, when an angler nearly knocked me off, I couldn't unclip my shoes fast enough and had to fall into the nettles to avoid going into the water!

Australia

L ike everything I do, I carried out a lot of research before I left. I flew to Hong Kong. I had a 12 hour stop-over, so I took the rapid train into the city and did the tourist bit. I rode a double-decker tram that went through all the sights and sounds of Hong Kong, for about 50p. I also went up the world's longest escalator (800 m long), up to the Peak on the tram to see fabulous views over the city.

Then I flew to Melbourne to stay with Mike Shove (from Columbia) who had married a second time, to Kirstin. They lived at St Kilda in an apartment where they had a swimming pool I could use in the day when they were working. I had a trip down the Great Ocean Road to the Twelve Apostles, visited a kangaroo park, rode on the Puffing Billy steam railway and went down to Phillip Island to see the penguins that come out of the sea at night. I hired a car in Melbourne and drove 450 miles to Sydney, via the Snowy Mountains, along the Alpine Way which circumnavigates the Snowy Mountains, and I stopped overnight at Lake Jindabyne, and when I pulled in for some petrol and told the attendant I was off to Sydney, he recommended the second turning on the left. Some 90 minutes later I still hadn't come to the first turning – the country is all on such a huge scale! Regarded as one of Australia's greatest scenic drives, I was fascinated by all the mailboxes made out of tins and oil cans at the end of their roads.

I arrived into Sydney and booked into a motel, just the other side of Kings Cross, where I could easily catch a bus into the centre. I'll never forget walking down to Sydney Harbour, seeing the bridge and the Opera House, almost unreal – suddenly I was there, it was incredible. I went into the tourist area, then drove up to the Blue Mountains, to the Three Sisters viewpoint. I walked from Bondi to Bronte Beach where I went swimming. I took a Darling Harbour cruise, went across to Manly on the ferry, and took two bus rides around the city sites.

I'd worked with WOM, and their manager in the UK had said there might have been a job for me in Brisbane, so I had booked to fly up there from Sydney. The booking didn't come off, but it was a good visit. I went to the Blue Lagoon, right in the middle of the city, with all these BBQs etc, and I was invited to join one of the groups there. My neighbour Geoff had suggested I visit O'Reilly's Guest House up in the rainforest, where I had three nights in one of the wooden cabins, surrounded by exotic birds etc. I came back from one walk covered in leeches – there was blood coming from my legs and arms and the leeches were difficult to remove! Nevertheless, I continued going out on these fantastic trails where I didn't meet a soul. (I looked on the internet recently, and the place has been ruined by progress; it had been a mountain home for 85 years). I had been told about the blue fresh-water crayfish, which weren't too harmful, but might make me jump! They stand on their back legs and hiss at you. Walking along a trail, suddenly one shot up and I leapt off my feet like I'd seen a brown bear!

I went from Brisbane up to Cairns for a week and stayed at a beautiful white wooden colonial hotel with a balcony, where I was dead lucky to meet three people in a bar, one of whom worked in a local travel agency. With their help I took a fabulous boat trip with the Billy Tea Bush Safaris to see crocodiles and flying snakes, and I was also taken to a forest area in the bush where I went wild swimming whilst they prepared a BBQ – there was only me on the trip being looked after by two others. Up in the Daintree National Park I went white-water rafting (what an experience!), and on the Great Barrier Reef I went snorkelling and had a 15-minute scuba experience that I loved so much that I booked to do it again the next day. Talk about adventures!

When I was in Sydney I also took a flying visit to see Pauline and Ray in Tasmania for three or four days (Pauline was the daughter of my landlady from the 1960s). They picked me up from Hobart Airport and drove me to their home up in the bush. Despite all the deadly snakes, all the years they had lived there walking around in sandals they'd never been bitten. They took me up to Mount Wellington and to Port Arthur, the former convict settlement, and we enjoyed a good number of counter meals (bar snacks). Their hospitality was tremendous.

Mont Blanc

At the end of September I achieved another major ambition – after months and months of preparation, planning and training, I flew to Geneva for the first part of my journey to walk the 'Tour du Mont Blanc'. Completing the Pennine Way adventure gave me a great feeling of satisfaction, so I had now set my sights on a greater challenge and bought the Cicerone Guide. Mont Blanc is 15,777 feet high, and the 105-mile walk is a circular route, right round the mountain, and with a height gain and loss of almost 33,000 feet. The route can be done in either direction, starting and finishing wherever you wish.

I decided to start at Les Houches, just outside Chamonix, and I walked anti-clockwise. I took a bus from Geneva and stayed in a pre-booked B&B right on the route. Rucksack packing was critical, as before; I asked for an early breakfast as the first day out of the B&B was a large climb. I was full of nervous energy and, as I climbed, I felt slightly light-headed due to the altitude. I reached Refuge de Miage after 3½ hours, even though the guide said it should have taken me 6 hours, so I was walking far too fast – hence why I was light-headed. I had reached the recommended stage for the end of the first day by lunchtime, so I pushed on and did half of day two. I continued the rest of the trip in this vein.

The walk left Switzerland and went through Courmayeur in Italy. I stayed at the Rifugio Bonatti at 2025 m (6643 feet). Chris Bonnington had written in his *Quest for Adventure* about Walter Bonatti climbing this great lump of rock. It was a solo climb that was going to take three days, so he had to camp at night anchored on the sheer rock face. On the first day he was in an awkward position, trying to hammer in a piton, when he missed and smashed the tip of his ring finger against the rock. Thankfully he was able to staunch the bleeding and carry on. On his second day, when he reached his stop, he opened his rucksack and discovered that his fuel bottle had leaked and contaminated all his food. However, he went on to complete the climb and it became known as the Bonatti Pillar ... and the refuge was named after him.

I pushed on and came to Champex in Switzerland, a beautiful Swiss lake resort. The walk was seven days long and, when I finally finished, I spent three days in Chamonix where I went up almost 4,000 m in the cable car to Aiguille du Midi. There's also a gondola that continues across Vallée Blanche down to Italy, and from that gondola you can see the Bonatti Pillar. On another day I took a cable car to Col de Voza, meeting all the climbers who were about to attack Mont Blanc. There's also a tramway which I took (full of these professional climbers), which had been planned to go all the way to the top of Mont Blanc, although the First World War brought an end to that idea. This fantastic trip gave me a taste for alpine mountains and it wasn't long before I went back.

Via Ferrata

Another of my dreams was fulfilled in September when I heard that Andy, a friend of Morag and John, was going to Italy to climb the Via Ferrata in the Dolomites. This is serious mountain adventuring using fixed cables, chains and ladders left over from the First World War. I'd heard and seen pictures of these for years, and had thought that these would be wonderful to do. Here was the opportunity! Via Ferrata means "iron path": many Via Ferrata were originally built to aid the movements of alpine military units during the First World War. They are in effect a range of protected routes comprised of fixed cables, ladders and even gorge-spanning bridges, and allow people like me to go to places normally reserved just for expert rock-climbers.

So I had to get the kit: helmet, a full body harness, Via Ferrata self-belay set (two pieces of cable, a metre long each, to attach to the cable and which acts as a braking system, so that the worst that could happen is a fall of 2 metres), carabiners to ensure one is always connected to the cables, and gloves, vital for a novice like me (the purists don't touch the cables, but a novice holds on to the cable like a monkey!). Andy and I flew to Venice and travelled to Corvara, not far from Cortina, and he very kindly taught me the techniques – he had climbed there a few times before. It was just amazing.

In May 2004 Andy and I flew to Northern Italy for our second Via Ferrata trip. We took a hire car to Arco and had another fantastic time climbing the mountains. (For that first trip, Andy had had a longer holiday than I and, as we'd hired the car from Venice, I caught the bus back to Venice on my own where I had a brilliant day out until my plane went later in the day). On both trips we camped in tents. Via Ferrata was everything I had hoped for and I would go on to enjoy a lot more of it.

Flying

Pete, a customer from my Alba days, told me one day that he had bought a share in a light aircraft as he was training to become a pilot. However, it was expensive on the fuel, so I suggested I go along and make a contribution to the fuel costs. There were three spare seats, so I invited Graham to join Sheila and I, but Graham let Judi go instead.

359

We took off from Leeds Bradford and flew to Carlisle where we set down for refreshments, and then flew off across the Lake District. Scafell Pike is 3,300 feet high, but the cloud level was at 3,000 feet, so we had to head back home. Pete followed the M6 for a while to get back to Leeds, but I could see that we were heading north – I didn't know what to say! Subtly I said to Pete, "If we keep going north, we will get to Glasgow." He replied, "Oh no, we're going the wrong way!" Not great when you're 3,000 feet up in the sky!

Paragliding

At the Outdoors Show I had been brave (or stupid) and booked a paragliding day at an airfield in Derbyshire. The day started with a classroom training session and safety briefing. We were kitted out with a huge, heavy backpack (which included the canopy, the seat and the harness), and then we were introduced to the winch. After preparing the canopy a steel cable is attached to the front of the harness, with the other end on the winch. When the winch takes up the slack and starts to pull you forward, you have to run as fast as you can as the canopy comes off the floor and up in air behind you. If you get it right, you are airborne and use the ropes to adjust direction and are towed down the airfield. Then the winch stops and you float to the ground and use your training knowledge to come to a stop and gather up your canopy.

That is if you get it right! I did not, and consequently was towed down the airfield on my face and belly before the winch was stopped. After a similar second attempt, I made it up into the air several times, and I have to say it is exhilarating. If you take further lessons, you are able to release the winch cable and fly freely around the airfield. I have seen many paragliding pilots carrying their equipment up hills to launch, but I knew that my long-distance walking rucksack was quite heavy enough for me to carry, so I retired, not so gracefully, from paragliding!

Corsica

The GR 20 is one of Europe's greatest adventure treks, and has a reputation for being the toughest of the GR routes at 118 miles with a climb of some 41,000 feet. I thought this would be a fabulous swansong for my mountain adventures. I trained very hard for this trip, but one day shortly before the trip I felt really awful. I went to the doctor who said that I had a touch of flu and needed antibiotics. Out in Corsica I continued to feel unwell and on the first day of walking I only went 100 yards and couldn't do any more. My legs were like lead, I was sweating and had no energy, so the guide rang for a taxi to take me to the second hut on the route, suggesting I wait there for two days to see if I could then go on. However, I was no better, and four other people dropped out because it was too tough.

They took me to the hospital for all sorts of tests, and it turned out that I had the Epstein-Barr Virus (a form of glandular fever), which was totally debilitating. I stayed in the hospital for two weeks and really thought my days were numbered! No one could speak English, I was on a drip and had a blood transfusion etc … I stayed there until the flight home two weeks later. Teresa picked me up from the airport and, after having short synacthen tests, it was discovered that I also had a steroid deficiency. As a result, for years I have had to carry round emergency tablets and injections for this condition. Back at home, I took a long time to recover. (Barbara Windsor also contracted this illness which debilitated her for two years.)

On Pen-y-Ghent with Jacko

A Bowland blizzard

CHAPTER 21: MUSIC MEMORIES

"**M**usic was my first love" is part of the lyric from the Top 10 hit 'Music' by John Miles and, along with mountains, it certainly is a tremendous love of mine and has played such an important part in my life. I have already written about the reasons for my happiness, but it is important to say that music certainly enhances my happiness. What wonderful memories music makes – Leonard Cohen said, "Music is the emotional life of most people." How true that is for me.

My earliest music memory was when I was eight in that Longfield cinema when I heard 'Answer Me' by David Whitfield and proceeded to sing it to my female companion on the way home. The majority of my earliest music memories were heard on the radio when I lived with my dad in Wales. Programmes like *Housewives' Choice* with that familiar theme tune, 'In Party Mood'. There were two other programmes on a Sunday, *Family Favourites* and *The Billy Cotton Band Show*, with his not-to-be-forgotten "Wakey Wakey" introduction. Sometimes the theme tunes are as memorable as the records, like *Desert Island Discs*, *The Archers*, and 'Hit & Miss' by The John Barry Seven, the theme tune to *Juke Box Jury*. Much later *Top of the Pops* had several introductory tracks – my favourite is still 'Whole Lotta Love'.

I have already mentioned the songs I sang to woo the girls at secondary school. 'Only the Lonely', a No 1 for Roy Orbison in 1960, is what I was singing when I went into the army. Lawrence tells me I sang almost all day in the factory all through the sixties, and of course I was privileged to be part of that Beatles, Rolling Stones emergence and the fabulous sixties, with the coffee bar, juke box era, part of which was 'Flower Power', immortalised by the No 1 hit in 1967 by Scott McKenzie, 'San Francisco (Be Sure to Wear Some Flowers in Your Hair').

These early music memories were courtesy of the BBC Light Programme, and later Radio Luxembourg, before the big revolution of the pirate radio ships in the sixties. Many of our well-known DJs were to be heard on Radio Caroline and London – Tony Blackburn, Kenny Everett, Emperor Rosko, John Peel and my particular favourite, Johnnie Walker. These were the days of the transistor radio, which you could take out with you – early versions of 'ghetto blasters'. In 1967 everything changed when the BBC launched Radio 1. I well remember waiting excitedly as Tony

Blackburn hosted the first breakfast show and opened proceedings with 'Flowers in the Rain' by The Move, who included Roy Wood and Carl Wayne.

In 1970, when I bought my mobile disco, I started collecting 45s and LPs new and old, and over the years many other favourite records of mine also include that magic word, 'music', including: 'Rock & Roll Music', 'Dance to the Music', 'Let the Music Play', 'Lost in Music', 'Don't Stop the Music', 'Let's Face the Music and Dance', 'I Love Music', 'I Can Hear Music' and of course, 'Thank You for the Music', a sentiment I wholeheartedly echo.

My spell as a DJ at The Pentagon was during the fabulous disco era, where dance floor favourites included 'Love Train' by The O'Jays, 'Rock Me Gently' by Andy Kim, 'Stuck in the Middle with You' by Stealers Wheel and 'Let's Go Round Again' by The Average White Band – I even played a huge favourite of mine, 'Way Down Yonder in New Orleans' by Freddy Cannon. When we travelled to Butlin's I remember we had a cassette player in our green Bedford van, and one of our favourite groups was Fox, and back at Butlins, 'The Hustle' by Van McCoy was a real crowd-pleaser.

David Bowie's *Aladdin Sane* was the first LP that Sheila and I bought together, followed by a very eclectic mix over the years with Reggae, Motown, Bob Dylan and the iconic *Tubular Bells*. Despite Sheila being much younger than me, she still enjoyed all the easy-listening artists like James Last, Perry Como, Bobby Darin, Dionne Warwick, Frank Sinatra and Andy Williams along with Paul Young, REO Speedwagon, Barry Manilow, Shakatak, Shalamar, Dusty Springfield, Simon & Garfunkel, Neil Diamond, Gene Pitney and Carly Simon among them. We also liked the three Chris's: Cross, Rea and de Burgh. By then CDs were replacing LPs and the 'Glam Rock' period produced some fabulous hits by the likes of T-Rex, Roxy Music, Slade, Sweet. They were followed by the 'New Romantics' with groups like The Human League, Ultravox, Spandau Ballet, Duran Duran and many more.

Memories of the charts in the 1990s onwards are vague. Like many people, as I got older my tastes changed. I changed from Radio 1 to Radio 2, with Ken Bruce and his PopMaster quiz and Steve Wright with his quiz in the afternoon. I also began listening to Radio 3 and Classic FM, as my classical music liking developed. My collection of CDs began to include

Mozart, Bach, Haydn and others. I never lost my love for any of the earlier music, but my musical tastes simply became broader. The audio cassette-playing Sony Walkman was replaced by the portable CD player.

The Hi-Fi industry is a perfect example of continuous reinvention to promote sales, from the wind-up gramophone to the record player, radiogram, music centres, Hi-Fi separates, midi systems, mini systems and micro systems – constantly finding new ways to take our money. I was very happy to give them some more for a unit I could load with five CDs which would happily play away for hours. Then along came iTunes, the iPod and the iPod dock – even my hotel room in Bangkok had one of these for guests. With the renovation of my home and the purchase of my Sonos System, coupled with the innovation of iTunes, my whole listening experience was transformed.

With 30,000 tracks playing randomly I am in musical heaven – all those genres I have mentioned along with audio books like the Complete Bible, poetry, books by authors such as Charles Dickens, Charlotte Brontë, Thomas Hardy, Ranulph Fiennes and all my motivational authors – even the speeches of Winston Churchill rubbing shoulders with Chas & Dave, The Vienna Boys' Choir, Buena Vista Social Club, *The Best of Bollywood* and *Blackpool Tower Organ Favourites*. I did try a couple of the streaming services but soon cancelled because I realised I wasn't getting to listen to my own music. (Robert also told me about Shazam, which I find brilliantly useful.)

Another benefit of my system is the ability to make playlists. So, at Christmas I enjoy all my festive season music, and on Sunday I can play my selection of hymns, gospel and sacred music. Other playlist choices are Northern Soul, Baroque with Vivaldi, Monteverdi and Handel, blues (a brilliant example is the track 'Muddy Water Blues' by Paul Rodgers), Stax and big band and swing (with Benny Goodman, Duke Ellington, Tommy Dorsey and Count Basie and their fabulous vocalists). Motown of course, but other playlists include Buddha-Bar and Café Del Mar, which include favourite tracks of mine: 'Maya' by Ravin, 'Twilight' by Blank & Jones, plus 'Light Signs' and 'Osiride' by Riccardo Eberspacher. Other playlists feature the sixties, disco, reggae, girl singers (like Lena Martell, Tanita Tikaram, Cilla Black, Madonna and Mama Cass Elliot, whose album *Dream A Little Dream* is full of meaningful and mindful tracks). Jazz is another category, with artists like Oscar Peterson, Fats Waller and those jazz divas like Dinah Washington, Billie Holiday, Nina Simone, Sarah Vaughan and Lena Horne. The groups list has the likes of REM, Fleetwood Mac, Dire Straits, ABC, Simple Minds, Runrig and Creedence Clearwater Revival. Whilst my world music playlist spans the globe, I enjoy it all, but a favourite of mine is 'fado', a music with its origins in Portugal. A CD I have recently bought is *Mundo* by the wonderful Mariza.

Other playlists include calm, relaxing and meditative music from artists like Llewellyn and *Buddha and Bonsai* by Oliver Shanti & Friends. The easy-listening list has two beautiful voices, Scott Walker singing 'Joanna' and Karen Carpenter with 'We've Only Just Begun' — what a duo they would have made. My soft-rock selection has artists like Bread, The Doobie Brothers, The Eagles, CSN & Y, Air Supply, Steely Dan and The Mamas & the Papas. This music has recently been given a new name by the industry: 'yacht' music — whatever it's called, it is some of my favourite sounds. But my 'go-to' playlist has to be 'happy', which includes many of those wonderful music memories from my life that I love to sing along and dance to, like the brilliant 'Reaching for the Best', by The Exciters, which is also a marvellous Memorable Maxim.

Dick Clark said music is the soundtrack of your life. It has a brilliant ability to produce a picture of a particular person and place, unlock that memory and transport you there. I have made a list of such memorable musical moments in my life, reminding me where I was and who with, and each has a story to tell, just like this advert for the Pentagon Nightclub does:

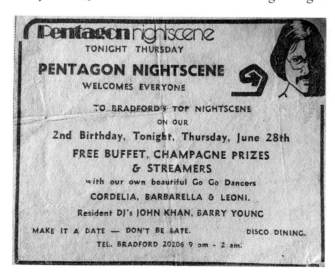

367

Sheila – Tommy Roe

Love Train – The O'Jays

Good Morning Starshine – Oliver

Let's Dance – Chris Montez

Twango – Laurie Johnson

Yesterday Man – Chris Andrews

1-2-3 – Len Barry

Be Young, Be Foolish, Be Happy –
    The Tams

April Love – Pat Boone

Can't Take My Eyes off You –
    Andy Williams

Everlasting Love – Love Affair

Love Me Do – The Beatles

Dance On – Kathy Kirby

Just One Look – The Hollies

(Don't Fear) The Reaper –
    Blue Oyster Cult

Only You Can – Fox

Friday on My Mind –
    The Easybeats

TSOP – MFSB

Tell Him – Billie Davies

Be My Baby – The Ronettes

Why – Anthony Newley

When It Comes Down to It –
    Tasmin Archer

She's About a Mover –
    Sir Douglas Quintet

I'm a Moody Guy – Shane Fenton

Working My Way Back to You –
    Detroit Spinners

Cherry Pink and Apple Blossom
    White – Eddie Calvert

Dream Lover – Bobby Darin

More than I Can Say – Bobby Vee

Pamela Pamela – Wayne Fontana

Can't Give You Anything (But My
    Love) – The Stylistics

Poetry in Motion –
    Johnny Tillotson

I'm into Something Good –
    Herman's Hermits

It Was So Easy – Carly Simon

Runaround Sue – Dion

January – Pilot

Hey Baby – Bruce Channel

Montego Bay – Bobby Bloom

Spanish Harlem – Jimmy Justice

Copacabana – Barry Manilow

Do You Believe in Magic –
    The Lovin' Spoonful

Wives and Lovers – Jack Jones

(Dance with the) Guitar Man –
    Duane Eddy

Wichita Lineman –
    Glen Campbell

Venus in Blue Jeans –
    Mark Wynter

Money – The Flying Lizards

My Silver Lining – First Aid Kit

A Picture of You – Joe Brown

The Twist – Chubby Checker

Love of the Common People –
    Nicky Thomas

California Dreamin' –
    The Mamas & the Papas

Young at Heart – The Bluebells

Language of Love –
    John D Loudermilk

Happiness – Ken Dodd

Sunshine Superman – Donovan

The Last Time –
The Rolling Stones

Answer Me – David Whitfield

Baby Love – The Supremes

Every 1's a Winner –
Hot Chocolate

Sugar Baby Love – The Rubettes

A Night to Remember – Shalamar

Wade in the Water –
The Ramsey Lewis Trio

Blame It on the Bossa Nova –
Eydie Gormé

Listen to the Music –
The Doobie Brothers

Rock Me Gently – Andy Kim

Sugar, Sugar – The Archies

It Might as Well Rain until
September – Carole King

Happy Together – The Turtles

Hang on Sloopy – The McCoys

Twist in My Sobriety –
Tanita Tikaram

Ernie (The Fastest Milkman in the
West) – Benny Hill

Two Kinds of Teardrops –
Del Shannon

Cry Like a Baby – The Box Tops

Say I Won't Be There –
The Springfields

Way Down Yonder in New Orleans
– Freddy Cannon

I Can Hear the Music –
The Beach Boys

Wishin' & Hopin' –
The Merseybeats

First Time Ever I Saw Your Face –
Lena Martell

Counting Teardrops – Emile Ford

How Long – Ace

Subterranean Homesick Blues –
Bob Dylan

Unforgettable – Nat King Cole

Night Birds – Shakatak

Polk Salad Annie – Tony Joe White

Killing Me Softly with His Song –
Roberta Flack

Diana – Paul Anka

Sweet Talkin' Guy – The Chiffons

Young Hearts Run Free –
Candi Staton

Search for the Hero – M. People

I Hear You Knocking –
Dave Edmunds

(If Paradise Is) Half as Nice –
Amen Corner

Reach out I'll Be There –
The Four Tops

A Certain Smile – Johnny Mathis

Light My Fire – José Feliciano

Misty – Ray Stevens

I'm a Believer – The Monkees

A Walkin Miracle –
Limmie and the Family Cookin

Some Other Guy – The Big Three

Rio – Michael Nesmith

The Boy from New York City –
The Ad Libs

(There's) Always Something There
to Remind Me – Sandie Shaw

The guests on *Desert Island Discs* have to choose just eight tracks to take to the island. When I get asked to go on the show, my eight will be:

1. 'Heartbreak Hotel' by Elvis Presley from 1956 when I was 12 and had my first job, selling the *Football Argus* outside pubs on a Saturday night in Wales.
2. It was 1962 and 'Wonderful Land' by The Shadows that has so many memories – our local coffee bar and the fabulous juke box and I got there on my first scooter.
3. It was also the year I first learnt to jive to the appropriately named 'Let's Dance' by Chris Montez.
4. My first musical memory of my disc jockeying days at The Pentagon in Bradford is 'Love Train' by The O'Jays.
5. 'Young At Heart' by The Bluebells was the first record I used when I started my training sessions.
6. Then when in 2000 I got my first big break as a speaker at the ISMM conference, the motivational record played to the delegates that day was 'Search for the Hero' by M People, and because of the importance of that day it will always be a fabulous music memory.
7. In my book I have made much of 'maxims' as guides to aid happiness and success; my final two very significant records with life-enhancing messages that I would take with me are 'Desiderata' by Les Crane, which has the most beautiful words that I would be happy to hear day after day on my desert island …
8. … as I would the brilliant messages in Baz Luhrmann's 'Everybody's Free (To Wear Sunscreen)'.

Robert Browning said, "There is no truer truth obtainable by man than comes from music." These wonderful lyrics from ABBA seem so appropriate for me:

Thank you for the music, the songs I'm singing
Thanks for all the joy they're bringing
Who can live without it? I ask in all honesty
What would life be?
Without a song or a dance, what are we?
So I say thank you for the music, for giving it to me.

Chapter 22: Contemplation, Contentment and Conclusion

As I look back and reflect on my life and my contribution here on earth so far, a wonderful verse from Patience Strong sums up many of my thoughts and feelings:

Make life pay dividends. You can if you choose —
for it's a business, you gain or you lose.
Though you have problems and trouble to meet —
Don't accept failure and loss and defeat.

It has been a life of circumstances, consequences and now contentment. I am often asked, "Why are you so happy Barry?" My reply is that I believe happiness comes from being content, and that is what I am … and of course, as Bob Dylan sang, "With God on our side," which I am blessed to experience. I believe happiness is being satisfied, grateful and content. Mind you, some of this is selfish – I am happy with my own company, I only have me to concern myself with and, as the title of the Muddy Waters song says, "I love the life I live, I live the life I love." Benjamin Spock argued that, "Happiness is mostly a by-product of doing what makes us feel fulfilled."

So, what is the answer to the question, "How did I get here?" I am sure my early formative years had a profound effect on my life. At an early age I had to organise, cater for and look after myself, make my own decisions and earn my own money. Living in digs I had to coordinate my affairs. When I was a salesman for Columbia, I worked from home without supervision, so I had to manage myself; I had to plan and prepare my days to make the best use of my time – in short, I had to accept responsibility for myself. After Sheila left and I became self-employed, then it was all down to me – self-sufficiency – no bookings, no money. I was paid on results, which is why I never 'just turned up' for a booking and why I always tried to be thorough in everything I did. What I was acutely aware of was in that ten two-letter word Memorable Maxim – "If it is to be, it is up to me." The great thing about working for yourself is that you only have to work for half of the day, but you do get to choose which twelve hours!

I learnt that success comes from desire, discipline and determination, and that life is about challenges, chances and choices: I could have easily become a victim of my circumstances. I could have just let life happen to me, but instead I seem to have made life happen for me. I grasped my opportunities with both hands and capitalised on them. George Bernard Shaw wrote, "Life isn't about finding yourself. Life is about creating yourself." For a lot of my life, I seem to have had to be the sole master of my attitude and attributes. Are these the things that helped build my confidence? I am sure it had a lot to do with my make-up. I learnt about commitment, concentration and competence; I became very competitive. I also had to be constantly creative. Yet if I had to identify one attribute that really did contribute to my successful and happy life, it would be application – the ability to organise myself. Success seems to be about getting the best out of what you've got. Sam Ewing said, "Success has a simple formula; do your best, and people may like it."

I didn't realise at the time, but I was obviously learning that, with a good attitude, we can turn negative experiences into positive lessons and that it is important to grab happiness in the passing moments of life. During the writing of this book, I asked friends, family and clients what they thought accounted for my success the most. The overwhelming reply was my "enthusiasm." I love the sound of laughter – as Charlie Chaplin said, "A day without laughter is a day wasted," and I certainly don't want to waste any of my days. I guess I was just doing the best I could with my life. I went from cutting up lumps of metal in a factory to standing on stage in Las Vegas. Now I really can't do anything but "Look on the bright side of life." "Success is getting what you want. Happiness is wanting what you get." And as Proverbs 17:22 says, "A merry heart doeth good like a medicine."

I have always said that if I had to, I could earn an adequate living without leaving the close where I live, doing DIY, cleaning windows, house work, gardening etc. Those early lessons from my dad meant that I have always been frugal and appreciated that there is no greater wealth than life. Henry Ward Beecher explained that, "The art of being happy lies in the power of extracting happiness from common things." This has perhaps been the story of my life. I haven't yearned for or chased money. I am happy with the common things. I appreciate the many ordinary things that make my life so valuable – my 86,400 seconds that are a blessing from God every day – and I celebrate that each day. One of my favourite hymns that I have chosen for my funeral is 'How Great Thou Art', and I find a great way to go to sleep is to recount my abundance of gifts from God. (See also Matthew 6.22-3.)

Another of my daily readings books is *The Golden Present* by Sri Swami Satchidananda. He explains that, "When anything comes to you, first ask yourself, 'Will I be maintaining my peace by getting this, or will my peace be disturbed?' If we are thinking of acquiring or doing something, ask, 'Will it rob me of my peace?'" I love this, and reflect on the past but, as they say, experience is a great teacher.

Two personal letters that meant a great deal to me were very rewarding and confirmed that my training objectives had been successful. They came from young female delegates – the first, in 2001 wrote:

Morning Barry. Now I am not doing this to crawl but I would like to say how much I enjoyed your course on Saturday, it genuinely had an effect on me. I have had the worst year of my life and after Saturday it made me have a totally different outlook on my life. Thank you. I even went out and bought Taken on Trust *by Terry Waite. I read 90 pages yesterday and already I feel lucky not to have been in the situation he was in years ago. I am not sure what my future holds but I do know that time is ticking away and I should enjoy every minute of it. Thanks once again. Wendi.*

The second letter in 2002 explained:

Dear Barry, my name is Gemma, we met yesterday afternoon when you entertained us all with your terrific training programme which I thought was absolutely amazing. Like yourself I would love to be involved in the enter-

tainment business. I think one of my magic moments yesterday was 'See your goal and aim for it'. I aim to become a well-known soprano and sing in the Royal Albert Hall. You probably wonder what all this has to do with your training session. Well Barry, you told us we need to have a goal and we have to see it, believe it and achieve it. Your training session has helped me believe I can go on this tremendous journey. Thank you.

My final piece of self-gratification is a note that my nephew Guy says I should finish my book with. I was on the upper deck of a bus from Stockton to Newcastle on the A19. It was very windy and the bus was swaying about a bit and moving from side to side. I had some fun with this, joking that people would have paid a lot of money for a ride like this at Disneyland, and generally enjoying entertaining my fellow passengers with my Frank Spencer impression during the journey. When a young female passenger got off the bus before me, she handed me this note:

Have a nice day Mr. Wonderful. You are a very nice person; your spirit cheered me up. The world needs more people like you.

My favourite short poem is:

Laughter is the remedy for sorrow and for care,
It brings joy to troubled souls and broken hearts repair.

I am aware some people find some of my antics embarrassing, but I think they are a gift from God – and as Sheila said, "You give a lot of people a lot of happiness Barry." A quote I read said that, "The noblest art is making people happy." So I feel obliged to continue using my gift. I also read about the importance of being happy with who you are and what you are, but remember happiness doesn't just depend on who you are or what you have; it depends solely on what you think. According to William Arthur Ward, "A cloudy day is no match for a sunny disposition."

When I am asked how I am, among my many positive answers is the fabulous word 'ebullient', which means being full of liveliness and enthusiasm – how could I be anything else? I have mentioned the power of positive thinking, and now at the age of 76 I am still employing it. As I reflect on those fantastic 76 years, I ask myself, "Have I done the best I can with my life?" It has truly been magical. This lovely poem puts it so well:

What have I sacrificed? What have I done?
What have I lost? and what have I won?
What have I given and what have I got?
How have I helped, just a bit or a lot?
Have I kept back what I might have bestowed?
Have I made easier somebody's load?
Have I been honest at work and at play?
What kind of a show have I put up today?

Of course, I didn't achieve all this on my own. I want to express my sincere gratitude to all those who have played any part of my life's rich tapestry – you have all enriched my life. Thank you for your hospitality, care and kindness; for your generosity of spirit; for the joy we have shared; and for putting up with all my idiosyncrasies, eccentric behaviour, misdemeanours, imperfections, my embarrassing showing-off moments, my Barryisms, my big-headedness, the streaking and the Frank Spencer impressions. To anyone who has touched my life, inspired and influenced me, given me so much joy and happiness, and those who are not here now, thank you. Thank you to those of you that have helped me directly with the writing of my autobiography, with information, dates and data, memories, recollections and reflections, ideas, thoughts and suggestions, especially my sister Rita who is now 90 and still going strong like me. (A glance at our family tree will show that we have sadly lost our two siblings, our wonderful brother Austin and sister Barbara.) You have been so wonderfully helpful and supportive, and your contributions have been invaluable. God has truly blessed me with you all. I would love to name you all but you know who you are – *thank you, thank you.* Johann Wolfgang Von Goethe said:

A man should hear a little music, read a little poetry, and see a fine picture every day of his life, in order that worldly cares may not obliterate the sense of the beautiful which God has implanted in the human soul.

Writing my story has prompted an enriched realisation and appreciation of how fleeting life really is. I have spoken about the importance of 'living in the now'. I believe it is also about 'living in the wow'.

My favourite poem has a powerful message for us all:

Leisure

What is this life if, full of care,
We have no time to stand and stare?
No time to stand beneath the boughs
And stare as long as sheep or cows:
No time to see, when woods we pass,
Where squirrels hide their nuts in grass:
No time to see, in broad daylight,
Streams full of stars, like skies at night:
No time to turn at Beauty's glance,
And watch her feet, how they can dance:
No time to wait till her mouth can,
Enrich that smile her eyes began.
A poor life this if, full of care,
We have no time to stand and stare.

W. H. Davies

Words from the song 'Happiness' sum up my life up perfectly: "I thank the Lord that I have been blessed, with more than my share of happiness." Writing the story of my life has been a marvellous experience, at times exhausting, enlightening, emotional, but most of all very, very enjoyable. Thank you for reading it. I hope you have enjoyed it as much as I enjoyed living it ... and don't forget to, "Always look on the bright side of life." Personally, I am also going to take the advice of the Tams and continue to "Be Young, Foolish and Happy."

God bless you all.

Barry.